YUCATÁN'S MAYA PEASANTRY AND THE
ORIGINS OF THE CASTE WAR

Yucatán's Maya Peasantry and the Origins of the Caste War

TERRY RUGELEY

UNIVERSITY OF TEXAS PRESS
AUSTIN

The maps on pages xi, 3, and 6 are by Christine A. Schultz.

Requests for permission to reproduce material from this work should be sent to Permissions, University of Texas Press, P.O. Box 7819, Austin, TX 78713-7819

∞ The paper used in this publication meets the minimum requirements of American National Standard for Information Sciences—Permanence of Paper for Printed Library Materials, ANSI Z39.48-1984.

Library of Congress Cataloging-in-Publication Data
Rugeley, Terry, 1956–
    Yucatán's Maya peasantry and the origins of the Caste War / Terry Rugeley. — 1st ed.
        p.   cm.
    Includes bibliographical references and index.
    ISBN 0-292-77074-X (cloth : alk. paper) — ISBN 0-292-77078-2 (pbk. : alk. paper)
    1. Mayas—Wars. 2. Yucatán (Mexico : State)—History—Caste War, 1847–1855. 3. Mayas—Yucatán Peninsula—History. I. Title.
    F1435.3.W2R84   1996
    972'.606—dc20   95-42405

Contents

Acknowledgments

Many individuals in different nations have contributed to this study: Anne Rugeley; John Hart, Tom O'Brien, Susan Kellogg, Steve Mintz, James Kirby Martin, Jim Jones, and everyone else at the University of Houston; Mark Saka, Ime Ukpanah, Barbara Angel, Matthew Restall, and Paul Sullivan; Margarita Peraza Sauri, Silvia López Córtes, and Rosaria Poot and everyone else at the Universidad Autónoma de Yucatán; Dra. Piedad Peniche Rivero, Andrea Vergoda Medina, Candy Flota García, and all the rest at the Archivo General del Estado; Michel Antochiw, Patricia Martínez Huchim, Yolanda López, and everyone at the Centro de Apoyo a la Investigación Histórica de Yucatán; Fr. José F. Camargo Sosa and Hermana Gladys N. Díaz M. at the Archivo Histórico de la Arquidiócesis de Yucatán; and the many archivists of Tulane University, the University of Texas at Austin, the University of Texas at Arlington, and the Clements Library at the University of Michigan.

Special thanks to Mr. Nelson Reed for an illuminating interview on his life and the Caste War.

Finally, I would like to thank Rinelda Cauich Ayora; she makes the Notary Archives notable.

Support for this research came from the Fulbright-Hayes Foundation, from the University of Houston Department of History, and from the University of Oklahoma Research Council and College of Arts and Sciences.

Divine Providence favors us with a brutal, fierce, and audacious people.
—Antonio Mais, *cura* of Tihosuco, on the
   Maya peasantry

Introduction

On the evening of October 18, 1866, the citizens of Mérida, Yucatán, gathered in a ceremony which for all its air of sanctity would leave the participants with a sense of bitterness, of lost opportunities and shattered dreams. The event was a benefit for the widows and orphans of men killed in the battle for Tihosuco, a town deep in the Yucatecan interior. Nineteen years earlier, Tihosuco had been a starting point of a rural revolt known to history as the Caste War (*la guerra de castas*). The village had remained an epicenter of fighting, repeatedly taken and lost in an endless war without quarter. But on this evening one could see little evidence of peasant jacqueries, only the respectable men and women of Mérida clad in Victorian coats and dresses, which Yucatán's barely perceptible autumn rendered no less uncomfortable.

The high point of the evening's commemorations was a reading by one of Mexico's most promising young poets, Juan A. Mateos. Following the classic poetic tradition, he began by invoking the spirit of his art and asking this muse to reveal to him scenes invisible to the mortal eye. The spirit complied. It spoke to him of the highest goals of nineteenth-century liberalism: progress and civilization. "I will sing the glory of Yucatán," it promised, the ballad of its heroic sons and soldiers past:

> *And by that beam of light which today illuminates*
> *Splendid recollections and memories dear,*
> *Before the altars of that generation*
> *DIVINE LIBERTY will fall kneeling!*

These were glories indeed. Of course, that Divine Liberty should kneel before human beings, and not vice-versa, presented an unusual metaphor and, to the critic, might have raised questions about the sort of society that had emerged here. But something more serious darkened this poetic vision. Some anomaly within Yucatán's march to glory was thwarting the poetic splendor. Midway through his invocation Mateos beheld a vision of Chan Santa Cruz—"Little Holy Cross"—the jungle stronghold where Maya rebels lived beyond the reach of Yucatecan law. Heeding the commands of his muse, Mateos suddenly cried out:

> *Chan Santa Cruz! Over your bloody temple*
> *Weighs a curse. Listen to your century:*
> *Accept civilization, or perish of contempt!*
> *You who have lived*
> *Amid the terrible bacchanal of crime*
> *In degradation and filthy airs*
> *Without feeling in your soul*
> *The faintest remorse,*
> *From the deep sleep of terror you awaken.*
> *The faith of Christianity*
> *Warring against your rude fatalism,*
> *Once, and yet again, calls to your door.*[1]

This, the rebel stronghold, the unspeakable barbaric Cross, the mere fact of peasant rebellion, darkened the vision of glory. Despite Mateos' prophesy of a Biblical destruction for Chan Santa Cruz, the rebel society would live on, both in actuality and in the vexed imaginations of Mérida's bourgeois gentlemen.

If Mateos sounded a note of bitterness in his poetry, he was to be forgiven. Much had been lost. In 1846 Yucatán stood on the threshold of destiny, ready to take its place among the favored nations of the earth. Its recent separation from Mexico, a separation which now seems merely to have been another case of the economic frustration and national disintegration endemic to nineteenth-century Latin America, then appeared in a far more positive light.[2] Yucatecan nationalists believed that they had carried out the latest momentous war of independence in the Americas, the culmination of a tradition which extended from the United States to Haiti to the Spanish colonies and, finally, to this peninsula, the "living rock," "*mayab t'an,*" "the land of pheasant and deer."[3]

Their destiny had been centuries in arriving. When the Spanish conquistador Francisco de Montejo arrived in 1526, he found the Yucatec Mayas fragmented into warring tribes. Montejo assembled a force of some four hundred soldiers, more than twice the number that Hernán Cortés had first brought to Tenochtitlán. But success proved elusive. One bemused Maya asked the con-

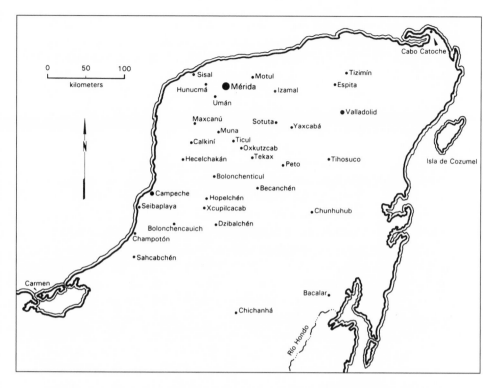

MAP I

quistador, "What will you do here, stranger, when you are set upon by as many Indians as there are hairs on the skin of a deer?"[4] The prediction proved only too accurate. The Spaniards spent their time repulsing Maya attacks or else foraging for provisions along the desolate northern coast. Ultimately the conquest required eighteen years and in the end yielded nothing but some parched real estate and a potpourri of traditional tribute—corn, beans, chiles, honey, wax, and cotton blankets—hardly a conquistador's dream. The Mayas regrouped under the protection of the corporate village or maintained a resistance in the Guatemalan Petén. Spaniards settled in the Europeanized towns in the north. But over time the two cultures gradually blended. Native demographic collapse, together with growing urban markets, tempted Spaniards to set up commercial estates in the countryside. Only in the eighteenth century, then, did Yucatecans see the first inklings of rural transformation.

By 1820 the hope of the future lay in sugar. For over three centuries sugar had been sweet gold, a dependably lucrative commodity on the world market. And what sugar had done for the Portuguese in Bahía, the British in the

West Indies, the French in St. Domingue, and the planters in Cuba, it would surely do now for the cultured and enlightened citizens of Yucatán. To pave the way for commercial planting, the creoles who controlled the state apparatus enacted legislation allowing over a million acres of land to pass from public domain into the hands of private entrepreneurs. New labor laws bound dispossessed peasants to the estates, while the national trade and political structures constantly changed as sugar producers and merchants maneuvered for the best possible terms.[5]

It was an age of progress in other ways as well. Yucatecans established their own legal and political institutions. They signed treaties and fielded diplomats as an independent nation. Successfully they defied the Mexican dictator Antonio López de Santa Anna. Yucatecans had their own primitive ports—Sisal, Bacalar, and the walled city of Campeche—and would soon construct another in the northern coastal village of Progreso. In the cities the elite of society enjoyed streetlights, theater, festivals, literary journals, and the fruits of modern medicine. Throughout the countryside, a network of schools was emerging which, the inhabitants hoped, would soon make the ideals of literacy and progress universal fact. Informed by the "spirit of enterprise," Yucatecans also boasted a special emblem of modernity, the steam-driven cotton mill, the first of its kind anywhere in Mexico. To hopeful creoles it now seemed they were about to join the affluent nations of Europe in nineteenth-century bourgeois affluence.[6]

But the sugar empire was not to be. Twenty years later, as Mateos recited before the crowd, the vision of independent Yucatán lay in cinders. During the Caste War, rural insurgents, originating primarily in the south and east, had pushed toward Mérida, destroying many of the towns and estates which lay in their path. By mid-1848 the worst was over, and in the face of reinvigorated military opposition the insurgents retreated into forest strongholds. But the damage was done. The upheaval had killed or dislocated as many as 200,000 people. Some died in battle, some in retribution at the hands of either of the two armies, many through starvation, and many more through the cholera epidemic which followed in 1853. Still others fled to outlying islands, to Tabasco, to the remote forests of Belize, or to the Guatemalan Petén. After the humiliating spectacle of offering themselves as a colony to various nations, Yucatecan creoles returned once more to Mexico, which would eventually sever off Campeche as a punitive measure and as a safeguard against future separatism. The many fine haciendas and even the churches, long-sacred icons of the countryside, were now burned-out rubble. In the south and east, much of the deep, fertile soils of the sugar territory lay uncultivated for years, and the entire territory of Quintana Roo, even with the entry of Mexican troops (1901), was to remain the province of unrepentant separatists long after revolutionaries had taken up arms against the dictator Porfirio Díaz. Sugar would return, but only as a secondary crop, and Yucatán would look elsewhere for its future.[7] Small wonder, then, that creoles issued a curse on the bloody temple of Chan Santa Cruz.

What provoked Yucatán's greatest conflict? I offer this volume as a social history of the decades preceding the Caste War, a survey of the varied human relationships which characterized rural life of the time and which ultimately gave rise to the war itself. The years between Mexico's independence in 1821 and the rise of the dictator Porfirio Díaz in 1876 were undoubtedly the nation's most turbulent period and remain its least understood. In the case of Yucatán, historians tend to read the years 1821–1847 as a coda to the eighteenth century, an extension of the restructurings begun by the Bourbon reforms of late colonial Spain.[8] Some, in a second approach, regard them as one more outbreak of an unchanging racial schism which continues to characterize Yucatecan society.[9] Others, in a third and closely related view, have chosen to emphasize the ways in which pre-Columbian Maya culture secretly circulated beneath the facade of the creole state.[10] Finally, still others read these years as an era which served merely as an entrée to the more familiar period of henequen dependency and revolution.[11]

As useful as these studies have been, I think that they have missed certain features which are all too apparent in the written record of the times. The first concerns our concept of the early national period. While sharing certain elements with both the colonial and porfirian periods, the first half of the century has much to characterize it as a period unique in itself.[12] Moreover, it is possible to reconstruct the history of this period beyond a mere recitation of the larger contours of polity and political economy. These long-familiar structures threaten to become sterile concepts unless we are able to establish how people lived and moved within them. And in *people* I include the majority of the people, the some 425,000 members of the Maya peasantry. We can rediscover peasants, both individually and in mass, as active agents in the annals of pre–Caste War history.

This brings us directly to a second point: ethnicity. Perhaps more than any other group in the Americas, the Mayas have remained the *elegidos* of gods and scholars alike. Their appeal derives from an ancient and exotic past, an apparent otherness, and a sheer persistence over the ages. These tendencies have heightened under the rage for ethnic study prevailing in late twentieth-century intellectual circles. The tendency, therefore, has been to interpret the

Caste War as a sudden collision of two hitherto separate worlds. I would suggest, however, that while ethnic and cultural identities did indeed exist, the lines separating the "ladino" and "macehual" worlds (that is, Spanish and Maya) were considerably less distinct than Nelson Reed or his academic successors have allowed. For all its neocolonialism, the world of Yucatán before Porfirio Díaz and henequen was a fundamentally interactive world.

In pinpointing the war's origins, I cannot entirely reject the long-standing argument that land alienation was a major factor. Between 1840 and 1847, an undetermined but significant amount of public land passed, at least on paper, into the hands of private developers. Haciendas gobbled up "vacant" public lands, and settled villages found themselves boxed into increasingly circumscribed and inadequate preserves. Peasants could no longer meet subsistence needs, let alone the continued tax demands of church and state.[13]

However, the simple appeal to changes in land tenure raises other questions. In transforming other parts of the world, land alienations have certainly generated local rebellions, but those rebellions have seldom approached the scale or success of the Caste War. Why rebellion here, and why rebellion of such striking success? These questions force us to explore the ways and means of the Yucatecan development, and the local and overwhelmingly rural context in which it transpired.

Yucatán's transition from peasant subsistence to commercial agriculture began in the northwest in the mid-eighteenth century and gradually worked its way southward and eastward. A consistent point of previous interpretations, then, has been that peasants rebelled when they lacked access to subsistence lands and could no longer avoid pressures by flight. But neither situation seems to have pertained exactly. Creoles had scarcely penetrated into the eastern forests, and there is no convincing reason why peasants themselves could not have continued to migrate there or to cultivate the eastern forest lands.[14] The same applies to the deep south of Campeche. The peasants were fully able to work this land with existing technology. Undoubtedly the land expropriations of the 1840s put enormous pressures on rural cultivators, but here as elsewhere, land tenure was not a purely independent variable. The pressures of the new land practices appeared within the context of specific social relationships and circumstances, which in this case favored peasant revolt to a remarkable degree.

The obscurity which covers the early national period partially results from lack of precise information about the people and institutions of the time. For that reason, I have found it necessary to say a great deal about the nonpeasant community as well. For example, we know relatively little about the church, a cornerstone of stability in rural Mexico. Existing scholarship tends to dismiss the church as weakened or committedly precapitalist or simply corrupt.[15] All too often these charges are misleading. Although one of the least studied institutions of Yucatán's early national period, the church is also among the best documented and in virtually all regards offers a key to understanding the pre–Caste War peasantry. Far more than the secular political structure, the church's parish system served as one of the key organizing principles of the countryside. Parishes divided the rural world into headtowns and outlying settlements. *Curas* (pastors) tabulated populations and ethnic distributions. Most importantly, the church provided the economic backbone of the peninsula, particularly in rural areas. In a largely pre-capitalist system of forced economic participation, church taxes comprised the principal device for prying money and labor out of the Indians. The private coffers of priests were some of Yucatán's main sources of finance and development capital, while individual clergy became formidable landowners in their own right. In all these features the church participated in the growth of agrarian commercial structures.

But the rural clergy's position was more ambiguous, both economically and politically. If rural priests funded nascent agrarian capitalism, they also perpetuated colonial tribute (in the form of peasant church taxes), while maintaining their accustomed prestige and paternal authority in an increasingly competitive milieu. They protected the Mayas in old ways but also exploited them in new ones. These ambiguities made the clergy a focal point for social tensions and later a target for peasant jacqueries. Did peasants see priests as allies, oppressors, or some combination of the two? To what extent did the colonial Catholicism instituted during the conquest, and continued after 1821, succeed in dulling peasant will for autonomy? These are only a few of the questions which need to be explored in tracing the Caste War's origins.

Similarly unexplored is the tax problem. The volatile issue of taxes remained the subtext of peasant relations with both church and state, each of which operated its own collection system. While not the material root of the peasants' difficulties, taxes were uniquely frustrating. They expropriated the farmer's wealth directly from his hands, after he had already expended the toil necessary to produce a jar of honey or a bushel of corn. Between 1800 and 1847, taxes generated more invective and spilled more ink than all other peasant grievances combined. It is impossible to overestimate the importance of this long-ignored issue in generating insurrectionary tension. For over three decades tax resistance and revolt would furnish the peasantry with ample occasions to rehearse its eventual role as a revolutionary force. In Yucatán the short-lived Spanish constitution (1812–1814) generated millenarian expectations of tax relief, even of tax abolition. Three decades of repression would fail to extinguish these expectations, and in the 1840s bitter murmurings over taxes would erupt once again, now as the language of revolution.

But there is more. None of these issues can explain the Caste War without a clearer picture of the nineteenth-century peasant community, a picture which includes not only strands of commonality, but of internal disunity and conflict as well. This is not to deny the centrality of the community to peasant experience, but only to observe that there were countervailing tendencies as well. A key argument of this study holds that Yucatecan peasant communities contained different strata of peasant interests held together not so much by a core culture transcending whole epochs, but by lines of power and authority which had evolved under colonialism. The diverging interests and aspirations of these strata conditioned their relationships to the colonial and post-independence regimes and also determined their roles in the eventual rebellion. Stated in another way, the decisive issue was not so much whether peasant villages were cohesive, but rather how internal cohesion was articulated with powers and opportunities beyond those villages. Ripples in the wider world could wreck havoc in the little community.

A key to the insurrection was the alienation of peasant elites, who were well accustomed to the benefits of commercial agriculture and the adventure of political machinations. This upper tier of peasant leadership, which included village caciques (in Maya, *batabs*[16]), lesser officeholders, prosperous peasants, and members of the Indian church staff, remained attached to certain structures of the colonial system. In exchange for their assistance in maintaining peace in the countryside, they enjoyed material rewards and social privileges which distinguished them from their fellow Mayas. The *batab* and other officeholders monopolized a disproportionate share of the peasant village's literary skills, organizational knowledge, and familiarity with creole institutions and weaknesses. They also enjoyed the traditional social status which enabled them to mobilize peasant energies: their word was sufficient to bring peasants to the town plaza. Perhaps most important of all, peasant elites controlled more material resources than their poorer kinsmen. Rebellion (at least successful rebellion) was an expensive business, and the more that rebels had put aside in reserve, the more likely they were to maintain armed struggle against superior powers. As long as Maya elites remained content, serious unrest was unlikely.[17]

The lower tier, the mass of poor Maya peasants who received little in the way of patronage from either the church or state, had a far different perspective. Maya commoners groaned under well-documented tax and labor burdens.[18] Peasants paid annual church taxes, fees for incidental church services, taxes to subsidize periodic church inspections, and taxes to subsidize mandatory catechism of their children. They also paid annual civil taxes (an updating of colonial tribute) and filled the labor rosters for state-decreed projects ranging from turning water-wheels to killing grasshoppers. In later years they provided military service, paid civil land rents on their own cornfields, and were expected to subsidize official measurements of their own village properties. Equally galling was the endless and unappeasable moral scrutiny which peasants endured, with the complex of church and state holding review on everything from marriage to personal travel to public speech. The grievances of poor peasants had always existed but remained secondary issues as long as peasant leaders and marginal creole elites were content with the larger political arrangement.

Prior to 1800 the Spanish successfully kept rural discontent under control. Spanish patronage coopted native elites, while a balance of repression and paternalism served to quiet the masses. Those rebellions which did occur were brief and localized. But once the old colonial system broke down, the status quo proved difficult to maintain. Yucatecan creoles quickly disposed of the Spanish monopoly on peninsular wealth and power. Like most decolonializing peoples, the creoles were fractious and incohesive, all the more so for their comparative poverty; their subsequent wars with Mexico and among themselves disrupted ancient customs and jeopardized many of the traditional fields of success for *batabs*. Growing disaffection of peasant elites after 1840 was to prove instrumental in undermining rural stability and ultimately in creating the conditions for the Caste War.

The years 1821–1847 caught rural society in a curious intersection of opposing tendencies. In some regards, poorer peasants witnessed the gradual deterioration of a moral economy, of understood limits of exploitation which had protected them for much of the colonial period. At the same time, however, a new impatience now colored their grievances. Troubles and disadvantages which they had borne patiently for centuries seemed intolerable now that the chance for their elimination was at hand. Peasants no less than creoles hoped to benefit from the accelerating changes of the late colonial and early national periods. They actively competed for the advantages of increased prosperity, government patronage, and material improvements such as hydraulics, orchards, and sugar distilleries. Peasants also expected (and actively worked for) the reduction or even elimination of taxes, a boon which creoles had learned to promise in the series of factional disputes beginning with the momentary abolition of church taxes and obligatory service in 1813–1814. In no small part, widespread discontent among the mass of the peasantry related to the failure of these expectations to materialize.

The contradictions implicit in the development of Yucatecan rural society reached a crisis only twenty-six years after independence. Beginning with a factional revolt in 1839, peasant expectations erupted once more as creoles recruited the Mayas with promises to eradicate church taxes. The moment of rebellion marked a collision of opposing tendencies: heightened expectations versus renewed assault on communal resources; mobilization of peasant masses versus the deteriorating prestige and economic position of the Maya leadership. The peasant elites who instigated this rebellion were only too well acquainted with creoles, their law courts, their military strategies, and their political quarrels. In some instances they were chums with prominent creoles and shared their entrepreneurial proclivities. Collectively they seemed to embody the prophetic Maya utterances of the *Chilam Balam,* which had predicted that before war would come a time when two people "tried on each others' hats."[19] Prior to the failure of the 1848 Caste War offensive they would never have considered the possibility of retreating to the forests on a permanent basis. And in the final analysis they rebelled because they had come to understand how rebellions should take place and found themselves at the precise cultural and geographical midpoint which favored their enterprise of war.

We should avoid reductionism in analyzing an event as complicated as the Caste War. For no part of this world was the development of insurrectionary consciousness a unicausal process. Land alienation was merely one facet of a larger evolution from a colonial tributary society to one based on agrarian capitalism. The transformation involved many aspects of social interchange which, while closely linked to land usage and ownership, nevertheless assumed symbolic and economic importance of their own. Were peasants free to move as they chose? What would be the conditions of their labor? Who would educate their children, and to what purpose? A more complete understanding of the Caste War's origins must therefore incorporate many related grievances and weigh those grievances as peasants themselves experienced them. Then as now, people rebelled for many reasons.

I have attempted to shift the emphasis of study as far as possible from the traditional sources. These consist of patrician historians of the nineteenth century,[20] state statistical reports,[21] Yucatecan literary journals,[22] and the accounts of foreign travelers, above all John Lloyd Stephens' *Incidents of Travel in Yucatan* (1843).[23] An unfortunate result of these familiar elite perspectives has been to emphasize peasant passivity and separateness. At the same time, I have tried to maintain distance from a recent and diametrically opposed reading, the idea that indigenous peoples such as the Mayas operated in an autonomous core culture that shared little with the outside world.[24] In my view, both traditional and revisionist perspectives encourage the notion that peasants and elites collided against one another only to bounce away unaffected—

in Eric Wolf's memorable phrase, "like billiard balls."[25] Economic rationalism often prevailed over cultural values. Those peasants best able to take advantage of new opportunities did so, *mentalités* notwithstanding, while those who could not remained committed by default to a communal ethic which provided them with moral vindication.[26] I have not avoided the traditional sources, but whenever possible I have tried to work from documentary material in the archives of Yucatán, Mexico City, and various repositories of the United States.[27] In conjunction with an emphasis on new source material I have tried to offer a skeptical treatment of many of the traditional readings of the Caste War and the social fabric which was its context. Peasant passivity, peasant homogeneity, peasant intransigence to all aspects of modernization, hermetically sealed indigenous communities and cultures, unicausal rebellion, a weakened or simplistic role for the church: we must question all these concepts.

Antonio Mais, the Tihosuco priest who witnessed the Caste War in its gestation, referred to the local peasantry as "a brutal, fierce, and audacious people." We do not normally associate the word "audacity" with peasants. And yet this accurately describes much of the behavior of the Mayas of the nineteenth century: an enterprising, competitive people as much at odds with elements of their own community as they were with the creole elites who strove to dominate them. What the documentation reveals is a rural world teeming with conflicts and contradictions. Like the poetic vision of Mateos, Yucatán of the early national period contained many voices, no one of which was destined to silence the others.

One   # A RURAL SOCIETY
IN THE NEW CENTURY

The Indians have not lost but rather gained considerably from the coming of the Spanish nation, as much in small matters as in the greater affairs.
—DIEGO DE LANDA, *Relación de las cosas de Yucatán* [1]

If it had not found in Yucatán physical and moral obstacles which have paralyzed its energies, the order deriving from the natural progress that moves societies to their perfection would have brought this province to the relative degree of prosperity that we desire.
—PEDRO MANUEL REGIL, on the social and economic conditions of Yucatán, 1811 [2]

At the dawn of the nineteenth century Yucatecan creoles lamented that the province of such potential should stagnate in poverty. Pedro Manuel Regil, deputy to the Spanish constitutional assembly in 1811, observed that any frank assessment of Yucatán ought to begin "by exposing the state of languor, depression, disesteem, and ignorance in which it finds itself." Regil and other elites believed that these deficits were the result of colonial policies that had failed to change with the times: the dead hand of Philip II still governed in the age of Jefferson.[3]

As events were to show, these criticisms were simplistic. Economic development would demand far more than the free-trade policies and the somewhat padded lists of natural resources which Regil and his fellow liberals so readily produced. But it was hard to deny that the colonial imprint lingered in most aspects of the society. Although the reforms of Bourbon Spain had stimulated commercial growth and had attacked certain traditional features of the

Americas, the wave of reform had left much of the colonial framework un-shaken. This included the political and ecclesiastical divisions of the province, the precapitalist labor conditions of the haciendas, the pervasive influence of the church in rural affairs, and the continued viability of the Maya peasant production in the face of commercial pressures. The rural society of the new century was a patchwork of the old and new, indigenous and European. It merits exploration in detail.

REGIONS

The Bourbon administrators modified but did not fundamen-tally alter Yucatán's long-established internal divisions. By 1786 the Spanish had created fourteen separate *partidos,* or administrative units. These were based on natural geographic boundaries, on the influence of the leading cities, on old colonial mission territories, and on the tribal administrative units which predated the conquest.

The *partido* of Mérida enjoyed the greatest social and economic develop-ment. Mérida boasted the oldest completed cathedral in Mexico and eventu-ally became the seat of an archbishopric which included Tabasco and the Petén. Most important of all, it had become a motor for economic develop-ment. Commercial estates producing corn and cattle sprang up in the regions which immediately surrounded it. By the end of the colonial period it was gaining the upper hand in its long rivalry with Campeche. Indeed, in virtu-ally all possible measures—administration, markets, imported trifles—Mérida functioned as the Rome of the peninsula, the hub to which all roads led and all gentility aspired. It enjoyed such curious refinements as sculptured animals used to identify streetcorners for the illiterate citizens. But the city also had an underside of poverty and abuse. To dispose of the excess of man's uncared-for best friend, the city kept a salaried dog-killer whose records, improbably enough, have survived two centuries of political upheaval. At the same time, there were unsalaried killers for Mérida's growing mass of underemployed hu-mans: epidemics, thriving on the town's unsanitary conditions, would ravage Mérida in 1825 and 1835. Later, this same *lumpenproletariat* would provide fodder for the peninsula's many coups and revolts.[4]

Along the western coast from Campeche to Sisal lay the two districts of the Camino Real (Alto and Bajo), so called because of the highway stretching between the peninsula's two principal cities. The cities of the Camino Real—particularly Umán, Chocholá, Maxcanú, Becal, Calkiní, and Hecelchakán—prospered from the commerce and travel passing between the two. But until

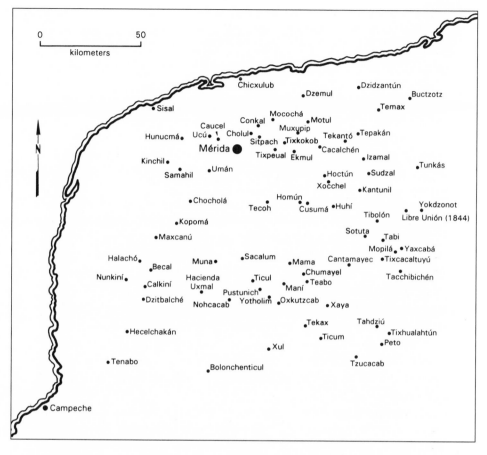

MAP 2

well into the 1850s Sisal, Mérida's port city, consisted of little more than pole houses with wattle-and-daub siding.[5]

The second colonial metropole and *partido* was Campeche. Smaller and less affluent than Mérida, this coastal city had walls to guard against the pirate depredations of earlier times. Campeche's feud with Mérida traced back to rival military captains of the seventeenth century and, indeed, to far earlier times, to the competing Maya centers of Kan Pech and T'ho. But the decline of Campeche's logwood trade was dampening economic growth here; at the same time, Mérida had come to dominate most of the new Havana markets, leaving Campeche to trade with the stagnant Mexican mainland. Far from serving as a healthy commercial rivalry, the Mérida-Campeche rift was symptomatic of colonial Spain's systematic underdevelopment. Internal infrastructure was lacking; poor roads and transportation kept the cities at a two-day's journey until the introduction of a sixteen-hour coach trip in 1840. *Campechanos* (those from Campeche) prided themselves in escaping the Indian influence which tainted Mérida, but this belief was more illusory than real, for the population remained heavily Maya. Campeche exercised the same relationship as Mérida over its surrounding countryside, in this case composed of Maya fishing villages and a few inland farm communities. On Saturday the beggars of these parts poured into town to receive distributions of alms. Campeche also became famous for the museum of the Camacho brothers, two priests who preserved a wide variety of archaeological and historical curios. Architecturally, the city consisted of one-story residences and a few more impressive public structures, all separated by narrow streets, and was painted so immaculately white that some believed the glare was responsible for the many *bizcas,* or cross-eyes, found among the citizens.[6] This was Campeche, "sweetheart of the sea."

The area now comprising the bulk of southern Campeche state was then divided between the *partidos* of Bolonchencauich and Sahcabchén. Sugar ranchos—small private commercial properties which for the most part are not recorded in the extant documents—would in time come to occupy these two regions. Development here began somewhat later than in the sugar regions further to the east, but contemporaries believed that in time its sugar production would reach parity. Despite their proximity to Campeche, the polities of these two *partidos* identified themselves with the *meridanos,* who absorbed the bulk of their commercial products.[7]

Another rural area to profit from Mérida's markets and commerce was the Costa *partido.* This covered the middle northern coastal area and extended southward to include Tekantó and Izamal. Lacking the soil depth and rainfall necessary for sugar, Costa lent itself to both corn and cattle. In time, its dependably dry climate would commend itself to henequen production, and Costa would become an epicenter of the porfirian economy. Izamal was able to grow as both a religious cult center and as a midpoint in the commerce between Mérida and Valladolid.[8]

Further to the east, Valladolid possessed neither the economic dynamism of Mérida nor the coastal sophistication of Campeche. Built on the Maya *cenote,* or limestone well, center of Sakí, it remained the virtual end of eastern development, a frontier town where retrograde elites lorded over the surrounding Maya tributary villages. The province was the former stronghold of the Cocom Mayas, who still persisted as a patronymic but no longer gave evidence of constituting a tribe per se. Underdevelopment was pervasive here. Quality of roads fell off from even the middling specimens of the west. In the town plazas Mayas performed dances and ceremonies which were only remotely Christian. The creoles, intent on their old conquistador status, took little interest in the public schools, hospitals, civic improvements, and progressive societies which were to flourish in the capital. Until 1821 the Franciscans maintained two Valladolid convents; however, these were neither beacons of progress nor keys to Indian control, but merely the vestiges of long-decayed power. Valladolid *partido* held few estates, most of these lying around the city itself and only a few in the domains of the surrounding towns. But despite its underdevelopment, several features would commend Valladolid *partido* to future generations. It contained the village of Ebtún, now famous for the extant litigation papers of the colonial era. Even more famous was Chichén Itzá, one of the world's great archaeological sites but then a private hacienda. Finally, the city would witness an armed uprising still celebrated as "the first spark of the Revolution" of 1910.[9]

The *partido* of Tizimín, north of Valladolid, faded into thinly populated forests of the extreme northeast. Mérida's economic strength failed to benefit Tizimín to any appreciable degree. The inhospitability of the terrain had limited settlement here, and Tizimín's principal growth would not occur until the 1840s, when rapid privatization of the *partido*'s public lands, taken by a small planter elite and by foot soldiers in Yucatán's civil wars, would make Tizimín a locus of conflict and unrest.[10]

The Sierra, or Puuc, was the old territory of the Tutul-Xiu tribe which had collaborated with Montejo in the conquest. It reached from villages immediately south of Mérida to the edge of a rainforest which extended into northern Guatemala. The deeper, richer soils of the Sierra commended it to production of fruits and sugar, but the greater rainfall made it too moist for henequen production and so would protect it from the cruel taskmaster of "green gold" in the second half of the century. By 1800 creole presence was strong in such towns as Ticul and Oxkutzcab and served to make the Sierra a locus of anti-peninsular liberalism.[11]

Of the two Beneficios *partidos,* the Bajos occupied the exact center of the peninsula and constituted the heartland of corn production throughout the nineteenth century. The name "Beneficios" apparently traced back to the early strong presence of the "beneficed" secular clergy, as opposed to a monopoly by Franciscan missionaries. Life in Beneficios Bajos centered around two principal towns, Sotuta and Yaxcabá. Both were of pre-Columbian vintage, life in the latter being focused around a prodigious if somewhat fetid *cenote.* Owing to its central location, Beneficios Bajos would suffer almost Biblical destruction during the Caste War.[12]

Beneficios Altos included the extreme southeast, its principal cities being Ichmul and Tihosuco. In 1540 the dominant clans of this region had been the

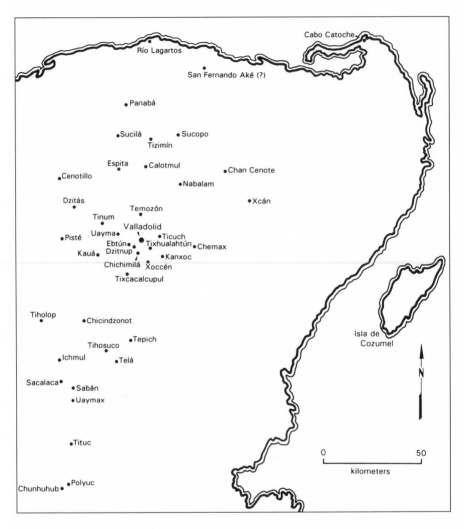

MAP 3

Cochuah, and although that particular patronymic had virtually disappeared from the name pool by the nineteenth century, others—including Pat, Chi, Chan, and Tus—had survived. Though given out in tribute grants known as *encomiendas,* Beneficios Altos remained a densely overgrown region which concealed numerous untabulated Maya hamlets throughout the sixteenth and seventeenth centuries. The peasants focused on subsistence production of traditional crops. Nevertheless, by 1800 sugar cultivation was well underway in its fertile, well-watered soils, and money-based trade both legal and illicit was common throughout. One town of Beneficios Altos, Ichmul, was and continues to be one of the great sites of peninsular religious pilgrimages, commemorated as the home of *el cristo ampollado,* or the blistered Christ, after a wood statue which survived a fire with nothing worse than a parched and blackened surface.[13]

Far to the south, and relatively isolated from other Spanish settlements, was the old fortress community of Bacalar. For Yucatecans Bacalar constituted the edge of the civilized world. It was, to borrow Joseph Conrad's phrase, "an outpost of progress," a garrison town set in the hinterlands and linked to the rest of Yucatán only by the poorest of roads and by whatever ships happened to pass into the reef-lined southeast coast. Beyond lay the Petén, conquered only a century earlier and now administered by the political authorities in Guatemala, though part of the Yucatecan archbishopric until 1865. On the Caribbean coast the Río Hondo, and an uncertain truce mediated between Spanish and British settlers, divided Yucatán from Belize. Parish letters from such villages as Chunhuhub and Polyuc suggest rough-cut settlements where stretches of tropical lethargy were punctuated by moments of crude, ungoverned violence and where Mayas abandoned their homes at the first sign of taxes or any other inconvenience. Labor shortages thus remained a recurrent problem throughout the deep south, with epidemics and hurricanes as close seconds. But the territory's lushness, its vast lands and exotic fruits, improved Bacalar in the popular imagination. Like many parts of the Yucatecan interior, it was fabled to conceal a trove of undiscovered mineral wealth. Apart from the usual tales of gold and silver, creoles speculated that the ground near Chunhuhub contained copper deposits, the smell of which they claimed to detect in airs rising from the village *cenote.*[14] These, of course, were little more than fables, and Bacalar itself remained a hinterland. But at least the undeveloped state of the fortress-town had one positive effect: the settlement escaped the hoards of beggars who overran Mérida and Campeche. It was easier for poor folk to stay in the countryside, living off such exotic indigenous fruits as *pox, pitaya,* and *ch'iich p'ut.*[15]

Prior to independence (1821) the population remained concentrated in the places that had first come under the domination of the conquistadors. Mérida, home to some 35,000 people, was the largest city, followed by the 20,000 of Campeche. But in terms of regions, the most populous place in 1806 was Sierra Alta, with 45,781 inhabitants. The coastal regions also enjoyed sizable populations, but the string of villages along the Puuc range consistently held more inhabitants. The *partidos* of Valladolid and Tizimín would remain economically underdeveloped and thinly populated until the 1830s and 1840s. However, growth had already begun along the strings of towns and villages leading to the southern interior. In the 1840s this increasing demographic shift to the south and southeast would help set the stage for insurrectionary violence in Beneficios Altos and adjacent *partidos,* areas where economic growth would outstrip the development of social and political controls.

Yucatán itself lay under the administrative control of the intendancy of Mérida. Governing individual *partidos* were the *subdelegados,* a class of political appointments whose responsibility was to mediate between Mérida and the village officials. Within each individual town the ruling figure was a magistrate known as the *alcalde* or, in smaller villages, the *juez español.* These appointments were often peninsular Spaniards, but once they had secured office, they used their power to incorporate themselves and their relatives into the local elite. They acquired revenues through various tolls and licensing fees and through internal sales taxes known as *alcabalas.* Peninsular control over local revenues inspired resentment among creoles and helped precipitate political squabbles which eventually served, among other things, to undermine rural stability and contribute to the long-term radicalization of the peasantry.

THE MAYA COMMUNITIES

The peninsula's macroregions had perhaps held greater meaning for the Mayas in older times, before the corrosive effects of *encomienda* and colonial governance had worn away the larger indigenous political powers.[16] In time regional authority gave way to an intense localism. Against this view, some have suggested that the Caste War began among the villages of an eastern tribe known as the Huits. But while the war did indeed erupt along the eastern frontier, the fact is that there was no such tribe. The name *"huit,"* originally a patronymic, merely applied to Mayas who were skilled in traveling and working in the backwoods.[17] Indeed, defined tribal structures of any sort were not particularly evident by 1800. The effects of colonialism, together with the Mayas' own tendency to migrate in search of better *milpa* land, had radically weakened tribal or extended-family networks such as the Xiu and the Cocom. If such macrostructures did play some role in Caste War organization, they were decidedly secondary to newer factors such as village political identities, regional economic interests, and even the (sizable) egos of the ambitious insurgent leaders.

For Mayas and non-Mayas alike, the most important administrative structures were the smaller and more informal units of parish and village. Between 1800 and 1847 Yucatán underwent a number of redistrictings, but the number of parishes always hovered between seventy and eighty. The parish-village construct—forced settlements from which Spanish colonizers could more easily access native labor and tribute—was largely artificial to indigenous culture. Nevertheless, over the course of centuries the village and secondarily the parish had come to be the center of Maya life.[18]

The rural parish divided into several components. Most prominent was the *cabecera,* or head town, for which the parish was named. The *cabecera* was a product of the colonial missionaries' policy of concentrating dispersed Indians into settled and more easily managed communities (*congregaciones*). These head towns served as focal points for civil and religious tributes, administrative nodes which gathered in the wealth of their surrounding hamlets.[19] Though practiced for centuries, the policy of *congregación* fundamentally conflicted with Yucatán's economic base of *milpa,* or subsistence farming, which forced peasants to change fields after a few years' cultivation exhausted the soil. The result was an ongoing struggle between peasants' tendencies toward dispersal and the centripetal demands of taxes, labor drafts, and moral supervision.[20]

Auxiliares, or secondary towns, received far less administrative scrutiny than did the *cabeceras.* At least until commercial expansion after 1821 cast an entropic effect on rural demographics, the *cabeceras* held considerably more taxable souls than did the outlying villages. To take an example from the year 1806, Tihosuco held nearly double the population of either of its two principal *auxiliares,* Tepich and Telá. Moreover, Europeans initially restricted their settlements almost entirely to *cabeceras,* leaving smaller towns in the hands of Mayas. Whereas Tihosuco was home to seven hundred non-Mayas, Tepich held only ten, and Telá had none whatsoever.[21] In part, geography accounted for their isolated character. Though some lay within six miles of the *cabecera,* others were as far as fifteen to twenty miles away. Roads to these outlying villages were no more than footpaths, while the villages' only permanent structures were their churches. At least in theory a parish minister said mass in the *auxiliar* every two weeks, but real conditions made this difficult, and peasants often complained of clerical neglect. Together these factors created troubling undercurrents in the political dynamics of outlying villages. While the *auxiliar's* peasants received poorer service at the same tax rates, and while its Maya elites often found themselves overwhelmed by the disproportionate power of elites in the *cabecera,* the outlying peasants also found themselves freer to assemble and converse without the scrutiny of the authorities. Significantly, both of Yucatán's last two great peasant rebellions began in *auxiliares:* the Jacinto Canek rebellion in Quisteil and the Caste War in Tepich.

There were other types of villages as well, notably the rancho. In Yucatecan parlance the term "rancho" had two meanings. To many the term conjures up images of the small individually owned farms of the Mexican Bajío.

These did exist, often in the dilapidated condition of the sugar rancho visited by the American traveler John Lloyd Stephens in 1841. In the more common usage, a "rancho" was a nascent village still too small to be considered an *auxiliar*. Ranchos appeared when a handful of migrant *milperos* settled on some choice piece of land. Some remained nothing more than collections of a hundred or so people; Xkuail, outside Ticul, held 117 inhabitants in 1828 and never rose far above that. Others, like Becanchén (south of Tekax), grew to formidable size with the discovery of water.[22] Yucatecans in fact had a variety of names for small, inhabited places: *"rancho," "ranchería,"* and *"sitio."* Locals applied these terms so indiscriminately that it is misleading to suggest hard-and-fast definitions.[23] To describe small, cultivated plots, Yucatecans used the terms *"paraje"* ("spot"), *"paño"* ("canvas"), *"callejón"* ("corridor"), *"tablaje"* ("plank"), and *"joya"* ("jewel"). More than one traveler was struck by the threadbare existence of these "ranchos and sitios, which may be likened to the huts and hovels of the Irish peasantry (without the starvation), or to the holdings of the Highland cotters in Scotland."[24]

Rural villages may have been corporate in some regards—much of colonial Latin America was—but by 1812 they were hardly closed and for this reason can only be called "Maya" in reference to the broader contours of population. Throughout the seventeenth and eighteenth centuries the towns of the interior had witnessed a steady trickle of Spaniards, creoles, blacks, and mixed bloods of all description. They came as priests and officials and as the owners and employees of estates. Indeed, only a select few in any town held large properties, a point evidenced by the 1811 censuses. As late as 1843, a foreign traveler in the hamlet Tabi could remark that the "few whites here, as is usual in many other places, principally maintain themselves by selling small articles, cotton cloth, and liquors to the Indians."[25]

The various communities had their own distinct racial patterns.[26] By 1814 the peninsula was still at least 75 percent Maya. Pure-blooded Europeans, whether peninsular or creole by birth, constituted 70,000, or 14 percent, with individuals of mixed blood numbering 55,000, or 11 percent. Aside from Mayas and Europeans, the most distinctive racial element was that of African descent. But the *cabecera* was the most racially mixed component of the parish. Contrary to the belief that peoples of mixed blood made their livelihoods as foremen on haciendas, they were far more likely to be found working in the small village.[27] They failed to exercise the kind of social control which the mixed-race ladinos of Guatemala did over those indigenous peoples in the nineteenth century, in part because institutions of native Maya leadership (described below) still sufficed.

Peasant insurgency in the late 1840s would drive many creoles into the cities while leaving rural areas in the hands of Mayas. This reflected the relative strength of the two groups in their respective domains. In the early 1800s Europeans still constituted an insignificant presence in the countryside. They scarcely mattered in Cansahcab and Tihosuco; only in the more Europeanized Ticul did they constitute more than 6 percent of the total population. The higher percentage of mestizos in Cansahcab may have reflected closer proximity to Mérida and older Spanish populations; stronger mulatto presence in Tihosuco almost certainly reflected the influence of Belize's slave society. In all cases, however, Mayas were a clear majority. Despite the growth of the rural economy, the European population still remained heavily concentrated in the peninsula's principal cities.

Here life was land. The viability of a village, and of Maya life in general, was inextricable from the lands which served for *milpa,* or subsistence farming. Acre for acre the largest component of any parish or *partido* was not titled village property or private estate but rather the vacant common lands: *terrenos baldíos,* in Spanish colonial parlance. Since the days of the Hapsburgs there had been a rent theoretically owed to the crown for the use of this property. But in actual practice Maya cultivators ignored the policy. Unless a private title existed, land was *baldío* and remained under the control of the first peasant to measure it for *milpa* and declare it his own.[28] Few issues in the coming decades proved as controversial as the fate of *baldío* lands. Yucatecan liberals, somewhat in advance of their central Mexican counterparts, attacked corporate and communal lands as an archaic vestige of the colonial economy, hence setting the conditions for a rural insurgency without precedent in the Americas. But in 1806 massive land alienation was still decades away.

Life was also the wife, or the husband. The Mayas considered marriage to be the necessary condition of adulthood, perhaps because *milpa* production mobilized the household as an economic unit. Maya peasants began looking for a spouse as soon as they reached the age for responsible labor, usually the mid-teens.[29] But unlike the predominantly male slave societies of the West Indies, Maya men and women lived in roughly equal number. Women slightly predominate in the village censuses, but this may simply reflect the husbands' practice of temporarily migrating out of the village in search of farmland. Even the hacienda neatly preserved this same ratio, for workers tended to live in family units on or near the estates.[30]

The Maya inhabitants of these communities were not socially homogenous. Above the masses stood Indian officeholders who wielded prestige and power and whose relationship to the colonial regime involved a unique set of

interests and expectations. The most important member of an Indian community, and certainly the most essential to the larger story of the Caste War, was
the *batab* (of whom I shall say a great deal in chapter 4). In precolonial days
the *batab* had been a village chief subservient to a regional commander known
as the *halach uinic*. The *batab* had wielded judicial power but had also regulated
local planting, seen to it that the priests maintained the calendar, and commanded village warriors in time of combat. The office of *batab* was usually but
not always hereditary and patrilineal. After the conquest, the *batab* stayed on
as the village chief, enjoying such privileges as (1) exemption from tribute,
(2) exemption from personal service, (3) preferment for colonial employment,
(4) permission to ride a horse, wear Spanish dress, and bear arms, (5) special
status in court, (6) a coat of arms, and (7) the title of "don." By 1800 all but
the first three had disappeared, and the "employment" had come first and
foremost to mean tax-collection duties.[31] The degree to which creole officials
took possession of this activity should not be overestimated, for *batab* tax collection, with or without the assistance of other Indian officials, remained the
norm and not the exception for the period leading up to the Caste War.[32]

For his services as tax collector the *batab* received a percentage of the revenues, usually in the vicinity of 4–5 percent. Supposing a mean parish revenue of 2,500 annual pesos, the *batab* could expect to take in 125 pesos, no small
fee for an Indian. But some did far better than this. *Curas* had enormous dis-
cretionary powers with church revenues, and some allowed the *batab* to borrow from, in advance of, his annual collection. For example, Jacinto Moo, the
batab of Sacalaca, borrowed out of the money collected for his *cura,* Fr. Juan
Tomás Brito. Moo then used the money to purchase and develop a small
property named Petulillo. However, Moo died before he could make good
the debt, and in his own will Brito stipulated that the money was to be collected by liquidating Moo's property, if necessary.[33]

The practice of using prominent Mayas to collect taxes addressed many
considerations. It was a matter of practical necessity, since the *batab* had the
necessary language skills, knowledge of the Maya community, and ability for
persuasion within his peer group. No matter how energetic a collector, a
Spaniard stood apart from the peasant community. But the *batab* was of his
people. His collections also allowed the *batab* to establish his own small niche
of power, since he served as a broker between two worlds and, if he was to be
at all successful, soon learned how to play off both sides. Finally, it created a
valuable ally for the colonial regime—provided, of course, that tax collections continued in orderly fashion. But latent in the arrangement were troubling, if still hypothetical, problems. If some political upheaval should disturb
the old tax system, then the *batab* would find his source of revenues suddenly

undermined. In the case of outright hostilities between creole and Maya, the *batab* would find that the role of broker and middleman was no longer feasible and that he would have to choose sides.

The *batab* did not work alone. Throughout the colonial era, and until the overthrow of Maximilian's empire in 1867, the Yucatecan Indian communities had their own form of authority, a civil hierarchy composed of some eight to ten of the most prominent members of the village. The Spanish used the *república de indígenas* as a mechanism for maintaining orderly control by working through indigenous middlemen. The *batab,* naturally, reigned as the head of this organization. Below him stood a Maya *teniente,* that is, a helper and *batab*-in-waiting, ready to stand in should the former be unable to fulfill his duties. Beneath him were two officials known as *alcaldes* and four of lower rank known as *regidores,* plus an *escribano* whose duty it was to record events and prepare letters, petitions, and so forth. As the occasion dictated, the *república* also appointed gendarmes and factotums known as *tupiles.* These bodies held limited power, and the functions they did perform remained under various checks and scrutinies. Meetings took place in the local *casa real.* In addition, the *repúblicas* had to apply to the *subdelegado* for funding their minor needs, including such basics as tables and chairs for their meetings and a strongbox with lock and key where they could store village documents.[34]

Succession in the offices of the Yucatecan *repúblicas* remains poorly understood. Indeed, it is doubtful that a unified pattern prevailed across villages. The most accurate statement we can now make is that in the early nineteenth century the *batab* was a fairly prosperous man in his community, usually with a proven record of ability in working with creole officials. There also appears to have been some degree of family succession, since patronymics reappear not only in the *batab* role, but also in other levels of the civil hierarchy. One example of this is the Pat family, who occupied numerous offices in Tihosuco between 1821 and 1847, eventually assuming leadership of rebel forces during the Caste War.[35]

Political and economic pressures had been testing the cohesion of the Maya village and its institutions since the eighteenth century. In 1811, for example, the *batab* and *república* of Calkiní came to loggerheads over coerced labor drafts for the sugarcane fields, with peasant villagers rousted out to work on sugar estates as far as eleven leagues away. The Maya had found impressed labor on cornfields acceptable if undesirable; but the same could not be said for sugar mills (*ingenios*), where peasants objected to the low pay, the skimpy rations, and above all "the harsh and dangerous work of breaking [cane] in the mill" ("*la tuerza de caña*"). The complicity of the *batab,* José Canul, forced lower-ranking members of the *república* into positions of leadership in order to resist the Calkiní system.[36] This episode was neither the first nor last skirmish between village and estate, nor the first intracommunity schism inspired by external pressures and opportunities. But the Maya *repúblicas* continued to function despite decrees of abolition in 1812 and 1820, and their letters, protests, and other communications remain instructive features of the historical record.

Other village institutions had not fared as well. Nominally converted to Spanish Catholicism, the Mayas focused most of their devotional energies on officially sanctioned religious sodalities known as *cofradías,* organizations which maintained a communal ethos and helped raise funds for the village through sale of its products. In the 1780s the bishop's office in Mérida began consolidating control over its rural parts by auctioning off the properties of the *cofradías* and by impounding the local village treasuries known as *cajas de comunidad*. Less successful were repeated calls to end pre-Christian religious practices, promulgate the Spanish language, and regather the Mayas in permanent and, from the tribute taker's point of view, more accessible communities. In order to put the colonies on a paying basis, then, Bourbon reforms such as these uprooted local bailiwicks, centralized control over colonial affairs and introduced changes conducive to commercial production; in so doing, they also alienated local Maya elites and other upwardly mobile individuals, reducing their role in political and economic affairs.[37]

The problem of expanding colonial pressures naturally leads to the subject of resistance and rebellion. Both phenomena are deeply rooted in the colonial situation, and in this regard Yucatán was no different. The first wave of indigenous resistance came in the decades immediately following the conquest, only to meet savage suppression at the hands of the Spanish.[38] A collection of smaller episodes related to the collapse of Spanish authority in the southeast after 1600, with rebels and runaways able to take advantage of the still-independent kingdom of the Petén Itzá. A tax revolt in Chichanhá in that same year seems to have been a final manifestation of the seventeenth-century power vacuum. Only in 1695 did a concerted Spanish war effort succeed in conquering the Petén. But the inhabitants, far from surrendering, simply dispersed into the tropical rainforests.[39] All in all, however, the often-detailed episodes of unrest after 1548 were fairly minor events; they erupted not as attempts at systemic overthrow, but rather from problems of personality, local quarrels, or small adjustments in the status quo.[40] Nor was revolt a viable proposition. The usual fragmentation of rural colonialized peoples prevailed, and while "Maya-ness" may have existed as a cultural concept, it certainly did not as a political entity.

The possibilities and limitations of colonial revolt were underscored in the episode of the Jacinto Canek uprising of 1761. Eighteenth-century economic and social transformations generated tensions which sparked the largest peasant rebellion in the colony's history, the Jacinto Canek uprising of the remote interior village of Quisteil (no longer extant, but then located between Yaxcabá and Ichmul). The underlying material tensions of the revolt were rooted in the events of October 1761, when the largest commercial estate in the region, the hacienda Huntulchac, suddenly changed hands. The Carrillo family had owned the property for well over a generation, but on October 23 sold it to the *cura* of Sotuta (Diego González), who had already acquired numerous properties in Beneficios Bajos. Huntulchac had become a significant cattle property and constituted the main economic influence over life in the village. For peasants, the sudden change threatened to upset standing arrangements between villagers and *hacendado*.[41] Tensions were therefore running high in November 1761, as the Mayas of Quisteil were celebrating their annual fiesta. The spark occurred when several of the carousers murdered a non-Maya merchant for refusing to sell them more liquor. Villagers then ran out the local minister. A clumsy show of force by authorities succeeded only in fanning the riot into a rebellion which encompassed villages throughout central Yucatán.[42]

Present at these jacqueries was one Jacinto Uc, not a villager at all but a Maya born in Campeche and educated by Franciscans. After a falling-out with his religious mentors, Uc abandoned hope for a more prestigious or lucrative career and instead became a baker. The fact that he was in Quisteil at all has lent credence to stories that Uc was touring the countryside to propagate a rebellion; but it is more likely that he was a rootless soul, at home neither in the town nor in the country, one of those marginalized individuals ideally suited for the role of radical leader. According to the account of a Jesuit who interviewed captive rebels, Uc had made impassioned speeches to the Indians, denouncing Spanish abuses, calling for insurrection, and promising a magic oil which would resurrect Indians killed in battle. Whatever the truth of these tales, Uc and other leaders seized on the energy of the rebellion to assume the lofty titles of ancient Indian heroes. Jacinto Uc became Jacinto Canek, after the last Maya king of the Petén. Francisco Uex, the chief of Tabi, now called himself the New Moctezuma. As would happen eighty-six years later in the Caste War, peasant rebellion became a means by which at least some Maya elites reasserted traditional claims to leadership and social ascendancy. But neither the appeal to lost Maya grandeur nor the initial peasant victories prevented Spaniards from putting down the revolt. Canek was taken to Mérida, tried, publicly tortured, and executed. The Spaniards hung and quartered eight other leaders, then whipped the additional captives, cutting off their right ears before releasing them. Between executions and military campaigns more than six hundred Mayas perished in this episode.

The various accounts of the Jacinto Canek rebellion contain gaps and inconsistencies. It is at least clear, however, that Quisteil did exist. Within seventy years of the revolt Maya peasants had reinhabited not only the village, but also the remains of the hacienda Huntulchac, where much of Jacinto Canek's drama had transpired. Peasants of the 1820s were anxious to prevent the long-abandoned hacienda from being revived as a cattle operation, and it is probable that similar anxieties contributed to the 1761 incident.[43] But whether real or fictive, downplayed or overstated, the Canek uprising left its mark on the Yucatecan consciousness. It was an occasional topic of Yucatán's literary magazines in the 1840s and seems in some ways to have justified draconian responses to organized Maya resistance. The revolutionary regime of the twentieth century adopted Jacinto Canek as a forerunner of everything from the Caste War to the Madero revolution; and as an art motif, Canek's torture has become the Yucatecan "Passion of Christ," particularly in Fernando Pacheco Castro's astonishing murals in the Governor's Palace. In 1830 dissident liberals likened conservatives to the Spaniards of 1761 by joking to one another, "You look like someone from Quisteil, old timer . . . they may cut off your ear!"[44]

HACIENDAS

As the Canek episode suggests, one of the more vital economic formations of the society in 1800 was the "hacienda": a private, landed estate varying in size but certainly larger than the tiny peasant plots of the Mayas. The haciendas incorporated their own social world composed of peons, tenant farmers, and hired hands, all ruled by the lordly owner and his immediate staff. The system had mixed purposes. On one hand, it made the owner a nascent capitalist by allowing him to take advantage of expanding commercial markets without the meddling of crown officials. On the other, it cast him as the feudal lord, with a resident force of dependent labor and a potential for self-sufficiency which cushioned him against hard times.

The evolution of these properties is now fairly clear. Toward the later seventeenth and early eighteenth centuries, the small cattle-raising operations known as *estancias* evolved into commercial haciendas, or large landed estates specializing in the cultivation of corn, cotton, rice, livestock, and sugar. The original impetus for haciendas was scarcity: the prolonged decline of the Maya population, together with Yucatán's many droughts, hurricanes, and other disasters, caused ongoing need for food in the colonial cities. Like such regional capitals as Guadalajara, Mérida and Campeche had grown steadily over time, and their urban markets now exerted continuous demand for products of the countryside. The need to control peasant labor, now made scarce by death and dispersal, also necessitated control of land, while the relative lack of Maya resistance created the opportune moment for land privatization. Spaniards enlarged their estates by piecemeal purchase and by moving operations onto unworked adjacent areas, thus establishing partial property right through the simple precedent of usage. For those willing to endure the bureaucratic hassles and a considerable outlay in fees and bribes, the colonial system allowed them to consolidate heterogeneous holdings through a reassessment of property titles known as a *composición*.[45]

Yucatán's soil and climate did not accommodate the traditional grains of Europe, but corn and cattle, whether alone or in combination, proved successful. Crops of secondary importance included honey, wax, chiles, citrus, and cotton, all of the old standbys of colonial tribute. Rice enjoyed some success along the Champotón River. The more well-watered soils of the southern and southeast interior invited sugar cultivation, principally directed toward the distillation of *aguardiente,* or "burning water," a crude, popular rum which brought tears to the eyes and comfort to the heart. Even though a royal monopoly on distillation restricted expansion of the Yucatecan sugar industry, haciendas specializing in the cultivation and processing of sugarcane (*ingenios*) were already proliferating by the late eighteenth century.[46] Private stills and *trapiches,* or small sugarmills, also abounded, and by 1812 the backlands of the peninsula were already knee-deep in *aguardiente*. Most towns had their grogshops and "fiesta stores." Moreover, the social havoc which spun out the liquor business was profitable in its own right. When town councils began to form after 1812, the towns took the opportunity to fine public drunks; creoles paid fines, while Mayas had to perform forced labor in cleaning the town plazas and sundry other projects.[47]

The principal type of hacienda labor was the *lunero,* or as some preferred to say, *lunesario*.[48] As Mayas returned to familiar territories after the mid-seventeenth century, they found that Spaniards had now established a base of property within the parishes. The hacienda provided attractive benefits at costs which were initially low, since for one day's labor the peasant could now obtain secure access to the estate's land and water. Originally the *lunero* received no wages but simply contributed a day's labor each week (on Monday, or *el lunes,* hence the name) for the right to work a portion of the estate's property. However, by the turn of the century economic growth had caused estate owners to expand their workforce, doubling the amount of services required while placing workers on wages and into debt peonage. The *hacendado* also assumed responsibility for paying his laborers' church taxes. In some cases this burden led *hacendados* to anticlerical agitations. But the actual state of affairs was more complicated, for many *hacendados* continued to use church taxes to their advantage, paying them in advance and thus gaining rights to forced peasant labor.[49]

In addition to resident peons, the hacienda also drew upon the services of *jornaleros,* salaried day-laborers who lived in some nearby town or rancho. The *jornalero*'s work included not simply the ubiquitous *milpa* farming, but also such artisan skills as carpentry and masonry. His wages were inversely proportional to the quantity of available labor. In populous regions the competition for land and water was fierce, and *hacendados* were more likely to pay low wages or to rely on estate peons. But in remote backwaters like Bacalar or Carmen the *jornalero* could hope to take in as much as 5–6 reales per day. *Vaqueros,* or cowboys, constituted a type of labor formation somewhere between peon and *jornalero;* resident on the estate, they nonetheless worked for wages and not for the right of access to *milpa* land. Finally, to supervise this heterogeneous collection of workers, the *hacendado* relied on a managerial staff. This included a *mayoral* who supervised the *vaqueros;* a *mayorcol* who supervised *milpa* farming; and a *mayordomo* who oversaw the operations of the entire estate and generally functioned as the *hacendado*'s proxy.[50]

At least until the sugar boom following 1821, haciendas remained concentrated around Mérida, Campeche, and Izamal. But the size of hacienda populations varied considerably. In Yaxcabá, 1828, only three of the thirteen haciendas held more than 58 people. The smallest, Kopteil, had only 13, while Kambal had 169. Assuming that the estates tended to take on larger labor forces over time, it seems likely that in 1806 few haciendas would have employed over fifty workers. Moreover, we seldom find many large haciendas within a single parish. More typical was the pattern of one or two estates with many workers, alongside of numerous other smaller properties with no more than ten or twenty.[51]

The hacienda also varied widely in terms of material size and value. Most were small in terms of acreage and heads of cattle, in no way rivaling the micronations of northern Mexico. Nevertheless, they represented a considerable expansion over the fifty-*mecate* (4.9 acre) plots of the Maya peasant. Huhbilchén, property of Diego de Rivas, was worth some 4,200 pesos. Probably the best estimate of a range for a late colonial hacienda value in Yucatán is 2,000–6,000 pesos. Usually one-half of this was the land value itself, followed by livestock value, material goods, and finally the debts of the workers themselves, often duly recorded in the sales inventories in order to be passed on to the new owner.[52]

Nestled among the cattle and sugar estates was another type of property: the peasant estate. Whether private or collective, corn or cattle or diversified production, these functioned as delicate miniatures of creole enterprise, rising alongside it and availing themselves of the same fledgling markets.[53] Peasant estates appeared wherever creole haciendas and *estancias* emerged. Developed properties were rare in both Champotón and Bolonchencauich, and each contained only one estate titled to a Maya or a Maya *cofradía*.[54] But even the small rice producers who worked along the Champotón River included a handful of Mayas. In more developed regions the patterns were clearer. In Costa and Valladolid, peasant estates comprised 14 percent and 12.7 percent respectively. In Camino Real and Sierra Baja, where roads and other infrastructure were more developed, and for whom Mérida's magnetic urban market lay closer at hand, as many as one of every four properties was in the hands of Maya.

Maya peasant estates were not evenly distributed throughout. In any given *partido,* about half the parishes had only one or two peasant estates; a quarter had none whatsoever. The remaining quarter contained a cluster of estates, some villages with as many as sixteen in their vicinity. These clusters almost invariably reflected larger patterns of development, with a corresponding multitude of creole haciendas as well. Thus, the mini-estates proliferated around such well-developed communities as Dzidzantún, Nunkiní, and Motul. But other late colonial towns, such as Temax and Valladolid, left no record of individual Maya properties. The reasons for this are unclear. Perhaps the Maya entrepreneurs benefited from a peer group more willing to share expertise, or perhaps the clusterings represent the retention of wealth in kinship groups. Indeed, in some parishes the estates lay almost entirely in Maya hands; we find peasant landholders as numerical equals or majorities in Becal, Bolonchén, Chumayel, Mamá, Nunkiní, Sacalum, Sicpech, Tepakam, and Xaya. With the possible exception of Nunkiní, these were secondary communities, smaller in size than the first order of rural communities and provincial capitals.

Less is known regarding the rice-growing properties of Champotón. Despite the very small number of landowners in the official census of 1811, three years later there were as many as 124 rice harvesters in the district, approximately 10 percent of them with Maya surnames. These harvesters were perhaps estate workers;[55] but it is far more probable that they were either sharecroppers and tenant farmers or else small producers working tiny properties along the riverside.[56]

Peasant properties tended to be smaller than creole haciendas, at least according to the only available measure, the number of cattle. While creole properties tended to run at 150 or more cattle, peasant properties operated on a far less imposing scale, usually less than fifty. Those in the market for horses need not have bothered to shop among the Maya, since they hardly ever raised them. We find notable exceptions to both these tendencies: Buenaventura Uxul of Mamá had 261 cows and 12 horses, making him the second largest rancher of the parish. In Nunkiní, Maya properties contained 511 of the 1,630 livestock head (31.3 percent). But for the most part, the peasant was content to work as a nickel-and-dime entrepreneur, operating fewer and smaller estates. These same properties doubtless produced corn, but on this score there are no figures.

Who owned these estates? A handful were *cofradías;* many others, simply listed as estates *"de indios," "del común,"* or *"del pueblo,"* were doubtless of the same or similar nature. But two-thirds of the identifiable peasant properties were privately owned.[57] Individual peasants seldom appear to have owned multiple properties, although the practice did occasionally exist.

To no surprise, *batabs* were among the Mayas who owned land. This practice merely continued precolonial customs of private lands for the Maya nobility and gained reinforcement by the imposition of Spanish property concepts. At least in some cases the size of estates exceeded what a single individual could work, thus placing the *batab* into an employer-worker relationship with other Mayas. A much-quoted observation from an 1813 ethnography suggests that these relationships qualitatively differed from those of Spanish estate owners and Maya peons. *Batabs* generally provided better treatment predicated upon a sense of community and redistribution of the fruits of mutual labor. One option for *batabs* was to pay their workers in specie at above-market rates; the other was to sell them produce from the estate at below-market costs. The latter practice was especially popular during times of shortage. In 1813, market corn prices ran at twelve reales per *carga* (160 pounds), while workers on *batab* estates paid only four reales. And, the ethnographer went on to report, "They feed them abundantly with this very Christian maxim, 'This comes from the sweat of my brothers, and it is not right that they should eat it at great cost.'" *Batabs* also loaned commoners money "when they are satisfied that they are not taking it on false pretexts." *Batabs* thus recognized the expediency of sacrificing a certain degree of profit margin and loaning out a portion of liquid capital in exchange for local political support.[58]

The dramas which attended these properties, the dreams and ambitions and petty triumphs of their commercial lives, are now lost to the historical record. They sprang up beside the larger estates like so many mushrooms under the shade of an oak tree. Creoles themselves seem to have discounted or ignored them and in sketchy accounts of country life were inclined to assert that the Mayas did nothing but plant corn. (A more typical phrase, "attend to their own labors," left room for the peasant commercial producer.) But the tradition of peasant-held private property would never entirely disappear. Village elites would continue to cultivate their lilliputian haciendas and in time would follow the creoles down the path of public land alienation as well.

Spanish and Maya property had different patterns of cohesion over time. Although the Spanish estates were fairly young, their owners enjoyed a useful legal device for keeping them intact: the *mayorazgo,* or entail. For a stiff fee the *hacendado* could place two-thirds of the estate in permanent entail, making it an inalienable and indivisible heritage, mainly passing through the eldest son. While a handful of creole families could afford to set up *mayorazgos,* for peasants the practice was flatly impossible. Instead, the Maya landowner left property to be divided by his numerous heirs. Another option was to leave a single piece of land to be held in common; this practice had approximately the same result, for it invited the heirs to subdivide into tiny plots or to sell outside the community.[59]

A few cases will serve to illustrate the overall dynamic. In the early 1800s Juan Tomás Tus, *batab* of Caucel, acquired a piece of land known as Kucab, which he and his wife stocked with mules and horses. In his will (c. 1813) Tus left the land to his wife but divided the livestock among his children.[60] Another example was that of Miguel Uc. Among the possessions which Uc held at the time of his death was a *sitio* named Santa María, near Hunucmá. Uc's will is now lost, but in subsequent documents his heirs described the property as having an irregular curved shape. Difficulties arose from the fact that Uc bequeathed Santa María to be held in common by no less than twenty-four descendants, a bewildering assortment of sons, daughters, grandchildren, and in-laws. To utilize this heritage the heirs decided to sell. In 1831 they hired a surveyor, then sold off Santa María parcel-by-parcel to creoles. Eight years later Lucio Coyi, "*vecino* of the town of Hunucmá" and one of the original heirs, sold yet another portion of Santa María (273 *varas* by 253 *varas,* for twelve pesos) to José María Castillo, a *vecino,* or neighbor, of Yaxcachalbac (near Hunucmá). Even with these transactions, family members continued to own mini-plots bordering on the sold property.[61]

One final case of multiple inheritance leading to sale dates from the year 1825. Pedro, Eusebio, and Mauricio Uh found themselves the coinheritors of a property located between Homún and Xocchel. Rather than attempting to subdivide the land or to work it communally, they instead sold it to Fr. Pedro Antonio Martínez. The land was of varied quality, since half sold for twelve pesos and the other half for five.[62] These inheritance patterns had the effect of weakening the Mayas' control of wealth, contributing both to peasant immiserization and, in the larger picture, to growing insurrectionary tension.

THE PARISH CHURCH

Just as villages and parishes were the social units most familiar to the average peasant, the local priests were the Spaniards with whom Mayas had the most contact. The number of priests active in Yucatán at any given time probably never exceeded three hundred, but because of their enormous role in the period leading to the Caste War, they deserve a close examination.

The central figure of the rural church staff was the *cura,* or pastor. Priests competed for the position by submitting applications and resumes and participating in subsequent examinations demonstrating their knowledge of theology and Latin (though not Maya). Distinctions between high and low clergy were fleeting. Rural and urban priests rotated frequently enough to be acquainted with both worlds. Even for those living their entire lives in Mérida, a half-hour's journey on horseback took them into a world that was heavily indigenous. Nor was Mérida, for all its cosmopolitan pretensions, a citadel of unadulterated European culture; as late as 1790, over half the total population (27,829) was still Maya.[63]

Curas retained their office for as long as they chose.[64] Several forces limited term of office. The most effective of these was death itself, for life in rural Yucatán was harsh. The *cura* enjoyed many privileges over the peasants which heightened resentment and, in the larger picture, contributed to insurrectionary hostility; these included better housing, better and more abundant food, and exception from manual labor. But rural priests also fell victim to many of the chronic maladies of the backlands, including malaria, typhus, cholera, venereal disease, and intestinal parasites, and complaints of ill health formed a leitmotiv of their correspondence.[65] Beyond this, a certain number of pastors chose to move on to more lucrative assignments. Finally, there were personal reasons to relocate: transfer wiped clean the slate of enmities and personal conflicts that had accumulated during one's tenure.

Once in office, the *cura* became the master of his domain, and only the most outrageous behavior could cause his removal. This was the case when Fr. José María Salazar was relieved of his post as *cura* of Hopelchén in 1804. Salazar had become so old and senile that the peasants themselves were maintaining the parish churches at their private expense and initiative. Moreover, the *cura* had provoked "continued complaints" by neglecting to pay his Indian servants.[66]

But for the most part, long curacies tended to be associated with harmonious relations between priest and peasants. Doubtless the two phenomena reinforced one another. For the *cura,* the surest way of keeping the peace was to reach an understanding with peasant needs and preferences. This implied negotiable tax rates, acceptable collection methods, a ready hand for community assistance, and a blind eye to the frequent violations of Catholic orthodoxy. It was the gift of flexibility, as much as any iron fist or mystifying chants, which made for a long and successful career among the peasants. The Maya too seem to have preferred long-lived *curas* who stayed in office year after year. In most instances the peasantry maintained a precarious existence, typically striving to minimize risk; personnel changes threatened unpredictable times, particularly when the case in point was the all-important office of *cura*. The preference for lifetime tenure was undoubtedly a vestige of colonial and even precolonial days. In 1848 Maya rebels negotiated a treaty establishing two presidents, one creole and the other Maya, each of whom was to serve for life; their demand was not so much hubris as an extension of long-standing peasant experience.

One *cura* whose career epitomized these tendencies was Raymundo Pérez. In 1804 Pérez, still a young man, fell into a long and public dispute with peasants in his backwater Tabascan parish of Macuspana. Grievances centered over allegations that Pérez demanded uncompensated domestic service and extravagant food contributions. From the peasants' point of view, the worst indignation was having to hunt alligators to satisfy Pérez' demands for tribute. The rumpus which followed these charges forced Pérez to abandon Macuspana for the curacy of Hoctún, outside Mérida. It also forced him to rethink his way of dealing with human beings. After a period of adjustment, whose nadir came during the 1813–1814 tax crisis, Raymundo Pérez seems to have adopted a more diplomatic touch with the Hoctún peasants. We find his name mentioned in a petition of 1837, in which the Maya signators cited him as an example of fair tax collection. Though now largely forgotten, Pérez used his years in Hoctún to become one of the most wealthy and powerful individuals on the peninsula. Here Pérez served as *cura* for the next thirty-nine years, moving into semi-retirement in 1843 and living on in the parish until his death thirteen years later at the age of eighty-eight. He served in his office well into the 1850s and may have played a role in muting insurrectionary tendencies within his own parish.[67]

In addition to the *cura,* most parishes employed various ordained assistants known as *tenientes,* or ministers. A *cura* seldom hired more than one or two ministers. As opposed to the *cura,* who pocketed whatever was left of peasant church rents once expenses had been paid out, the minister worked on salary. The slightly later evidence of 1828 reveals annual ministerial salaries of 240–300 pesos, while *curas* in middle-level parishes might expect to clear five or six times that much. We occasionally find reference to a *coadjutor,* an assistant administrator somewhat above the minister in status but still his equal in salary. Some parishes also had scribes, musicians, and archivists who did occasional work for small pay. Ministers stood at the absolute bottom of the ecclesiastical hierarchy. They amounted to little more than itinerant workers who labored in a parish for a few years before local conflicts, or the hope of a better position, drove them on again. After a year or so, the minister would only begin to grasp the multiple conflicts, factions, and ancient grudges—to say nothing of the subterranean world of pre-Hispanic beliefs—which characterized these seemingly tranquil farm towns. More often than not he was the *cura*'s enforcer, a collector of fees and confiscator of idols.[68]

Social differences between *cura* and assistants were important. The system functioned smoothly as long as the assistants could aspire to their own curacy. But an obstruction in social and institutional mobility had the potential for embittering this sector of the priesthood—numerically far greater than the *curas* themselves—and bringing them into sympathy with the radical demands of local creoles and peasants. This tendency revealed itself time and again during the politically troubled decades before 1847.

Finally, each parish supplemented its ordained ministry with a Maya religious hierarchy in which prominent peasants served as caretakers to the church and assistants to the priests. Literature on the Maya communities of highland Chiapas and Guatemala have described "classic" civil-religious hierarchies as consisting of alternating service in lay and religious organizations, but there is no evidence that this was the case in nineteenth-century Yucatán. The two realms of secular *república* and religious staff appear to have been separate. However, since we have virtually no clues as to the backgrounds and identities of the religious helpers (who left no documents of their own), the conclusions must remain tentative.[69]

The Maya religious staff consisted of two basic tiers, each with a variety of offices. Uppermost was a group of paid and relatively skilled assistants, specialists who constituted unique professions within the peasant community. The *sacristanes mayores* were professional acolytes whose duties were to assist in serving mass and to care for church ornaments. The upper tier also included the *fiscales de doctrina,* who taught church doctrine to Maya children. Finally, there were the *maestros cantores,* who sung at masses and other religious services. According to documents from Ichmul, the *maestros* sang every Sunday, Thursday, and Saturday, as well as on holy days and specially contracted masses.

The lower tier consisted of multitudinous unskilled assistants who acted as gravediggers, musicians, extra singers, and general help. (We have no record of what instruments the Mayas played, although guitars, violins, and pre-Columbian log drums certainly existed in the remotest villages. Tekax enjoyed the services of an organist, although the individual's race is unknown.) The *cura* of Izamal used a living peasant to play the role of mechanical clock-striker in the city's turret clock![70] In 1815, Tihosuco *cabecera* employed two *sacristanes ma-*

yores, four *fiscales,* and forty assistants. All work was done on a rotational basis, since each week the pastor required only one sacristan and three assistants. *Maestros* and *fiscales* worked more or less regularly. In their off-time the other members of the staff worked their *milpas,* "the common occupation of all Indians."[71]

One important issue in terms of the coming social upheaval was the salary of the Indian religious staff. Whatever else the church hierarchy may have been, it was also a means of patronage whereby these rural churches established a base of support. In this regard we find a sharp difference in the interests of Maya specialists and general assistants. The latter simply appeared for periodic labor service as in any other form of corvée. The upper tier, however, drew real material benefits. Like the *batabs,* the *sacristanes, fiscales,* and *maestros* enjoyed exemption from church taxes, an exemption also valid for the wives of these officials. *Sacristanes* and *cantores* enjoyed a percentage from their participation in ceremonies like baptism, marriage, and special masses. Similarly, the *fiscales* took in a percentage of what was known as *doctrina,* or a contribution of eggs and castor oil which peasant children brought when they gathered at the church door for catechism.[72]

Salary was important to these Maya laymen. Despite occasional claims that no church paid its staff, we do know that the Tihosuco *maestros* received an annual stipend of fifteen pesos, while the *maestros* of the parish auxiliaries took in a combined sixteen pesos. In addition, the upper tier received "various perquisites and regalia of dress," indications of the prestige values common in peasant communities. Other samples from the existing fragmentary evidence suggest that the Maya religious hierarchy expected and even tried to increase the material reward they received for their services. Numerous Mayas serving as *fiscales* and *maestros* in Cholul petitioned unsuccessfully to be exempted from civil taxes, while peasants of Yaxcabáb (a small settlement near Peto) complained that the *fiscal* of their village had retired for lack of salary.[73]

During the heyday of church rents in the colonial period, this class of professionals remained a bastion of support for the rural status quo. But in the 1840s, as Yucatán's ecclesiastical tax system began to deteriorate, the religious staff lost one of its major incentives and thus became a locus of parish discontent. This fact carried troubling implications, since *curas* depended on amicable relations with peasant leadership in order to maintain stability.

PARISH REVENUES

Despite the growth of commercial agriculture, church parishes continued to base their incomes on numerous extractions on the peasantry, the first and most important revenue being the obvention (*obvención mayor*), a head tax imposed upon adult Mayas of both sexes. The obvention was a device created by the Franciscans. Because of the Indian exemption on tithes, the regular orders of the sixteenth century had to cover their expenses in some other way. The Franciscans always maintained the fiction that these were *limosnas,* or alms, spontaneously given to the church. However dubious, this claim exempted the friars, at least to their own minds, from opening up the matter to review by the state and the secular orders. Rather than imposing an adjustable tax like the tithe, the Franciscans held the Indians to a strict obligation: in 1800, 12½ reales annually for men and 9 for women. Those subject to the obvention tax were males from the ages of fourteen to sixty and women from the ages of twelve to fifty-five.[74]

Late imposition of fixed-rate taxes has been identified as a leading factor behind peasant revolts of the nineteenth century in Southeast Asia.[75] But in Yucatán the practice had existed from the moment of spiritual conquest, and more than one priest would become addicted to "the mellow liquor of obventions," as a critic would later call it. This form of tax threw all the risk on the peasantry, who had to place the obvention before all other concerns, and who could escape it only by death, flight, or short-lived rebellion. The obvention remained one of the most hated features of peasant life. Its coming is recorded in that encyclopedia of sorrows, the *Chilam Balam,* or Maya book of prophesies, alongside of fire, famine, and pestilence.[76] Conversely, the fixed-rate tax minimized risk for the Franciscans. They enjoyed a steady revenue with largely accurate projections of future earnings, so that they could plan and budget in advance. This practice, as much as any advantage in zeal or education, accounted for their extraordinary success in the sixteenth and seventeenth centuries, but it also provoked endless tensions among the peasantry.

Whatever the relative justice of the system, it was clearly profitable. In 1803 and 1804 the average rent of the Yucatecan parish was somewhere around 2,500 pesos. The most lucrative parishes lay in two regions. First, there were the *cabeceras* along the Camino Real: Calkiní, Hecelchakán, Umán, and Kopomá. In addition, a group of affluent parishes lay in a string extending southeastward from Mérida into the Sierra Alta: Ticul, Oxkutzcab, Tekax, and Ichmul. These trade routes apparently succeeded in drawing peasants through the promise of urban markets, social interchange, and supplemental earnings. Not including the rents for Mérida and Bacalar (which do not appear among the parish inspections, known as pastoral visits, for 1803–1804), obventions were annually yielding some 166,000 pesos, enough to cover the price of a fully operational cattle hacienda in each of the sixty-five *cabeceras.*[77]

Other significant sources of funding included the minor obventions (*ob-venciones menores,* also known as *derechos de estola*). These were clerical fees charged for incidental religious services. Mayas did not have to pay for routine acts of worship like confession or communion; but any religious service associated with an event of life-passage, such as baptism, marriage, and burial, required payment. Mayas also paid for commemorative masses. Minor obventions brought in only about 10 percent of the funds generated by the religious head tax.[78]

Like all Spanish priests the staff of Yucatecan parishes enjoyed income from private endowments known as *capellanías*. The terms of these endowments stipulated that in exchange for a sum of investment capital, whose interest would support the priest, a wealthy Spaniard would receive posthumous prayers and masses in his name, thus hastening his soul's passage through the fires of Purgatory. The returns on this principal were private monies and were not pressed into the parish account. Records on *capellanías* are extensive. Among the most common documents in the Yucatecan collections are priests suing to collect on *capellanía* loans. It appears that as many as half of the parish priests in 1800 were thus endowed, with an average principal of two thousand pesos.[79]

The tithe represented the non-Indian contribution to church finances. This was a 10-percent cut on all forms of agricultural production. Shortly after the conquest of the New World, the Spanish crown exempted Indians from tithing for a period of time. The eventual imposition of this tax on the indigenous peoples was different in each region; the Yucatecan Maya, however, never paid the tithe. Officials consistently worded the instructions so as to exclude the fundamental indigenous products—corn, beans, honey, wax, squash, and so forth—while concentrating on lucrative, creole-controlled businesses like cattle ranching. There were two important exceptions to the Indian tithe amnesty, however. The first was a special class of titled Maya known as the *indios hidalgos,* for whom obligation to the tithe reflected one's status as a quasi-Spaniard. Tithes also applied to money generated by Indian religious organizations or *cofradías,* since they raised commercial products.[80]

There remained still one more source of revenues. An important feature of rural Yucatecan development was that *curas* developed extensive hacienda properties of their own, becoming, in effect, another part of the agrarian bourgeoisie. Exactly when this practice began is unclear. Legal documentation relating to priest-owned haciendas dates from the 1720s, but by 1800 the practice was common in all parishes. The reasons are not altogether mysterious. Yucatán's Franciscan monopoly dominated rural obventions for an inordinately long time, leaving the secular priests to find alternate sources of income. Relatively small for the first two hundred years, the secular clergy grew up as an extension of the *encomendero* class, often brothers who failed to inherit the family property. As the *encomenderos* gradually shifted to hacienda practices in the eighteenth century, the secular clergy shared these aspirations and accompanied them.

By 1821 priests were formidable men of property. Consider, for example, Fr. Miguel Antonio Estrada. In his 1817 will, Estrada listed no fewer than nine haciendas, all in the region of Conkal. If the number was exceptional, the basic phenomenon was not. Priests were also in the vanguard of sugar cultivation. When José Gouyoun, *cura* of remote Chunhuhub in Beneficios Altos, died in 1814, he left one hundred *mecates* (9.8 acres) of sugarcane, canoes, mules, one hundred pounds of copper for distillation mechanisms, and the mortgage on "a shed of aguardiente." Fr. Juan Tomás Brito of Sotuta owned forty *mecates* of sugar and the mortgage on a distillery in Tecoh. Although *curas* often did own haciendas within the confines of their own parish, priests who served as administrators in the cathedral in Mérida also owned rural estates, and absentee landlordship was a common practice among this class of rural entrepreneurs. Clerical hacienda ownership increased, not diminished, in the coming decades.[81] And despite repeated waves of anticlerical politics, the elite families of Yucatán continued to place members within the church establishment.[82]

It was the combination of family networks and access to liquid capital through peasant rents which linked the priest with commercial enterprises like sugar cultivation. The history of Fr. Miguel Cabañas illustrates these mechanisms of economic development in a remote Mexican region. Cabañas arrived in Hopelchén in 1800, accompanied by numerous dependent relatives, including an aged mother. In order to support this collection Cabañas began to set up loans for commercial development, the most favored recipients being, of course, his own family members. One brother-in-law used Cabañas' money to invest in a still which would make *aguardiente* out of locally produced cane juice. (Royal prohibitions were no impediment to the determined entrepreneur.) After the distiller's death in 1807, the operation passed to another brother-in-law named José Baqueiro, but he in turn died three years later, leaving it to his widow (the priest's sister), Dolores Cabañas. For reasons unexplained Dolores Cabañas "lost" her sugar crop for the years 1810–1815 and was thus unable to succeed as an independent producer; she moved back to the house of her brother and appointed him manager of her financial affairs. So empowered, the priest proceeded to rent the distillery to other local cane growers. In 1815 jealous neighbors accused Fr. Cabañas of having operated an illegal distilling operation for nine years, to a total profit of 5,400 pesos. But since he had not performed the distillation himself, Cabañas argued that he was not responsible.[83]

The case of Fr. Cabañas documents the way that capital remained concentrated within close family networks. Central to these networks was the relative who had entered the priesthood and who was thus able to draw in liquid capital through taxes on the peasantry—acting, in effect, as an economic battery which stored up wealth and periodically discharged it into the system. As economic development proceeded under the liberal policies after independence, these same exclusionist devices allowed creole entrepreneurs to monopolize new resources and markets, marginalizing the aspiring Maya elites and creating a class of insurrectionary leadership.[84]

The economics of the parish intermeshed with the Mayas in an intricate manner. Church taxes were a business of volume, so that a collector's profit depended on his ability to effectively pressure the indigenous masses. After the two obventions had been summed, the *cura* deducted ⅐ for the *fábrica,* a fund used for the maintenance of central operations in Mérida.[85] In addition to this, the *cura* also had to pay his staff, usually at the rate of three hundred pesos for every minister. Next came the pension fund, a minor deduction averaging somewhere around 1 percent. *Curas* also listed small deductions for operating expenses such as paper. Of the sum that remained, the largest deduction was the *cobranza,* a fee which went to the pastor's tax collectors, usually Maya elites whose loyalty related directly to this patronage. The *cobranza* does not appear to have been a set rate, but fluctuated from place to place. The collectors in the parish of Tekax picked up 15 percent for their work, although this was clearly a group salary and gives us little idea of individual earnings. Elsewhere we find individual salaries of 10–11 percent, while in Homún, scene of a later tax revolt (see chapter 3), the amount was as low as 4 percent. The remainder was the *cura*'s as the profit from his office.[86]

How did the peasants of 1806 pay their church taxes? A portion came through forced donation of agricultural produce. In nearby Guatemala these donations were known as *raciones;* the term does not appear in Yucatecan records, but the practice was common enough. The amount of tax obligation met by payment in kind probably varied according to place and circumstance. In 1815 the peasants of Yaxcabá donated half a *carga* (80 pounds) of maize and one *almud* (13.3 pounds) of beans at harvest time, each of which was worth one real; "in time of want" (such as the war-induced grain shortages in late 1846 and early 1847) they found themselves compelled to give three reales in place of the two crop donations.

However, most evidence suggests that peasants paid the lion's share of their obventions in hard cash. Accounts of Mayas using chocolate beans as money

TABLE I   *Parish Revenues of Tihosuco, 1818*

Type of Payment	Value in Pesos	Percentage of Major Obventions	Percentage of Total Revenue
Major obventions			
Cash	416	62.3	34.5
Species			
Wax/honey	71		
Chickens	39		
Corn	35		
Beans	35		
Chiles	35		
Thread	20		
Salt	17		
Subtotal	**252**	37.7	20.9
Minor obventions			
Baptisms	31		
Marriages	25		
Masses	9		
Subtotal	**65**	**na**	**5.4**
Musiles	80	na	6.6
Remainder from previous year	392	na	32.5
TOTAL	**1,205**	**100.0**	**100.0**

Source: AHAY, "Cuentas de fábrica del curato de Tihosuco compresivas desde 23 de marzo hasta 30 de abril de 1827."

are misleading, for while such beans were common in small transactions, peasant communities also expended large amounts of coin money for church taxes. Though peasants had pittances of money, available coins probably went to larger official transactions like taxes and legal fees. In an 1844 legal investigation from Chichimilá, a Maya who had witnessed two men brawling over a card game was able to specify the amount of money on the table, explaining that "although an Indian he was accustomed to having money and to seeing it." But the comment was clearly misleading: given the number of peasant grievances over issues like wages, tallies of hacienda exit papers, and, above all, taxes, it is clear that peasants used and understood coin money.[87]

Detailed parish inventories from Tihosuco, 1818, provide clearer information on how peasants paid taxes (see table 1). Of their total yearly obventions (668 pesos), the peasants of Tihosuco paid the majority (62.3 percent) in cash.

The remainder was paid through combined donations of corn, beans, chickens, thread, wax, honey, salt, and chiles. Obventions in specie also constituted the plurality of total parish revenues. By contrast, a mere 77 pesos, or 6.3 percent of total parish revenues, came from minor obventions. Finally, Mayas paid a small additional church tax called the *musil,* intended to defray the cost of pastoral visits.[88]

Money came into Yucatán from foreign purchases of agricultural commodities, initially from Seville and later from such ports as Veracruz, Tampico, Havana, New Orleans, and New York City. Peninsular businessmen regularly trafficked in sums of several thousand pesos. Peasants themselves made money by hacienda labor, domestic service, laundry, selling crops in the towns, and by artisan trades such as bricklaying, well digging, and candle making.

There was also the curious enterprise of *koché.* In this system, a type of rural taxi service, six or eight peasants carried travelers through the countryside on palates.[89] Not everyone used *kochés.* Rather, their clientele was heavily weighted toward the old and the infirm, as well as the indolent foreign traveler. In the sprawling northern parish of Tizimín, for example, one minister rode circuit on horseback for nine years, a mode of travel made preferable by the fact that horses were swifter and less quarrelsome than the native porters. When rheumatic illnesses made riding impossible, he continued his twenty-six-league journeys by *koché,* until those same maladies forced his retirement eight years later.[90]

Donations of produce often exceeded what the priests could actually consume, a point which served to heighten peasant indignation. In fairness to the fathers, however, three factors probably kept food surplus from reaching this peak. First, actual donations undoubtedly lagged behind projection, a result of inability or simple unwillingness to pay, while in famine years payments ceased altogether. Second, a certain amount would have been lost through spoilage, pests, and so forth. Third, the fathers may have set aside some of this grain for charity, since each parish had its indigents. Food doles in times of crisis could easily exhaust the surplus of the previous year's bumper crop. These mitigations aside, however, it is clear that forced donations spared the priests from using their own salaries to pay board.

SUMMING UP

This was Yucatán on the eve of the new century. Old tributary devices like the hated *repartimiento de mercancías* had been abolished. Others, like *encomienda* and mercantile trade restrictions, were gradually disappearing as well. In their place had come the commercial hacienda. But despite a half-century of change, the colony still retained many of the features which characterized rural Latin America prior to the Bourbon reforms. Local peasant governments persisted, and rural Yucatán was still Maya.

While ideas of economic liberalism were incubating in Mérida and Campeche, two sectors of the society remained rooted to the older colonial traditions. The first was the rural clergy. On one hand, the church structure was well on its way to economic diversification within the tolerances of society. In addition to serving as banker, the entrepreneurial priest was now a property owner as well. His land was typically in the northern center of the peninsula, one of the small cattle ranches catering to the demand for meat and leather goods in the urban markets or on the sugar plantations of Cuba. Well aware of the success of Cuban sugar, and connected through trade and loans with the island planters, priests had also begun setting up small sugar mills in the less-developed southeast. On the other hand, the Yucatecan clergy retained a commitment to tribute. Head taxes, payment in crops, church fees, personal service, and donations by school children remained the rural church's undergirding.

The second bastion of conservatism was the upper tier of peasant society. The *batab*'s status derived from his ability to broker between Maya needs and Spanish demands. In addition to the status he drew from these activities, he also took in his livelihood from church taxes. As long as these taxes existed, and as long as the *batab* collected them, he would remain an ally of the old colonial system. Similarly, the prestigious *sacristanes, maestros,* and *fiscales* expected real material benefits for their association with the church. Because both the loyalty of peasant leadership and the integrity of the church's parish structure had been fundamentals of rural society, their interests could not be jeopardized without provoking hostility and unrest, and perhaps violence, in the countryside.

But the years between 1800 and 1810 were relatively quiet. Yucatecans fought no wars, suppressed no rebellions, suffered under no ruinous factionalisms. Their wrangles with pirates and Belizean interlopers were largely behind them. Peasants gathered the corn. Priests carried out rites and ceremonies and tallied the parish accounts. Cattle grazed on the haciendas. The shrewdest observers could hardly have guessed that within ten years the long colonial calm would end and that Yucatán would begin its descent into decades of political turmoil and peasant revolt.

| *Two* | # THE RETURN TO PAGAN ANTIQUITY |

Every day the insubordination continues to increase, until they reach the point of insurgents.
—PEDRO GUZMÁN, *cura* of Uayma, 1813, remarking on the attitudes of local peasants[1]

The Indians fled from the church as though it were a gallows; entire hundreds fled to the mountains, if not to return to the pagan adorations of their antiquity, then at least to live in the freedom of corrupt conduct, without religion, without culture, without civility, without laws and without the delights of human society.
—Rural *curas*, on the peasant initiatives of 1813[2]

The year 1808 may have been a quiet one for Yucatán, but the same was not true for Spain. Far away, on the other side of the Atlantic, events were stirring which would forever change this backwater colony. In May of that year Napoleon Bonaparte sequestered the Spanish Bourbon monarchs and installed his own brother Joséph to rule the Iberian peninsula. The turbulence of these dramatic events rippled into all corners of the Latin American colonies, even to the land of the pheasant and deer. While Spanish loyalists battled their French occupiers and struggled to implement their own constitution, Maya peasants seized upon the confusions of the colonial regime to strike out against elite hegemony. Their initiatives, petty compared to the Napoleonic wars to which they were linked, were nonetheless unprecedented here. For a time the Mayas threw off elite dominance and boldly asserted their own social and economic demands. Brief though the incident was, Yucatecans would never entirely put it behind them. The crisis of the years 1813–1814 first taught the peasants about organized resistance and laid the groundwork for future agrarian revolt. It was the Caste War's first rehearsal.

ECONOMIC AND POLITICAL BACKGROUNDS

A half-century of economic growth had preceded the constitutional crisis. Since the installation of the Bourbon family in 1700, and more particularly since the reign of Charles III (1759–1788), Spain had implemented a series of reforms designed to put its colonies on a paying basis. These structural changes and the resulting economic growth had stimulated competition and initiative among all groups of the countryside, including priests, landowners, and the urban merchants and professionals whose wealth came directly or indirectly from the proceeds of Yucatecan agriculture.

Initially most of the economic and political maneuverings were confined to elites. As part of the legacy of Spanish colonialism, the rural parishes suffered from conflicting legal domains; for example, the age-old conflict between secular versus clerical authority in judicial matters still cropped up on occasion. This was the case when the *cura* of Hocabá shielded Bacilio Noh, a peasant who had allegedly murdered his wife, from the extradition claims of the *subdelegado* of Beneficios Bajos.[3] But rural social conflicts failed to break down into simple patterns. Secular and clerical authorities could also be allies and kinsmen. Fr. Juan José Barrera of Peto was the brother of José Alejandro Barrera, magistrate in the nearby village of Tituc. The two worked as partners in a sugar rancho, *trapiche,* and distilling apparatus located in Chunhuhub, until falling into quarrels and litigations over rights of ownership.[4]

Perhaps the deepest potential for conflict lay between a parish's two greatest powers: the *cura* and the *subdelegado.* The point of contention between them was almost invariably control over peasant labor and loyalty. But rather than falling into a single pattern for all parishes, relationships between *curas* and *subdelegados* evolved over time and were informed by such features as the tenures and personalities of the people involved. The career of Antonio Solís, *cura* of Peto, provides an example of a career running the spectrum of these changing relationships. During his long (thirty-year) tenure, Solís acquired considerable influence over the Maya peasants, as well as considerable property in the process. Prior to the 1813 crisis he had managed to work in concert with civil authorities. But the arrival of a new and headstrong *subdelegado* named Liborio Anteguero upset this arrangement. With Solís now in his seventies and near retirement, it seemed an opportune moment to challenge the *cura*'s supremacy in the parish. Anteguero staged a series of confrontations in which he accused the *cura* of interfering with peasant labor allocations. This dispute in turn mirrored another conflict, the shifting of labor needs from tribute to coerced labor on commercial estates. Solís' enormous wealth and prestige could not fend off the changing times; as if possessing a sense of the timely exit, he drew up his will and died.[5]

The dawning spirit of competition also touched peasants. Previously Mayas had resisted the encroachment of large estates on village lands, but increasingly they found themselves in competition with other peasants, villages with other villages. Hence, in the extensive records of Ebtún, a Maya village near Valladolid, one recurrent theme is the land dispute between Ebtún and the nearby village of Cuncunul which occasioned a process of charges, countercharges, land occupations, and seemingly endless review of titles.[6]

Economic quickening had brought determined peasants, now hungry for alliances, into new relationships with the Spanish elite. Seeking patrons among the gentry had always been a peasant strategy, but it now became all the more crucial as rival villages squared off over disputed and increasingly valuable lands. In November 1811 the *batabs* of Tixcacaltuyú and Tacchibichén formed a string of alliances to help them in their long-standing property dispute with the village of Tahdziú. The *batabs* solicited José María Domínguez, *cura* of Tixcacaltuyú, who in turn persuaded one of his own kinsmen, the military captain José Luis Durán y Domínguez, to act as their legal council.[7] Peasants did not compete on equal terms with other rural elites in these episodes but were nonetheless active participants in the quest for control of rural resources.

For many creoles the most problematic feature of the late colonial years was the monopoly which peninsulars and their immediate allies held on highly lucrative appointments, and on church and state affairs in general. Key positions reserved for the Spanish-born included not only the governorship, but also much of his administrative staff, together with the intendancy's military command and many of the positions of *subdelegado* and local judgeships. Ironically enough, in 1812 the constitutional government had appointed as governor an adherent of Spanish monarchism, Brigadier General Manuel Artazo Torre de Mer. Elderly and indecisive, Artazo was doubly confused by his role as colonial proconsul for a once-absolutist empire now moving toward reform. His inability to decide where his loyalties lay ill-suited him for dealing with the controversies which were to come.

Peninsulars also monopolized the highest positions of the religious hierarchy. We only need to point to Pedro Agustín Estévez y Ugarte, who had assumed the Yucatecan bishopric in 1797. Born in the Canary Islands, Estévez y Ugarte had spent his formative years in Grenada and had brought with him an

entourage of staff assistants from that province. Although a visionless care-
taker much like Artazo himself, Estévez y Ugarte was also a political survivor
who would hold his seat well past independence until his death in 1827. Colonials were far more reluctant, at least initially, to violate church sanctity by
expelling the bishop.[8]

Policies regarding colonial revenues also generated conflict. Integral to the
system of peninsular control was a series of taxes and revenue-generating
practices which restricted free enterprise and soaked the small creole business
class. With or without open ports, Yucatecans paid a 1-percent import tariff
and a 2-percent export tariff on all commodities except basic foodstuffs and
minted silver. The Spanish crown continued its ancient tobacco monopoly,
while in order to protect the rapidly developing Cuban sugar industry, it
maintained exclusive right to sell *aguardiente* (always a popular commodity) in
the Yucatán peninsula. Local Spanish magistrates of the northern coast controlled the lucrative salt business; salt itself carried a stiff exportation tax of
two reales per *fanega* (1.6 bushels), roughly one-third of the total value. Spanish officials appointed agents to govern commerce along the Palizada River
and turned a blind eye to the agents' practice of charging selective and often
extortionate tolls. The internal transportation and sale of corn remained under the control of the *subdelegados*. In practice this amounted to private taxes
imposed on the corn supply to major cities like Mérida and Campeche. Finally, the colonial bureaucracy also drew off the lion's share from Yucatecan
tribute. Of the 1803 collection, the Real Hacienda pocketed 69,244 pesos,
leaving 51,878 pesos for local pensioners and *encomenderos*. Figuring in additional small charges, including the cut from tithes, the bureaucracy was ab-
sorbing almost two-thirds of the provincial tribute proceeds.[9]

Equally vexing was the *subdelegado*'s control over rural labor. *Fagina,* the
practice of forced peasant labor, supposedly applied to projects of benefit to
the general public. But in reality it was the politically appointed *subdelegado*
who decided when and for whom the peasants worked.[10] Their power to direct workers constituted an obstacle to the estate owners' goal of implement-
ing greater discipline over their own labor force. Thus, at the turn of the century we find the *ayuntamiento* of Campeche, a body composed of local elites
with investments in the surrounding countryside, appealing to the crown to
limit the *subdelegado*'s authority over *fagina*.[11]

Those who dreamed of an economically vital Yucatán had still another
reason to resent the colonial system. For all its exploitations, Spain did grant a
certain degree of protection to peasant rights. Peasants enjoyed access to legal
council and to the Spanish justice system; by the end of the sixteenth century
their proclivities for litigation had become notorious. In part these protec-

tions reflected the continued need for peasant taxes and services, the understanding being that extractions on rural Mayas remained an essential component of colonial revenues. Destruction of the peasants' means of subsistence jeopardized those extractions. In part, however, royal paternalism also constituted a check on creoles, who otherwise might have assumed a too-independent hand in their own affairs.

One episode illustrating the type of restraints which colonial procedure threw upon entrepreneurs was the sale of Yaxleulá, a small property near Yaxcabá. By 1815 Yaxleulá had come into the possession of two Maya women, the sisters Leandra and Juana Kantún. José Francisco del Castro, a creole living in Yaxcabá, succeeded in purchasing the property from them for eighty-five pesos. But in so doing he was forced to endure a four-month process involving the review of all relevant Maya land titles; moreover, he was forced to submit the sale to review by the local *batab* and *república,* who eventually gave Castro permission to proceed. The sale generated no fewer than twenty documents in both Spanish and Maya.[12] The ultimate solution to such red tape was the state-sponsored alienation of public lands, a policy which would raise storms of conflict not only in Yucatán but throughout rural nineteenth-century Mexico. But the first step in the process was relaxing the legal grip exercised by Spain and its Yucatecan loyalists.

Creole disaffection emerged in two factions. First, some estate owners and their local allies resented the rule of *subdelegados* and other officials linked to the Spanish regime in Mérida. Many rural elites also resented the clergy for their success in the competitive world of agrarian capitalism. By custom the *hacendados* paid church taxes for the peasant workers on their estates. The practice sufficed in earlier times but had grown more onerous as estates multiplied in size and number. Of course, this point must be weighed against other considerations. Advance payment of church taxes also served as a legal pretext for coerced labor practices, while the church still provided a generous amount of indoctrination and social control. But these benefits were rapidly losing their appeal. For a substantial portion of the estate owners, the priest had become a cumbersome middleman who now impeded direct control of the peasant workforce.[13]

Equally important was the fact that the rural clergymen used their status, capital, legal skills, and organizational contacts to dominate access to labor, all to their own benefit. Examples of this include the running feud between Fr. Raymundo Pérez of Hoctún and Felipe Baldos, another landowner in the same parish. In a series of litigations which raged throughout the 1810s, Pérez accused Baldos of illegal land usurpations, while Baldos countered that Pérez was monopolizing the supply of peasant land and labor. Pérez eventually won the case. Though the verdict in part reflected his own superior legal expertise, it also underscored the fact that the crown, through its support of the clergy as a privileged body, at times served to uphold the rural status quo against entrepreneurial development.[14]

The second and far better documented faction was the small body of intelligencia present in the Yucatecan cities. The *sanjuanistas,* so called because they met in the rectory of the church of San Juan in southwest Mérida, were a diverse bunch who directed their discontent against Spanish political absolutism and its ideological trappings. The organization included liberal urban clergymen as well as secular men of talent: lawyers, teachers, and bureaucrats, the most capable being the multifaceted Lorenzo de Zavala, who went on to achieve fame in Mexico and Texas. Other leading figures included the lawyer Francisco Bates; a philosophy professor named Pablo Moreno, whose deistic beliefs had earned him the nickname "the Voltaire of Valladolid"; and attorney José Matias Quintana, father of the noted Mexican statesman Andrés Quintana Roo.

The *sanjuanistas* were few in number, but they enjoyed an inordinate influence as the elite of Mérida's professional class. They also proved adept at whipping up support for their positions through public rallies and the uninhibited use of a printing press, the first in Yucatán. Pablo Moreno in particular came to exercise power through his position as advisor and chief secretary to the indecisive Governor Artazo. One *sanjuanista,* the radical priest Vicente Velásquez, carried on the tradition of Bartolomé de Las Casas by advocating the restoration of indigenous autonomy, but other members of the group either ridiculed or politely ignored such enthusiasms. To some degree the *sanjuanistas* also represented, or at least allied themselves with, Yucatán's discontented estate owners; but the details of the alliance remain unexplored.[15] The club's more fundamental goals centered on political and economic power for urban creoles. Like many of the estate owners, the *sanjuanistas* resented the rural clergy for their competitive advantages, while as vanguards of the new ideology, they also despised the *curas* for their resistance to secular education and to the general tenets of liberal discourse.[16]

For creoles, however, many issues clouded the political waters and thus tempered sentiments for independence. Creoles themselves suffered divided interests; some were loyalists and occupied key positions of power. More important, it was not always clear how the colonials could survive without the material and ideological assistance of Spain. In colonies such as Mexico, indigenous peasants produced the wealth through labor or tribute. Control over peasant surpluses often required legal coercion backed up with military force;

both in turn depended on capital resources and on the assumption that creoles could effect a transition which would leave the old social mechanisms intact. The ideology of Spanish dominance had also established allegiance to authority as an absolute rule. The examples of the Haitian revolt (1791–1804) and the Hidalgo uprising (1810–1811) had already shown what could happen when creole political quarrels awakened the masses. How then could creoles separate themselves without passing along unintended lessons to the peasantry? The answer, of course, was that they could not, as subsequent instability was to prove. For the moment these considerations meant that demands for Yucatán's independence came about in slow and often contradictory motions.

But events in Spain played directly into the hands of Yucatecan discontents. With the venal and reactionary Bourbon monarchs now out of the picture, Spanish liberals convened a representative body called the Cortes, which in turn produced the 1812 constitution. As part of its bourgeois agenda, the Cortes issued decrees limiting the most important powers of the colonial traditionalists: peasant taxes and labor drafts. This furnished the *sanjuanistas* with the ideal political path. The constitution allowed them to bludgeon their provincial enemies while proclaiming loyalty to Spain and, with a little luck, to retain control over the rural peasants through the terms of estate labor.

Predictably, local officials did not rush to implement such reforms as the abolition of peasant tribute and the end of personal service. In Beneficios Bajos, for example, Governor Artazo repeatedly had to reissue the edicts throughout the first six months of 1812. But obstructions only delayed the inevitable. By April the Maya *república* of Sotuta was already making reference to the constitutional decrees in its documents, revealing that, while the reforms may have not become a common practice, peasants were aware that changes in the political system were now opening the way to new initiatives. Before the year had ended, peasant communities were receiving regular news regarding the decisions of the Cortes.[17]

The opportunity for a coup of sorts arrived on November 9, 1812, when the liberal Cortes issued a decree emphatically restating the abolition of tribute and personal service for Indians and mandating the end of all forms of racial distinction among Spanish citizens. Under an intense media and lobbying campaign by the *sanjuanistas,* Artazo was forced to acknowledge, correctly enough, that obventions were a form of tribute. On February 27, 1813, he issued his own decree to that effect. In each town, officials assembled the peasant masses and read them the governor's proclamation in Spanish and Maya. While *curas* looked on in horror, the peasants beheld a world turned upside down. Tribute, taxes, beatings, and personal service—the very stuff of their historical experience—had suddenly disappeared from this parched, forgotten corner of the earth.

PEASANT INITIATIVES

The events of the constitutional crisis raise broader interpretive issues. What is the attitude of weaker members of a society to their stronger and more privileged counterparts? What joins the two together in times of peace? And what causes their occasional conflicts, as in peasant rebellions such as the Caste War? One way of explaining why the underprivileged majority tolerate an overprivileged minority is ideological hegemony, the argument that institutions such as the colonial church impose upon peasants a way of thought which blinds them to their true interests and renders them docile subjects.[18] The difficulty of this argument has always lain in trying to interpret subaltern behavior while this hypothesized hegemony was in operation—that is, in extracting the attitudes of subalterns from the larger matrix of dominance and power. A counterview is to argue that the subaltern's docile demeanor conceals a resentment of unequal power; that subalterns defer out of necessity, but their true hostility can be read in small acts of daily resistance.[19] The significance of Yucatán's constitutional crisis is that it allows an unusual test of subaltern behavior when social structures of dominance have been partially withdrawn. The case carries implications not only for reading peasant behavior during the Caste War, but also for understanding the larger sphere of peasant rebellion.

Seen thus, the *sanjuanista* episode provides little evidence for a theory of cultural hegemony. Rather, the 1813 proclamations provided the opportunity for peasants to assert themselves along a wide spectrum of issues.[20] The first effect was that peasants withheld the hated obvention payments. They also curtailed forms of participation which did not involve money, such as attendance of mass and *doctrina* classes. In Espita, for example, Mayas abandoned the schools which the *cura* Fernando Rosado had recently opened. As a further show of resistance, local Mayas were taking leave of the village and going off to live in the backwoods. Rosado's only recourse was to send a sergeant-of-the-guard to various peasant homes, advising them that Providence would frown on those who kept their children out of school. As to the effectiveness of this early truant officer we can only guess.[21]

Ichmul, a parish in the very heart of the southern frontier, suffered identical problems. Peasants ceased to attend the *doctrina* classes. Nor were they in-

clined to provide *cura* José Gerónimo Espinola with food. Espinola's lieutenant in the satellite communities of Tiholop and Timun could not maintain
church control in that region. The parish's geographical size and large population (some seven thousand people) made it impossible for minister José
Marcos Martínez to tell how many were avoiding church sacraments. Since
the publication of the royal decree, the Maya had abruptly pulled their children out of the Christian schools, taking with them the contribution of castor
oil necessary for lighting. Martínez was still able to persuade servants to work
for him, "but not as they ought." [22]

In Tixcacaltuyú, peasant noncompliance forced the *cura* to draw three
hundred pesos from his own pocket in order to pay his staff. Moreover, economic injury combined with dissent: he now had to endure the "scant obedience, subordination and respect shown by the Indians." Nonparticipation
tended to obstruct the *cura*'s role as information gatherer, a role which had always been instrumental not only for church control but for the larger colonial
regime (even after independence, the government continued to utilize *curas* as
sources on such topics as local populations and the progress of epidemics).
Hence there were frequent complaints that *curas* had no idea where the villagers were or what they were doing. [23]

Geographically, the collapse of parish control extended far beyond frontier
regions such as Valladolid and Tekax. Izamal, one of the oldest and most
Hispanicized regions of Yucatán, also became a scene of discontent. Diego
de Landa had overseen construction the city's famous outdoor convent, the
largest in Mexico, in 1553. Since that time, Izamal formed part of Mérida's
commercial network; and in times of plague and pestilence citizens of Mérida had often borrowed its famed virgin, in reality a syncretic adaptation of
the sky god Itzamná. But despite Izamal's role as center of hegemonic colonial religion, Maya audacity surfaced here as well. *Cura* José de Jesús Texera
reported:

> *Since the right of citizenship was proclaimed for the Indians, and
> tribute was abolished for them, along with obventions, many of
> them have disappeared, and go wandering two, three, and even four
> months without attending the Divine Offices, nor do they comply
> with the precepts of Our Mother the Holy Church. Children have
> abandoned the doors of the churches, where daily they were instructed
> in the rudiments of Our Holy religion; and even though I had reme-
> died this harm with provincial elementary schools which I have set up
> in all the annexes, the alcalde . . . closed them, dispersing the chil-
> dren and influencing the Indians, in effect, so that they do not visit*

those who look after them and say mass on holy days, and that their
conditions and foods are not made known to the said priests.[24]

There was an attitudinal change as well, or at least a greater freedom in
venting long-suppressed resentments. The value-laden descriptions which
shocked elites applied to Mayas—"cavilous," "audacious," "insubordinate,"
"unruly," and so forth—implied that those Mayas were now acting with a
new aggressiveness and self-assurance.[25]

However, peasants did not confine their attacks to the clergy. They also
seized the opportunity to settle scores with local landowners, officials, and
even rival factions within the community. Without the underlying mechanism of church debt, hacienda peons found less reason to linger on the
estates. Gone too was the fear of beatings, the time-honored means of rural
discipline. In Maxcanú, for example, peasants left the haciendas to take up
residence near some water wells which happened to exist in the parish. The
exodus took place in spite of the local *ayuntamiento*'s efforts to keep them
away from the wells. Peasants also abandoned haciendas in Espita, Ichmul,
Teyá, and Tizimín. However, the operative principle here may not have so
much been hacienda flight as simple freedom of movement. While the peasants of Maxcanú fled to surrounding vacant lands, there were other cases,
such as in Ichmul, where hacienda peons opted for life in the town, now suddenly made congenial by the absence of taxes and labor drafts. Peasants were
now living where they chose.[26]

The new attitudes manifested themselves in one small rebellion which
took place in Xocchel, two miles southeast of the *cabecera* Hoctún. Conflict
here arose over the eggs and castor oil which the Maya children had given
at *doctrina* classes. Despite Artazo's decree, certain *curas* continued to demand
food and labor donations with the full blessing of the local civil authorities.
Among these was (once again) Raymundo Pérez, *cura* of Hoctún. In Xocchel
three Indians—Francisco Dzul, Nicolas Chay, and Salvador Mas—complained
to the bishop that Pérez had failed to end the practices as ordered. Pérez
justified his continued extraction on shaky legal grounds, then contacted Luis
Gamboa, the local *alcalde*. Gamboa wrote back announcing that he had punished the miscreants. He identified Dzul as the ringleader who had roused
"almost all the Indians of Xocchel into rebellion." Dzul dared to question
the authority of both the *alcalde* and the *ayuntamientos*, "saying that he
would not even allow his children to give eggs and castor oil, that the King
had freed him, and that [Pérez] and [the *alcalde*] wanted to rob him." In this
case peasant daily resistance meant expounding the belief that they had been
delivered by the distant but all-good and all-powerful king. These glittering

visions shattered when the peasants sought to practice them, but they demonstrate only too well the predominant themes within peasant culture: the inherent justice of peasant causes and the obligation of the powerful to protect and favor the weak. The Xocchel grievance also demonstrates how quickly peasants learned to manipulate the new political climate: by continuing to charge outlawed fees, *curas* themselves had become outlaws, enemies of the constitution.[27]

A second incident concerned burial fees for dead peasant children. The rumpus began with the death of the daughter of Diego Pech, a peasant from Cusumá. Pech took the body to the church for burial, but the *cura coadjutor* refused to perform the service on the grounds that Pech lacked the requisite 3½ pesos burial fee. In other times priests might well have deferred this fee, but in 1813 clerical income was growing scarce, and relations between rural pastors and the peasantry were strained. Denied credit, Pech went to Mérida and laid the dead body at the feet of Governor Artazo himself as a protest over his dilemma. The fate of the cadaver is unknown; but the village *alcalde,* incensed by the fact that a peasant had gone over his head, promptly jailed Pech on the return trip. Trivial in itself, the incident provided grist for the liberal press, which seized on it as a means to discredit the more reactionary elements of the clergy as part of their campaign to assert control over regional revenues for state and private initiatives.[28]

The question of non-peasant instigation is problematic. To some contemporary observers, the peasant resistance of 1813–1814 was the work of "jacobins," the estate owners and urban intellectuals disenchanted with old colonial strictures. Doubtless there was much truth to this. After all, the Mayas operated under the same patron-client relationships which constrained peasant autonomy throughout rural Latin America. In many cases their creole patrons were hostile to the power of parish priests, and peasant activities reflected many of those intraelite conflicts. But it would be an exaggeration to say that peasants acted solely upon the direction of their patrons—then or now. Maya villagers received all the information they needed from the proclamations which had been heralded in every town. Part of the distortion in historical reporting lies with the patrician historians, who tried to discredit peasant initiatives and who preferred instead to argue that Mayas took their motivation solely from *hacendados, sanjuanista* meetings in Mérida, and even *sanjuanista* newspapers, of which the mass of peasants were certainly ignorant. Similarly, the *curas,* operating under a self-deception regarding the loyalty of peasants and the ultimate justice of peasant-priest relationships, often convinced themselves that a conspiracy was afoot. Moreover, the rural clergy had to admit that they could not prove the complicity of "irreligious men."

Comments to this effect came from the pastors of Espita and Teyá. Bartolomé José del Granado Baeza of Yaxcabá, a *cura* who maintained a particularly long relationship with the local Maya, acknowledged that "in part it may be the effect of the influence of certain seducers, but I believe the principal cause to have been the removal of the fear of punishment."[29]

Although peasant resistance was widespread and multifaceted, it was not total. It is true that the attitudinal changes at times passed beyond mere candor and into millenarian expectation, in which peasants believed that all taxes were nullified and that all social obligations to the dominant classes were at an end. But the rural masses did not move to armed revolt, incendiary raids, or any of the wholesale mobilization found in the 1847 uprising.

Why? The non-appearance of some 1813 caste war owed to many circumstances, including geographical fragmentation, lack of arms and military experience, and the relative stability of material pressures confronting the average peasant. But it also related to class divisions within Maya society. On one hand there was the lower strata of peasant society: poor masses who surrendered their surpluses to both church and secular society. And on the other there was an elite tier which prospered in no small part from non-Maya patronage. The cohesion of these two groups in colonial times had owed not to purely Maya cultural features, but had intimately related to the presence of Spanish/creole power; when that power was withdrawn, village cohesion began to fragment.

And indeed, in this early rehearsal for rebellion, peasant leadership showed itself to be confused, opportunistic, or at best tentative. In most cases, *curas* suffered the desertion of the peasant religious staff. Sacristans, *fiscales,* and *maestros* quickly abandoned the church when traditional sources of patronage disappeared. The desertion of the religious staff was in fact a preview of the years before the Caste War, when disruptions in the parish revenue system once more alienated supposedly loyal peasant elites from the creole authorities. The link between peasant loyalty and material rewards also demonstrated itself in other ways, as, for example, in Chichimilá, where the Maya peasants rehearsed some of their later Caste War rebelliousness by refusing to provide the *cura* with uncompensated *koché* service. Only at Izamal was the *cura* able to report that "the servants of the sacristans and churches of all the *partido* still continue to serve under freedom of the law, they and also their families, and they continue receiving emoluments, despite the influence of the ill-intentioned." But Izamal, given its character as a religious supercenter appealing to all classes, had a better prospect of surviving the crisis. Desertion by the Maya religious staff was the norm, not the exception.[30] The newly liberated subalterns also pursued ancient folk religious cults with new openness.[31]

Other elites, such as *batabs* and high-ranking members of the *repúblicas*, reacted with uncertainty. In some instances the *hacendado's* loss was the *batab's* gain, as was the case in Espita, where people of a rancho owned by Pablo José Peniche were flocking to the estate of a local "wealthy Indian." But in other cases, peasant factions were openly demanding the dissolution of their *repúblicas*, bodies which they identified as inimical to their own interests.[32] Nor did the Mayas of Peto mourn the passing of their own *república*, recently dismissed for grafting off hard-earned tax money.[33] In the light of Spain's momentary power shifts, village institutions which had once seemed essential now began to look exploitative and vulnerable.

Perhaps the relative absence of *batabs* from the 1813 documentation resulted from attempts to suppress the *repúblicas*, a reflection of official discourse but certainly not of the very real status of Maya elites in rural communities. The influence of the November 9 decree on old colonial modes of organization was at most superficial. Despite the fact that the dictates of the Cortes abolished the old *república de indígenas*, in actuality these bodies continued to meet and generate documents throughout the decade. References to *batabs* also appear in Spanish documents of 1813. In all probability, it was impossible for either Mayas or Spaniards to imagine rural life without these ubiquitous middlemen. Indeed, with the sudden shortfall of revenues *curas* found it all the more necessary to cling to their remaining means of leverage, while local officials also needed to shore up their weakening grip over peasant behavior. The most privileged tier of peasant society appears to have been caught unawares by the sudden crisis. Uncertain as to how or whether to exert leadership, they retreated or tried to turn the opportunity to their advantage, as suggested by the lawsuit against the Maya *alcalde* of Tixcacaltuyú. Others resorted to inchoate protest. This was the case when the authorities of Nohcacab discovered that the *batab* of nearby rancho San José Chac spent all of his time drinking and calling up rabble-rousing meetings against all local officials. Those same officials promptly dismissed him.[34]

Beyond this, some Maya and non-Maya elites preferred to involve themselves in legitimate political openings created by the constitution. Before 1812 the residents of small towns did not enjoy the same political rights as colonial metropolites, for only Mérida, Valladolid, and Campeche had *ayuntamientos*, town councils which to some degree negotiated the rights and interests of their constituency. But the constitutional decrees allowed all towns to establish these bodies as part of the process of liberal democracy. As a result, many towns throughout the peninsula drew up *arbitrios*, or plans of incorporation, designating community assets, necessary expenses, and proposed revenues—

that is, taxes. The surviving *arbitrios* offer a guide to town features and aspirations in 1812–1814.

Who participated? While creoles dominated in matters of politics, the Maya presence was more than nominal. At least eight of the *ayuntamientos* were entirely or predominantly Maya.[35] Numerous other towns included one or two Maya signators, possibly the *batab* or some other peasant elite. At least in one case, Nunkiní, the would-be *ayuntamiento* members also happened to be Maya estate owners, a natural convergence of polity and political economy. Local Maya interests made themselves felt even when peasant elites were not immediately present. In Sihocho, which lacked any Maya signators, the *arbitrios* still contained a provision that the *batab* and *república* would be allowed to continue in their accustomed roles as tax collectors.[36]

These municipal tax proposals were largely of a piece. The towns planned to fund themselves through taxes on livestock and estates and on the ever-popular liquor stores, taxes which fell heavily on the creoles; there were also plans for a capitation tax aimed at the numerically vast peasantry, usually to the figure of six reales per year. Proposed taxes also varied according to region, conforming to the strengths of local economies. Towns along transport lines placed a rate upon *koché* users, upon hiring mule trains, and upon visitors who stayed overnight in the village. *Aguardiente* taxes were also common, an indication of how prevalent—and overt—illegal distilling operations had truly become. In Bacalar, where river travel was virtually the only travel, a tax on canoe construction seemed a good bet: one real for small crafts, two for the large ones.[37] Had the proposed tax changes taken shape as planned, with church taxes declining and reduced local taxes taking their place, the constitutional system would have meant a significant decentralization of power and resources, with locally generated monies remaining in the control not of priests and *subdelegados,* but of a broader local elite which included affluent and ambitious Mayas.

In addition to political maneuvering, Maya elites tended to work through legitimate legal channels. In March 1814, Maya representatives from five of the largest towns of the southeast interior appeared in Mérida to appoint attorneys to protect their interests. These were not small bands of twos and threes, but sizable and well-organized delegations led by members of the *república.* Yaxcabá employed an attorney to defend the interests of the village. The Tihosuco delegation sought to prosecute "Alcalde Don Francisco Reyes for violating the articles of the political constitution of the Spanish monarchy." The peasants of Dzitbalché revealed economic concerns, demanding "that the 57 pesos 1 real which D. Nicolas de la Cucba took from us be restored, along with the well and property." The inhabitants of Sacalum brought suit against the *alcalde,* Juan Barrera, for failing to observe the articles of the constitution, presumably a reference to the new prohibitions on tribute, corporal punishment, and forced service. Tixcacaltuyú demanded "that *alcalde* Don Santiago Tzeb receive the punishment he deserves for violating the articles of the constitution, and as a known despot."[38]

The suit was revealing in several ways. First, it demonstrates how quickly the rhetoric of high-level political issues filtered into the rural communities. The plaintiffs denounced Tzeb in the name of the "articles of the constitution" so recently promulgated in the colonies. Second and more importantly, it testified to the internal fragmentation of the Maya community. One faction of the Mayas, led by a *regidor,* or lower-ranking official, was assailing another party, the *alcalde.* The fact that none of the forty-five plaintiffs had the last name of Tzeb suggests that village hostilities had a dimension of kinship. The sudden upheavals of the constitutional years not only gave peasants license to abandon the old religious taxes and services, but also raised the lid from old village conflicts. High-ranking peasant village officials, men who would have had the most extensive contact with Spanish society, now found their position undercut by a weakening in support from above and a corresponding lack of support from below.

Peasants were not a homogenous class, nor should we reduce their interests or initiatives to the single demand for land. In a more accurate assessment, peasants of every level found themselves tied to many diverse interests and social institutions. By 1813 the Maya lived in a world formed by contributions of both pre-Columbian and European cultures. Economically, peasants remained tied to subsistence, but many now participated in larger commercial networks as petty grain suppliers, part-time wage laborers, mule drivers, artisans, and so forth. Even the most isolated peasant made periodic connections with his more interactive kin through local and regional markets. Religion too was a syncretism which entailed contradictory impulses: promotion of communal solidarity but, just as importantly, a connection to the money economy and a symbolic vocabulary which linked peasants of one village to those of other villages and to non-peasants who used portions of that vocabulary. These points as much as anything conditioned peasant responses during the crisis of 1813–1814. The mass of poor peasants were able to discern the inequalities of their relationship with elites and were similarly aware of the community mavericks—peasants or otherwise—who were too closely tied to the regime or who tried to exploit the new situation.

Rebellion in 1813 was thus problematic. In light of the massive rejection of the church and its various extractions, it does not appear that participation in the hegemonic colonial religion rendered the peasants docile or ignorant of their true interests. But at the same time, certain very real facts restrained massive, violent upheaval. A lack of leadership among peasant elites kept the sudden spirit of confrontation to the level of local, individual protests. Peasants also moved in too many directions: some against the *cura*, others against a hated official, still others against a rival peasant faction. Mayas retained enough autonomy to enjoy amicable relations with numerous non-Mayas and, if we are to judge from their attempts to work through such nonviolent means as lawsuits or migrations, still felt that they could act competitively within the local sphere. Finally, and perhaps most importantly, the coercive apparatus of the regime was still in power. The militia remained standing. Cracks in colonial control had yet to reach the point of true systemic failure, which in fact was the only real way in which a peasant revolt could ever have succeeded. Those inclined to revolt would have to wait three decades for such failure—less than a lifetime. For the moment, however, too many diverse interests and an all-too-real state force kept a restraint on social conflicts.

THE REACTION OF 1814

The crisis of rural instability came to a sudden and expected end. On May 4, 1814, the arch-reactionary Ferdinand VII returned to the Spanish throne and revoked the constitution. On August 26 Governor Artazo, long under pressure from conservative factions, published a decree restoring all obventions to their former state.[39] The most immediate victims of this policy reversal were the *sanjuanistas* themselves. Triumphant conservatives arrested Velásquez and paraded him through town in a spectacle of humiliation, an impromptu auto-da-fé. The three most vocal *sanjuanistas*—Lorenzo de Zavala, José Matias Quintana, and Francisco Bates—all went to the fortress of San Juan de Ulua for three dismal years.

Of more importance to the unfolding process of peasant insurgency was the attempted reaction in the countryside. "If we were now to detail individually the things which took place in the parishes of Yucatán after the reestablishment of obventions," wrote one contemporary, "there would be enough material to fill volumes." In rural areas the reversion to monarchy infuriated the peasants. But it also antagonized rebellious creoles, who tried to break up royalist public ceremonies by "expressing themselves with the crudest and most insolent words against the sovereignty of His Majesty." In Valladolid, unrepentant creoles attacked the drum-and-bugle corps which performed reveilles in the king's honor. Nor were these malcontents the hoi polloi of rural society, but rather local elites who had rushed in to assume titles of office.

Needless to say, they quickly found themselves deposed. But the hostility and resentment which the restoration provoked at all levels and among all races did not auger well for Ferdinand's continued reign.[40]

Clerical methods of reasserting control ranged from conciliatory to draconian. Some curas pretended that the episode never occurred. Others chose more punitive measures. Father Castillo of Sabán summoned the peasants to the church; after reading them both the May 4 and August 25 decrees, he abused the república members, who had been instrumental in fomenting resistance, then tore up a copy of the constitution and threw it in their faces.[41]

Personal service returned. So did corporal punishment, a disciplinary method which had found new popularity in the wake of the Canek rebellion but whose use had declined once the immediate panic of the rebellion had subsided. Others talked of putting the countryside back on a mission footing, with peasants congregating at the doorsteps of the church each morning to receive their daily tasks from the curas.[42]

However, peasant resistance did not end with the constitutional revocation. Having tasted momentary liberation, Maya communities were in no mood to surrender. It was a case of relative deprivation: old injustices which the peasants had borne with patience for centuries now seemed intolerable once the possibility of their removal was at hand.[43] Peasant reaction in Tabasco was so hostile that General Félix Calleja, then at war with Mexican insurgents, intervened to postpone temporarily the restoration of taxes. In Abalá, south of Mérida, peasants greeted the return of obventions with "such violence" that the local cura declared any further extension of peasant taxes or services to be flatly impossible.[44] However, even in cases in which elites managed to coerce peasants into submission, the sentiments of assertion and initiative loosed by the constitutional crisis continued in other forms of low-level resistance. For one thing, peasants were less inclined to accept whippings. When Teodoro Camal, second alcalde of Hunucmá, suffered a beating from the cura, he assembled an open-and-shut legal case which included the testimony of two surgeons. Camal apparently acted independently and with great indignation, since the cura insisted that "in addition to being an ungovernable Indian, habitually drunk and impudent, he is also disobedient and insubordinate." Only the timely death of the cura spared him a humiliating investigation.[45]

In hopes of hanging on to briefly held rights, one peasant strategy was to carry out campaigns of complaint and slander against rural elites such as the curas. In Hampolón, outside Campeche, the peasants accused the cura of tying one of the maestros to a pillar in the church and laying into him with one hundred lashes. Despite the evident exaggerations of the account, the complaint found its way to the desk of the governor, who commissioned an investigation. The results are unknown, which may be some indication of the accusation's validity. Nevertheless, it is significant that the peasants felt sufficiently secure and assertive to lodge such a grievance.[46]

This spirit of litigation and resistance had penetrated deep into the countryside. The Chichanhá Maya, a poorly documented group living far to the south of most Yucatecan settlements, appeared briefly in 1819 when they filed simultaneous suits against their *batab* and Spanish judge. Complaints about the former centered around high-handed tax collection. Indeed, it was not sufficiently irritating that *batab* Lucas Cocom left the parish for extended periods to loaf about in Bacalar, showing up at planting time to collect his revenues; he was now boasting that only death could separate him from his work. Peasant litigants attacked the judge for ordering illegal labor drafts on Mayas and for whipping those who chose to resist.[47] The Chichanhá complaints remind us of the fragmented quality of this rural world: peasants found themselves in conflict and competition not only with priests and landowners—the usual villains of historical narrative—but also with other elements of the community who, in the atmosphere of growing economic life, were forging links with forces outside the traditional peasant sphere at the expense of traditional peasant interests.[48]

Another way to combat the restoration of pre-1813 privileges was to deny them by appealing to the almost supernatural level of expectation. Millenarian beliefs have always provided peasants with the strength to resist colonial exploitations. Indeed, millenarian rumors did surface among the peasantry at this time. Ylario Cen, a peasant living in Sacalum, began to circulate rumors in early 1821 that all taxes had been outlawed. Although such reports were his own invention, they found a willing audience by appealing to fundamental peasant conceptions of justice. Cen's fellow villagers refused to pay either church or state taxes. The authorities brought Cen before the bench, declared him guilty of malicious rumor-mongering, and fined him six reales (half a year's church tax) to be given to the town's *ayuntamiento* for the maintenance of schools for the poor.[49]

Peasants seized on many pretexts for quarrels and foot-dragging. The church had always exempted certain handicapped peasants from the obvention, although depending on the nature and severity of their condition might still expect them to contribute in other ways. Far from placating the peasants in question, this special consideration only tempted them to bargain for further exemption, a tendency which became all the more pronounced in the wake of the constitutional upheaval. Yldefonso and Damián Pech were brothers who had been born deaf and were thus excused from the annual head tax.

With the aid of their wives ("two haughty cavilous women"), the brothers repeatedly feigned fractures and dislocations in order to avoid doing unpaid labor for the local *cura*—this, in spite of the fact that the Pech brothers could often be seen working their own *milpas*. In addition, the two "overbold" wives went to the *cura* arguing that the term "exemption" meant exemption from any fees or contributions whatsoever.[50] The argument was a noteworthy example of peasants stretching a legal point to cover all bases.

Nor did the reaction of 1814 put an end to alliances between peasants and non-peasant elites. Although the indignities suffered by Lorenzo de Zavala and the other *sanjuanistas* suggested that their experiment had failed, the strategy of building a popular base against one's enemies remained a staple of Yucatecan political life. Numerous smaller imbroglios continued to rehearse peasants in the years before 1847, accustoming them to popular mobilization and even military skills and acquainting them with the benefits to be drawn from intracreole quarrels.

One case of rehearsal which closely followed the tax crisis was that of Fr. Juan Esteban Rejón, *coadjutor* of Ichmul. Rejón had attended the original *sanjuanista* discussion groups in Mérida in 1812. After Ferdinand's restoration the church banished him to remote Ichmul, an understaffed parish whose massive Maya population participated only minimally in church-directed activities. This was particularly true of the *auxiliar* Tiholop, whose Mayas had passed their entire adult life without attending the sacraments. But if the hierarchy had intended Rejón's assignment as part of an effort to extend church control, they were seriously mistaken. Rejón quickly realized that Ichmul's lopsided power structure had alienated the peasant masses to the benefit of a small circle of creoles and their Maya adherents. It was an ideal situation for populist agitation. Rejón began organizing local Mayas for such improvements as the construction of a well for communal peasant use. For a mere parish assistant this sort of initiative was presumptuous. But Rejón's real offense was to turn against Ichmul's traditional elites, the landowners and his fellow clergymen. Rejón encouraged peasants to boycott local estates, using his command of the Maya language to explain to crowds the legal safeguards available to them and making clear that peasants were not obligated to pay above the minimum prices specified by the church for clerical services. One creole complained that, under Rejón's encouragement, "the Indians have begun to despise me. . . . He entered with a sword in hand, clashing with everyone." That is to say, Rejón warred with fellow priests as well, encouraging peasants to shake off their traditional habits of deference toward the clergy and insulting that pillar of church support, the peasant religious staff. A concerted letter campaign, including the participation of priests, landowners, and

the *batab* and *república,* succeeded in removing the troublesome *coadjutor* from
Ichmul. His later fortunes are unknown, but the parish of Ichmul, and particularly the *auxiliar* Tiholop, maintained a tradition of popular agitation which
would continue until the Caste War, an uprising in which the peasants of
both villages took an active hand.[51] Though defeated for the moment, Rejón's methods foretold the future of Yucatán.

The restoration of rural tranquility was thus difficult and in the final analysis incomplete. When the Caste War erupted in 1847, it followed decades of
heightened expectations brought on by the brief liberation of 1813–1814.
Abolition of church taxes—in effect, a return to the freedoms of 1813—provided a recruiting platform for peasant insurgents and remained a peasant goal
throughout the conflict. The crisis also proved a central experience in the
lives of future revolutionary leaders, who as young men witnessed how easily
popular resentments could burst into open confrontation.[52]

TAX REVOLTS

At the center of the constitutional storm stood the issue of taxes.
And indeed, the most common form of resistance after 1814 was tax dodging.
This took many forms: slanderous gossip, lawsuits, continued deferral of payment, and flight from the parish. All had the effect of postponing and even reducing the taxes which peasants handed over to their *cura.* Several cases merit
examination. In addition to providing a glimpse into Yucatecan rural society
in the 1810s, they illustrate peasant strategies in dealing with what would remain one of the fundamental sources of alienation leading to the Caste War.

The story of Homún epitomizes the problem of reestablishing obventions.
In 1813, Homún was a moderately large parish with a total population of
4,700, including the 1,500 of Cusumá. As in other communities, the freedom
from contributions and clerical services utterly disrupted the old social fabric. The *cura* at the time was Fr. Anselmo Texero; but the man who bore
the weight of this sudden power inversion was his *coadjutor* and collector,
Fr. Bernardo Reyes. Without his annual 5 percent commission, Reyes' income would have been low. Using the 1804 estimate of two thousand pesos,
Reyes could expect to bring in one hundred pesos annually, no great sum. In
this case, abolition of the constitutional experiment did not mean a return to
business as usual. In May of 1816, Reyes complained that "since the publication of the decree of obventions, many Indians of Homún and Cusumá have
resisted paying what they owe to my *cura.*" The sum in question was seven

hundred pesos. Reyes appealed to the intendant to command the *batab* and members of the *república* to aid him in collection. The intendant promptly complied, but in the requested message added a clause stipulating equity and good treatment for the Indians. Unfortunately for Reyes, the intendant's decrees made little effect, and the debtors continued to fall into arrears. When Texera died in late 1816, the peasants still owed him 1,171 pesos.[53]

Into this unhappy situation walked the new *cura,* Fr. Francisco Bravo, one-time philosophy professor at Mérida's seminary of San Ildefonso, an urbane liberal whose studies of cartesian science had in no way prepared him for dealing with the obstinacy of peasants.[54] Repeating the habits of the past, Bravo hired out the collection to the new *coadjutor,* Miguel Ortiz, and to cover the arrears, Bravo borrowed money from a local woman, through the agency of her brother. But the peasant debtors continued to prove intractable. Their first strategy was simply not to pay, claiming the support of the constitutional decree. When this failed to dissuade collectors, peasants adopted a new tack: they informed Fr. Ortiz that they had already paid their fees to the *batab,* Bartolomé May. The would-be collector Ortiz consequently faced contradictory testimony on one hand from the masses, whom he could not control, and on the other hand from the *batab,* whom he could not afford to alienate. As Bravo pointed out, postponing the debt long enough meant a forgiveness of sorts, since the debtor would eventually die or in many cases move to parts unknown; or if they did continue to live in the parish, various illnesses and infirmities would legally exempt them, as would age itself, since the few men who reached sixty years were not, and could not be, expected to contribute.[55]

The peasants, in Bravo's words, were "cavilous," "quarrelsome." They had instituted a campaign of slander and malicious gossip against the *coadjutor,* spreading tales that he was extorting and beating them. They constantly gathered in juntas to plan ways of thwarting the collection. While pleading poverty before the collector, they produced money only too readily for lawsuits, and when the day came to appear in court, these same peasants "studiously" dressed themselves in rags and tatters to dramatize their poverty. When Mayas did pay, the *batab* tended to graft away large portions and could not be induced to part with them. Finally, there was the problem of flight. Should the collector press too insistently for the back obventions, he risked provoking the peasants into pulling up stakes and removing themselves to some other parish. If this were to happen, the overzealous collector would lose not only the back taxes, but returns for the current year as well.[56]

The official response to these tricks varied. Fr. Ortiz had tried passing the collection to another minister, Fr. Gregorio Balladares. Bravo himself clearly favored the sanctioning of corporal punishment, for "they are never led by honor, and always by fear." But forbidden to employ the rod, Bravo wrote numerous letters to the bishop, hinting some sort of debt forgiveness might be in order. From where Bravo stood, this made sense. The long overdue obventions could not legally belong to Bravo unless his predecessor Texero had bequeathed them to him which was not the case. When Texero died, he was in debt to the *fábrica* of the church for the entire sum and left specific instructions for his executor, Fr. Bernardo Reyes, to make good the debt by collecting it from the peasants. For Bravo, then, it was expedient to write off past debts to the church hierarchy in order to collect his own rents. Naturally, the cathedral office balked at this suggestion. Its own interests lay in collecting the back debts in order to draw off its share, and its responses to Bravo continually ordered him to stand up to the peasants.[57]

Thus constrained, Bravo enjoyed little success. He reported that his minister had now farmed out collection to a local creole. But local Mayas, sensing the change of the wind, had shifted strategy as well. They now claimed that they had already paid all taxes due to the *coadjutor* Bernardo Reyes, who by this time had washed his hands of the collecting business. Furthermore, they claimed that the minister's long and frequent absences from the parish were a violation of religious duties and consequently exempted them from paying. Where no service was rendered, the implication ran, no fee could be due.[58]

At one point Bravo, frustrated by his lack of progress, filed a complaint against the *alcaldes* of both Homún and Cusumá, charging them with "lack of activity and efficiency." He simultaneously tried to circumvent the colonial administration by having a special commission established solely for the purpose of gathering his obventions. The strategy, presumably, was to allow him to cut through the mish-mash of conflicting authority and excessively broad responsibilities which characterized rural government. However, the Yucatecan government replied that it had no authority to create such commissions and directed Bravo once more to rely on the "zeal" of the *alcaldes*.[59]

Bravo pleaded to be "released from the weight which such an intricate labyrinth poses." But his words were in vain. By 1822 the conflict was still raging. By now it had spread to Cusumá, five kilometers directly to the west of the *cabecera*. There, six Mayas were writing directly to the bishop to urge that some sort of restraint be placed on Balladares. They complained that Bravo and Balladares had thrown them in the "dungeon," and they appealed to all the traditional standbys: their poverty, the hardship of separation from their families, and the afflictions of a recent epidemic which had caused grain shortages throughout the parish. Bravo's response only partially refuted these claims, but in other ways shed light upon the events of Maya community life.

He denied putting them in a dungeon and even procured a letter from the *al-calde* of Homún stating that "in this village there is no dungeon separate from what constitutes the jail." This was something of a sophistry, since it seized on the word "dungeon" when admittedly he had incarcerated them. The Mayas frequently overstated their grievances, hoping for compromise. Their adversaries understood the strategy, and it exasperated them to no end.[60]

Bravo also dismissed the claim that recent epidemics had caused shortages within the community, although here too his argument was suspicious. While there was a shortage of grain, he admitted, the peasants had exaggerated its proportions. The price had not passed twelve reales per *carga*. And in a sense, he believed, the shortage benefited the parishioners, for being something of a corn basket for the territory, Homún was able to take advantage of increased demand and could draw on outside labor to help with the harvest. The argument tended to stress the peasants in the role of entrepreneurs rather than in their simultaneous role as subsistence farmers. As usual, peasants' ability to pay taxes depended on who was doing the reporting. One interesting facet of Bravo's discourse was the information it provided about local peasant leadership. In the case of Cusumá, the "caudillo" of the six offenders was a certain Francisco Chim, described in terms which suggest social banditry. This Chim was "cavilous"—that is, we must assume, he chose to argue with the authorities from time to time. He was "a horse thief, tried and imprisoned, in past times, in the jail in Mérida for cattle theft."[61]

In 1825 Bravo and the peasants of Homún were still haggling over back taxes. By now, his worst fears had come to pass: the Mayas were fleeing in droves, a response to the crackdown on debtors. In all, some 800 obvention-payers had fled, leaving a mere 1,838, a population loss of 30 percent. Some of this flight may have come as a response to the epidemic of that year.

Feelings between the Indian population and their *cura* hardened in July of 1827.[62] At that time, Bravo assumed responsibility for liquidating the goods of the parish's two *cofradía* haciendas, Chenkuch in Cusumá and Santa María in Homún. The former had been operating as a cattle hacienda, albeit a small one, for the public auction of its herd yielded a mere 196 pesos. Livestock of the latter sold for 121 pesos. These were hardly the endearments which would bring the local peasants rushing to pay taxes. In November peasant tax resistance forced Bravo to hire a "dragoon" to do his collections. The terms were 12 percent plus expenses, a considerable increase over a *coadjutor's* 5 percent and a clear index of Bravo's growing desperation. Bravo was not the first *cura* to employ dragoons in order to expedite collections. Six years earlier (1821) the peasants of Sanlahcat, in the adjacent parish of Hocabá, had used the same methods of debt-dodging, causing the *cura* to use force against them. This particular show of force had been even stronger than Bravo's, since it employed two dragoons instead of one. The new collection force used methods that were predictably ungentle. Arriving at the house of one Marcelino Ek, they demanded his ten-real debt. When Ek could produce no more than four reales, the dragoons applied lashes, then carried him before the *alcalde*. Ek forcefully complained to the governor's office, which cautioned the *alcalde* regarding his men's use of excessive force but otherwise took no action. This final show of force served its purpose. Within a year Homún was back to some three thousand inhabitants, with a gross revenue of 2,324 pesos. With revenues back in place, the *batab* and *república* were cooperating once more; among the items deducted for parish expenses that year were 358 pesos for their services as collectors. However, many of the old debtors were now dead, while others had reached the age of exemption or had simply left Homún, never to return.[63]

The Homún tax revolt shows that Maya parishioners had their own ways of resisting elite domination when they were undergoing unusual stress. Once relieved of taxes and service in 1812, the Indians quickly seized the initiative, so that rescission of the constitution in 1814 did not mean an immediate return to the colonial norm. Given the complex business of collection, it was simple enough to play off one collector against another. Gossip and over-dramatized poverty all proved trusty weapons. Peasants resisted by litigation, charging the priests with unjust tax collection and breach of religious duty. Finally, the debtors developed methods of forcing debt forgiveness: by out-living the debt, by running away, or by simply holding out until absolved by death.

Homún established the pattern for later tax resistance. One evidence of this point comes from Tahdziú, where peasants employed similar strategies during a four-year tax rebellion in the 1820s. Located five miles north of Peto, Tahdziú had experienced considerable growth in the last decade of the colonial empire. In 1804 its income of 1,000 pesos ranked it as one of the poorest of parishes; by 1828, however, the annual rent had increased to 2,505 pesos and even after various deductions still left the *cura* with 2,147 pesos net income. The problem lay in collecting these rents. In 1821 a small nucleus of determined peasants began to withhold their obventions. The proximal cause is unknown, but the protest had an electrifying effect, for "with their example, and the hopes which the rest of the population nurses regarding the demands they have posted, the resistance has become general, and the efforts of justice in consequence useless." In this case, the rebels succeeded in gaining legal protection, including an injunction forbidding the *cura*, Fr. Miguel

González, from using force in his collections. In November 1823 González and the peasants settled on a compromise solution from the bishop, recognizing the debts but allowing the peasants to pay them through installments. However, the peasants soon found that they could withhold installments as easily as lump sums, so that when the debt was scheduled over a series of payments it merely gave them more opportunities to drag their feet. After producing the first installment, the peasants informed González that they had paid in full and now owed him nothing at all! Others chose to interpret the bishop's intervention as a blanket amnesty on all back debts, thus further hindering the *cura*'s progress.[64]

Like Fr. Bravo in Homún, González eventually resorted to force. When Teodoro Coyi refused to pay up, the *cura* expropriated and sold two of his cows in order to liquidate the debt. Other debtors received jail threats. In retaliation, the Tahdziú peasants launched complaints to the bishop. Stressing their humility in "prostrating" themselves before the bishop (and thereby reminding him of his obligation to protect them), they recited all their old grievances. Was it possible, they asked in a typical flourish, that having received the bishop's "benign decree," Fr. González should still persist in his heavy-handed tactics? That he should reject monthly installments out of hand and even threaten to dispossess them of their homes? In this case, however, González does seem to have prevailed, since parish rents reached an all-time high three years later.[65]

These cases of tax revolt reveal the wide spectrum of strategies which peasants used to resist extractions. Of equal importance, they document popular notions of justice, notions which reversed the normal social order of the "great tradition," in which officially sanctioned priests, officials, and estate owners ruled over the Mayas. The recurrent strategy was to invest some high and distant authority such as the bishop with a personal interest and pro-peasant sympathy which certainly did not obtain. The orders of this infinitely just sovereign were thwarted by the wicked intermediaries who ruled the poor in the sovereign's name. In a related vein, peasants interpreted the bishop's orders selectively, almost intuitively, as their needs dictated. Correspondence arriving from Mérida, even if it was only a simple letter of inquiry, gave rise to reports of tax amnesties, favorable legal decisions, and so forth.[66] In addition to promoting tax evasion, this type of selective popular reporting also succeeded in infuriating the *curas* and extracting, as it were, a certain measure of revenge. Far from isolated incidents, the tax rebellions in Homún and Tahdziú reflected popular sentiment throughout the Yucatecan countryside.

INDEPENDENCE

The *sanjuanista* episode had ironic conclusions. Among other things, it taught the clergy that revenues and social power depended on the increasingly unreliable support of imperial Spain. Consequently, the more ambitious and insightful conservatives began to insinuate themselves into the liberal party; their strategy was to gain control over the party which would dominate Yucatecan affairs when a breach with Spain became necessary. Crossovers included Francisco de Paula Villegas, ex-*cura* of the wealthy parish of Hecelchakán and now promoted to San Cristóbal in Mérida. Another new liberal was Raymundo Pérez, whose sudden conversion generated sarcasm for years afterward. Thus, when imprisoned *sanjuanistas* returned to the peninsula and to political life in 1817, they found that many of their former adversaries had become allies.[67]

The reorganized liberal party did not have to wait long. An army rebellion forced Ferdinand to reinstate the constitution on May 4, 1820. Among colonials this turnabout revived memories of 1813 and an ungovernable peasantry.[68] Forces now fell into place for Yucatecan independence. The liberal party had come to represent a broad coalition of local and regional interests. After a decade of rural insurgency, central Mexico itself everywhere hailed a bonapartist general named Agustín de Iturbide, whose Plan of Iguala promised to uphold the rights of church, army, and oligarchy in a sovereign nation. The new Yucatecan governor, Juan José Echéverri, realized that political forces now favored separation, and rather than resist the change, he offered his own services as leader of the new nation. Yucatecans politely declined: local elites had waited too long for power to accept a foreign head. Thus, after months of conspiracy and intrigue, the Yucatecan congress declared its independence on September 15, 1821.[69]

Political arrangements in Yucatán made concessions to almost all parties. Most peninsular Spaniards made their exit, and the mechanism of state now opened to creole elites, who lost no time in occupying the roles of *subdelegado* and judge that they had once so harshly criticized. Lorenzo de Zavala went on to serve in the Mexican government and in the new nation of Texas, until an accidental midwinter fall into Houston's Buffalo Bayou brought about pneumonia and a premature death. Francisco de Paula Villegas moved on to even greater riches as the bishop of Puebla. After a brief fling with politics, Raymundo Pérez gave up elected office to concentrate on his haciendas and urban real estate interests. Members of the liberal party would dominate the first decades of Yucatecan politics. The rural clergy enjoyed the full restoration of its privileges. Their hated competitors the Franciscans were formally banished

from Yucatán in January 1821. More importantly, the obvention system returned in full force.[70] The 1813–1814 crisis had reminded liberals and *hacendados* that they were a privileged minority situated among hostile peasant
masses. Yucatecans would have to wait twenty-five years until the lesson of
1813 had been forgotten and political exigencies once more tempted them to
tamper with the mechanisms of rural control.

The sudden volte-face prior to 1821 proved to be one of the church's most
remarkable feats of adaptation. But at the same time, it left enormous contradictions. By 1821 the Yucatecan clergy was well on its way to economic diversification within the bounds of its society. Tithes, obventions, service fees,
personal loans, *capellanías,* institutional salaries, commodity investments, and
commercial estates all provided varying sources of income.[71] The constitutional crisis, temporary though it was, vindicated that strategy. Indian collections depended in large part upon the old Spanish state—hardly a model of
stability—at the very moment when the emerging talent of peninsular society
was straining to eliminate Spanish rule. To the entrepreneur-priest, it was clear.
Yucatán was moving to a more complete form of agrarian capitalism. The
hardy perennials of the colonial economy might wither. Or, should they survive, they might be dwarfed by revenues from newer forms of production,
such as commercial sugar. Above all, the key to working the new economic
devices would likely be control of land, not of souls. Labor discipline would
demand that peasants no longer "escape to the hinterlands" as they had done
so often in the past. For all these reasons, the Yucatecan clergy continued to
maintain itself in the vanguard of commercial agriculture.

But other considerations tempered the clergy's commitment to reform. As
in all times of changing economies, the entrepreneur faced uncertainty. Prices
rose and fell; markets could vanish overnight; a year of drought could dry up
a lifetime of capital accumulation. The relationship with Mexico also heightened insecurities, for favorable trade depended on the whims and humors
of the ever-mercurial central government. But amid this confusion one fact
remained clear: the peasantry would continue to grow corn. Urban markets
would continue to demand it. Consequently the clergy sought to retain control of the one feature which gave it an edge of competition, namely, forced
contribution. If possible, they would maintain it through the obvention; if
not, then through the tithe. Thus the sector of entrepreneurial priests, while
key to Yucatán's internal development, also perpetuated certain practices of a
precapitalist society, practices which would be pivotal in the unfolding process of peasant radicalization and insurgency.

The events leading to independence also had an ambiguous effect on the
Mayas. Except for fringe elements like Velásquez, the *sanjuanistas* had no real

commitment to peasant interests. The standard assertion of liberal discourse, from 1810 to the Caste War and beyond, had held that the liberal economic agenda was in fact something undertaken on the peasant's behalf. The argument ran that old colonial mechanisms such as tribute, *repúblicas, cofradías,* and subsistence farming had kept the Maya in a state of degradation and arrested development. With or without the peasants' consent, the new regime would see to it that those features were abolished. The mass of poorer Mayas now faced a renewed erosion of the traditional institutions of rural life. But the recent years had also acquainted the middle and lower strata of Mayas with new possibilities—social and geographic mobility, the abolition of taxes, and so forth—while the expanding economy seemed to hold out opportunities for ambitious peasants.

Maya elites faced many of these same ambiguities. Their hopes for mobility were greater than those of the Maya masses, but they had also learned something about insecurity. As long as certain colonial status quo persisted, as long as taxation and church patronage continued, there would still be room for middlemen. But if that old status quo were to vanish, then individuals who had prospered as middlemen would risk alienation and downward mobility. In 1814 serious crisis had been averted. But as for the future, in the age of independent Yucatán, as new social pressures would begin to fragment the creole community without simultaneously eliminating key peasant strengths, Maya elites would think long and hard over the lessons of the constitutional years.

Three   THE OTHER SIDE
OF THE GOLDEN AGE

> *The government of Sr. López, which lasted four years in accordance*
> *with the Constitution, was one of the most tranquil and happy*
> *that the peninsula has enjoyed since its emancipation from Spain.*
> —ELIGIO ANCONA, on the Yucatecan political system
>   of the late 1820s[1]

> *Lacking the wherewithal to satisfy the obventions which we owe to*
> *our pastor who incessantly presses us for them, it is hard for us to*
> *pay him. For as we have said before, we find ourselves in the utmost*
> *misery.*
> —A group of destitute peasant widows from Hocabá,
>   complaining about their tax difficulties[2]

Yucatecan liberals remembered the 1820s as a golden age.[3] Between 1821 and 1839 creoles mapped out a new Yucatecan state unfettered by
Spanish or Mexican control. The political and economic aspects of this tran-
sitional period are straightforward; less clear is the role of the peasantry. Peasants issued no manifestos and published no periodicals; when they did complain to the authorities in Mérida, it was usually to address some symptomatic
issue and not to formulate broad statements of policy or philosophy. Nevertheless, it is still possible to retrieve much of their history by examining peasant roles in the material conflicts which to a large degree defined them in the
new society. The 1820s and 1830s had their golden side, but like all miracles,
windfalls, and *épocas doradas,* they had their other, less enchanting dimensions
as well.

POLITICAL DEVELOPMENTS
AFTER 1821

Initially the peninsula remained aloof from the rest of Mexico. Many Yucatecans considered Mexico a greater liability than Spain: an extractive and monopolistic central government which lacked the old empire's wealth, stability, and trade connections. Yucatán's principal cities squabbled endlessly over the issue. Mérida was tied through trade connections to Havana and New York and consequently favored strict regional autonomy; Campeche traded primarily with Veracruz and wished to preserve relations with the new metropole of Mexico City. With Iturbide's overthrow in 1823 and the proclamation of a federal republic, Yucatán joined the larger nation. Led by their first governor, José Tiburcio López, the peninsula's new leaders began constructing a modern state apparatus which would allow them to direct the region's economy and attendant social relations to their own interests. They laid the legal groundwork for road building, education, and the political apparatus—enthusiastically, if not always to great effect.

In many ways the new state constitution (1825) was neocolonial. It guaranteed the church's institutional status and perpetuated traditional labor practices of binding workers to the estates through debt.[4] But it established key changes as well. Political authority passed from Spaniards to the creole oligarchy of propertied, literate males, their power secured in the institutions of governor, congress, and *ayuntamiento*. Of equal importance, the constitution established a goal—privatizing Yucatecan land and transforming it to commercial usage. The federalists' economic program promised social power and political stability through the control of export profits.

But success eluded the Yucatecans. They had no product of real value on the world market and for the time being had only limited power to alter the social relationships which centered around subsistence farming. Continued revenue shortfalls intensified intraelite rivalries, destabilizing the government. Pondering these political convolutions, the irascible French traveler Frederick de Waldeck could only conclude that intrigue was bred into all Yucatecans.[5] The breeding, however, was more structural than genetic: the limited opportunities of a weak economy encouraged a restrictive political system, making coups and cabals the shortest way to power.

In 1834 a centralist revolt handed the government to more traditional elements within the tiny elite class. Viewed from the distance of more than a century, the federalists and centralists are rather difficult to separate. Although they tended to divide between Mérida and Campeche respectively, both parties included priests, urban merchants, and rural estate owners, all tied to agricultural wealth. The centralist forces allying themselves with general and frequent president Antonio López de Santa Anna enjoyed particular support among the Campeche clergy, who on Mexican Independence Day displayed large blue-and-white flags replete with slogans linking the dictator with religious piety.[6] With Mexican support, the centralists succeeded in placing an ultramontaigne young cleric, José María Guerra, in the bishopric left vacant by the death of Estévez y Ugarte seven years earlier. Until his death in 1866 Guerra presided over the greatest crises of the Yucatecan church: the Caste War and the period of liberal ascendancy.[7]

Moreover, the two parties maintained certain policy continuities. Though remaining in power until removed by a federalist revolt in 1840, the centralist leaders brought little meaningful social change, so that in terms of its effect on rural peasant life the centralist period merely continued the ways of the early federalist government. The years 1821–1840 thus formed a coherent period characterized by the creation of a state apparatus and by uncertain attempts at unregulated, physiocratic developments in which the new elites tried only tentatively to overturn many of the rural society's traditional structures.[8]

THE ISSUE OF LAND

The most important issue concerning peasant culture was land. The 1840s would witness a Yucatecan land grab foreshadowing later dispossessions in central Mexico under the Ley Lerdo. But this still lay in the future. For the most part the 1820s and 1830s kept faith with the late colonial period: process dominated expediency, while estate formation and growth continued largely through piecemeal acquisitions. Peasants thus found the new Yucatán not so different from the old.

Estate formation continued throughout the 1820s and 1830s. Corn and cattle remained the popular staples, but new cash crops were gaining a foothold. Henequen was gaining some popularity in the dry north-central region, although its boom lay several decades in the future. Most important of all, planters in southern and eastern Yucatán were choosing to put their property into sugar cultivation. It was the southern sugar expansion, more than any other economic trend, which characterized the first decades of independence.

The enabling legislation which was to bring Yucatán such grief was over half a century in maturing. Indeed, the issue of privatizing Yucatán's *terrenos baldíos,* or public lands, had been in the air since the late colonial period. It was one of the keys to estate growth in the second half of the eighteenth century. The privatization controversy surfaced in 1813 with the numerous proposals for town funding under the Spanish constitution. And it remained at least theoretically possible in the 1820s. But given such problems as low profits, scarce capital, and uncooperative peasants, it was difficult even to sell properties which had already been alienated from public domain. Hence the government's inability to find buyers for *terrenos baldíos* around chronically dry Temax in 1823.[9] Needless to say, not all lands were choice, and the property most easy to alienate was that which no one wanted, peasants included.

Foreshadowings of Yucatán's land-alienation crisis were evident at least as early as 1813. In many of the *arbitrios* of the brief constitutional experiment, the would-be town councils, or *cabildos,* proposed selling off *terrenos baldíos* which lay within town jurisdiction. In a few instances these *terrenos* were designated by name. In Tunkás, for example, the intended target was the *cofradía* property Tocbas, worked by some *indios hidalgos* but, alas, merely used to support "their drunken revels." Privatization and sale of property had also included urban lots (*solares*). The struggle for control of these latter properties generated an enormous amount of controversy prior to the Caste War as priests, Mayas, and *vecinos* alike fell into prolonged quarrels over the rights to various urban *solares,* a sign that commercial values were transforming the older and more traditional culture. The *ayuntamiento* of Tekit justified expropriating three lots on the grounds that they were places "in which thieves and pickpockets are hidden, and young virgins are violated."[10] However, it does not appear that the municipalities envisioned immediately privatizing anything beyond the immediate boundaries of the community. The larger plans for selling off surrounding *baldío* properties were temporarily shelved during the Spanish restoration and subsequent independence debates.

Liberals presented a new and national statement of intentions in the 1825 constitution, which declared that *terrenos baldíos* were public property and that the proceeds from their sale would accrue to the state. But agrarian transformation also stumbled over the same exclusionist social networks which characterized societies like Brazil. That is, land laws were designed not so much to facilitate homesteading as to keep property within the hands of the well-to-do. The few surviving petitions (*denuncias*) for "empty" land for this period suggest that family connections served to facilitate legal process, as when Francisco Polanco of the prominent Polanco family secured land on the recommendation of kinsman Salvador, president of the *ayuntamiento* of Cenotillo.[11]

Compounded to this were the vestiges of colonial land-use concepts. Prior to the advent of agrarian capitalism, all Spanish lands theoretically belonged to the king; those who held title to them and who worked them did so only by his permission. The crown always reserved the right to prohibit various forms of land use (as for example in Cuba, where planters possessed titles but were only allowed to plant tobacco).[12] Such restraints persisted into the neo-colonial regimes that followed independence. For example, once the would-be entrepreneur had received a property title, he still had to obtain special permission to stock the land with cattle. Petitions had to specify the land's proximity to villages or ranchos which might suffer depredations from wandering cattle. For example, a priest named Luis María Escalante sought to stock the hacienda Santa Cruz, equidistant from Ichmul and Chikindzonot. Escalante assured that his cattle would present no danger to the rancho community T'bob, one-half league away and with only "six or seven individual rancheros."[13] Safeguards such as these harkened back to the corporate paternalism of colonial Spain; though beneficial to the peasant, they inhibited the development of agrarian capitalism.

The first attempt to bring the matter down from rhetorical clouds came in December 1833 with a law governing the sale of the *terrenos baldíos*. It defined such properties not only as empty lands (fallow, to the *milpa* farmer), but also the *cofradía* properties, a handful of which were still operating after a century of attempts to liquidate them. In theory the policy was designed to prevent latifundia, for it allowed a maximum purchase of one thousand square *mecates*. The new property had to lie at least one league from an existing hacienda in order to prevent growth by agglomeration. In order to prevent a disruption of the peasant agriculture upon which the society still depended, the law dictated that workers currently occupying the lands (and who were presumably to be evicted once the transfer was completed and the crops were in) were for the moment sacrosanct and were not to be impeded by either the surveying or the sale.[14] The law made no provision regarding distance from community property (*ejido*) and thus invited conflicts between estate owner and peasant.

But despite the high hopes of the new elite, the 1833 law produced only modest response, and the Yucatecan economy continued to stagnate. The first problem involved certain key provisions which discouraged purchase and thereby continued to work in the peasant's favor. Terms of acquisition remained prohibitive for the average Yucatecan. *Baldíos* were to be sold at public auction, a condition which elevated the government's sale price by forcing bidders to compete with one another. Once purchased, the new owner paid 5 percent down, with the full amount coming due in two years. Second, the government stipulated that, while the land became private property, "wells, *aguados, cenotes* or springs" which by tradition had been used as common sources were to remain as such. Rather than a fit of generosity toward peasant culture, this clause was more a concession to reality. The conversion to commercial agriculture was likely to be gradual, and while awaiting prosperity,

Yucatecans still needed to keep peasants in the field. Like the clause protecting the *milpa* farmers from being molested by the workers during the surveys, then, the water clause was a case of keeping a foot in both worlds.

A third and equally important factor obstructing land commercialization was peasant opposition. The complaints of the *repúblicas* of numerous villages suggest that the villages were still able to retard alienation through legal maneuvers, land invasions, and daily resistance. Piecemeal encroachments met with equally piecemeal counterstrikes such as cattle theft, land invasions, and sabotage.[15] Conflicts with peasants who defended *baldío* lands forced the would-be entrepreneur into a variety of unpleasant stratagems, including burning down their huts and provisions when they were off working in the fields.[16] But such heavy-handed tactics could backfire by provoking retaliations as well as costly and interminable feuds.

Land measurements in particular invited long and bitter court disputes in which both *hacendado* and peasants struggled to establish settlements most favorable to their own interests. Among the more decisive displays of peasant legal tenacity was the suit of the *batab* and *república* of Ucú (Mérida *partido*) preventing Felipe Gil from claiming *baldío* properties within their territorial limits. Over the course of a month the courts reviewed the matter, at last commissioning an investigation by the magistrate of Canquel, who was forced to admit that "the specified lands, far from being *baldíos,* as was supposed, are visibly found among the *ejidos* of that town."[17] But Ucú was not exceptional. Peasants of towns such as Tsilam, Buctzotz, Cenotillo, Sucilá, and Panabá had previously managed to obstruct *denuncias* through lawsuits and petitions.[18] Land-related litigations also turned up in Yokdzonot, Hecelchakán, Sudzal, and Kinchil.

Certain areas enjoyed a notoriety for peasant resistance via the law courts. One of these was the Nohcacab region of Sierra Alta, now straddling the state borders of Yucatán and Campeche. The area possessed rich soil which made it particularly suited for sugar cultivation. On November 2, 1830, the peasants of San José Chac—the place where the drunken *batab* had staged rabble-rousing meetings seventeen years earlier—reached an extraordinary compromise with one of the local landowners. Trouble had erupted over the question of who owned certain lands around San José Chac: the Maya residents or Juan Pereza, who claimed them as part of his estate? Pereza's cattle had invaded the *milpas,* and the peasants had retaliated by raids on Pereza's two properties, Tabi and Santa Ana, and then initiated a lawsuit. In an effort to stop "this prolonged litigation" and "further costs," the two parties agreed to the following. First, the people of San José Chac would pay Pereza the sum of six hundred pesos, a fortune for a peasant community and a clue that Pereza's claim may have been legally sound. The money would come in two payments, half in November of 1831 and half in the following November. To obtain this money, the peasants agreed to mortgage portions of the rancho's properties. (Apparently the local peasants were not merely subsistence farmers, but rather expected to make some profit from their property.) Third, the peasants promised to curtail their raids on the estates. In exchange for all this, Pereza abandoned all claim to the rancho property.[19] This complex compromise suggested that estate hegemony was still far from complete.

Finally, it is important to consider the quality of development after 1821. The land alienation laws did not uniformly engender a latifundia process in which vast estates dominated the land. In many regions rural properties remained small. Thus, although a few large haciendas did exist in all *partidos,* the more common formation, particularly in the sugar region, was the humble rancho. To an extent the difference was one of scale. A viable hacienda typically contained granaries, livestock corrals, irrigation, an *ingenio,* or mill, for making sugar, and a distillery for conversion to *aguardiente.* While the rancho may have had storage facilities and some livestock, it usually lacked the more sophisticated sugar technology. It enjoyed the same relation to the hacienda that the Cuban small sugar cultivators (*colonos*) did to the great *ingenios:* small properties of individual entrepreneurs supplying cane for centralized and highly capitalized processing units. Creoles by no means monopolized ranchos, for we find accounts of ownership by individual Mayas. In fact, the rancho offered an ideal pursuit for Maya entrepreneurs, since it required little capital but allowed Maya elites to take advantage of their rapport with the indigenous community in times when labor was required.[20] The numerical strength of ranchos vis-à-vis haciendas in the south and east was a pattern which prevailed until the time of the Caste War and in certain ways served as a predictor of insurrectionary violence (see table 2).

The progress of land alienations of this time was therefore mixed: neither a land grab nor total stagnation. The virtual absence of land *denuncias* from the notarial records before 1843 does not necessarily indicate that alienations were not taking place: as argued in chapter 5, the land rush of the 1840s to some degree simply ratified titles to commercial properties which entrepreneurs had already developed and were working without benefit of proper title. Until 1843, however, the neocolonial features of the government still held out the hope that peasants might counter these advances. Hoping for the most favorable returns possible on the sale of public lands, the government kept credit terms fairly high. Moreover, key provisions still protected the peasant subsistence producer. In combination, these factors allowed peasants to mount an effective resistance to commercial transformation. These factors

TABLE 2   *Number of Haciendas, Ranchos, and Sitios by Partido*

Partido	No. of Haciendas	No. of Ranchos and Sitios	Rancho/ Hacienda Index
Hopelchén	11	116	1,054.5
Bacalar	11	27	900.0
Peto	3	317	674.5
Espita	47	215	581.1
Tekax	61	289	473.8
Tizimín	37	170	435.9
Ticul	47	42	111.9
Valladolid	117	115	98.3
Sotuta	77	72	93.5
Campeche	12	32	89.4
Hecelchakán	59	37	62.7
Motul	191	95	49.7
Mérida	207	99	47.8
Tecoh	100	43	43.0
Maxcanú	92	39	42.4
Seibaplaya	33	8	24.2
TOTAL	**1,105**	**1,716**	——

Source: CAIHY, Expedientes, VII, 60, Nov. 29, 1845, "Estado que manifiesta las leguas de distancia que tienen entre sí los pueblos y ranchos de población . . ." I have excluded the anomalous *partido* of Carmen, which was simply undeveloped *and* lacking in significant indigenous population.

helped to ensure that land alienation programs made only limited headway in the first twenty years following independence. Indeed, as late as 1837 we find 101 aspiring but frustrated creoles (and two Mayas) placing their names on a waiting list for *terrenos baldíos* in anticipation of further enabling legislation.[21] This state of affairs would not change until massive deficits and instabilities of the 1840s forced the government to permit land *denuncias* on far easier terms.

DEBT AND TAXES

It was hardly surprising that taxes should continue to number among the most important of peasant grievances. Following the break with Spain, the new creole government adapted the old tribute system into a new civil tax called the "patriotic contribution," a name which implied voluntary and perhaps emotionally charged gifts to the fatherland. Although the one-

peso annual tax fell upon everyone, the bulk of the contributors were peasants, for whom the single-rate tax was a far greater imposition. In addition,
the complex hodge-podge of church fees and taxes remained in operation,
despite the momentary crisis of the 1810s.

However, ongoing peasant resistance to taxes helped to limit revenues of
both church and state. Nature also played a hand in this resistance. No sooner
had the parishes reasserted some measure of discipline over the peasantry than
they were struck by a combined smallpox-measles epidemic in 1825 and 1826.
Effects were uneven (and as yet unstudied), but in the most severely affected
areas the revenues from peasant taxes virtually disappeared for these two
years.[22]

Economic hardship was the most common grounds for seeking tax relief.
Often this was on an individual basis, but community-wide hardship, usually
related to epidemic and crop failure, provided justification for petitions of
blanket amnesty or reduction.[23] The exemptions list from Becanchén, 1844,
excused people "for lack of air" (asthma?), "suffering from fistulas," "visible
impediment," "for paralytic airs," and so forth.[24] Peasants were quick to perceive the usefulness of ill health and sought exemption for such physical maladies as failed eyesight, incapacitated limbs, and even deafness. The validity of
these complaints raised new controversy at every turn.

At other times Maya peasants simply refused to recognize the special incidental fees which confronted them. One of those was the (stiff) three pesos
required for a church dispensation allowing marriage between close kinsmen.
Given the frequency of Maya marriage with cousins, or remarriage to in-laws,
this fee was fairly important.[25] The need for such a practice stemmed from
the bureaucratic ways of the church, for a dispensation involved inquiries into
each party's family tree, inquiries often carried out by long-distance correspondence, given the peasant propensity to migration. The priest who was to
perform the ceremony had to draw up a genealogical chart which showed the
two parties' relation to a common ancestor, then write a petition for dispensation which in turn went to the bishop for approval. Like virtually all the
colonial church practices, the dispensation process imposed moral and ritual
standards on peasants which it then required them to subsidize.

These incidental fees provoked ad hoc resistance. The unnamed Maya who
arranged the matrimony of Pedro and Elisa Be, two cousins, simply refused to
acknowledge the dispensation fee, probably because it was not part of regular
marriages and thus appeared as a contrivance. To settle with this obstinate
matchmaker, the *cura* of Sudzal sent him to carry the request for dispensation
to the bishop in Mérida. Otherwise, the peasants would assume that all special
fees had been concocted on the whims of the local clergy. As the *cura* remarked,

"In this way I freed myself from the suspicion of the claimant, and of the other Indians, who like idiots have malice and distrust in their nature."[26]

The natural consequence of taxes was debt, the condition which rendered the peasant susceptible to innumerable manipulations. Debt justified coerced labor. Because of owed money, the peasant was forced to tie himself to an estate or, conversely, to travel to far-away cane fields or salt pools. The peasantry understood money values as well as anyone; borrowing and lending, together with obligations of repayment, were a normal part of the peasant's life experience. But while elites owned money, peasants were owned by it, with their entire lives and identities revalued according to figures in the debt-ledger books and tax rosters.[27]

Significantly, once the Caste War was underway, the rebels consistently demanded total forgiveness of their debts, thus rendering them free agents. This must have seemed a temeritous claim to creoles. Indeed, how *did* the peasants reach this demand for debt forgiveness? Certain dimensions of the problem appear obvious. Mayas could hardly have failed to recognize the maldistribution of wealth. Loan capital, especially in larger quantities, was a resource almost entirely in the hands of elites. The natural assumption, then, is that rebels seized upon the anarchy of the Caste War, when all values and practices were up for grabs, to attack the validity of debts. But it is also a fact that debt forgiveness had precedents within the historical memory of these same communities and that the Maya were calling for restitution of something which had always been theirs: a *privilege* from the elite viewpoint, but from the peasant perspective a *right*.[28]

The demand for debt forgiveness had its origins in colonial days. Exactly when the practice began is unclear, but by the beginning of the nineteenth century it had become a gesture among certain wealthy individuals, especially those who had made their wealth from dealing with the Mayas, to return some of that wealth at the time of their death through special legacies of money, property, and debt-forgiveness. The practice calls to mind those occasional bursts of noblesse oblige associated with European feudalism or with the planters of the American South. Such fits of largesse, voluntary and sporadic, were the exclusive privilege of those who held lord-like control over peasant labor.

In Yucatán the practice of debt forgiveness through legacies was already pronounced by the late colonial period, when political stability meant large clerical incomes. Between 1813 and 1822 we find six sizable legacies for the indigenous poor, together with two impressive gifts to Indian domestic servants.[29] Manuel Francisco Olivera, *cura* of Temax, stipulated that all the debts of the servants and *luneros* on his estates be reduced by one-third. Miguel Antonio Estrada also specified that the debts of "the *mayordomos, vaqueros,* and servants of my haciendas" be cut; long-time employees were to receive a one-third reduction, recent employees a mere one-quarter.[30] Men who were not priests almost never indulged in these displays, but women, who closely identified their social role with virtue and religiosity, were more likely to imitate the priests by reducing or eliminating servants' debts.

The most brilliant display of clerical largess was that of Antonio Solís, long-time *cura* of Peto. Peto lay in the deep interior, at the edge of colonial penetration. By the time Solís composed his will in 1815, he had presided over the local peasantry for thirty-two years, and in that time his wealth had become considerable. He held mortgages from various haciendas totaling eight thousand pesos, additional monies in assorted outstanding loans, five houses in Mérida, the cattle hacienda San Antonio Xiel, the hacienda San Antonio Aranjuez in Peto, and the sugar rancho Animex Dzucpat, complete with sugar-refining apparatus, in the same town. The basis for this wealth, as in all other forms of Yucatecan wealth, had been peasant labor and taxes, the latter in this case running at some 3,500 pesos annually.[31]

At the brink of eternity Solís was generous. He left the local peasants his hacienda and rancho in Peto, rare gifts indeed for simple farming communities. But there was a catch: rather than reaching the legatees directly, the lands were to be sold, and the returns divided among the parishioners. In the stroke of a pen, these gifts went from being peasant resources to being church resources. Property remained within the orbit of commercial development, while the money, now private and alienable wealth, was available for subsequent church rents and fees. The story of Fr. Solís and his munificent will had an even more suspicious conclusion. A certain Manuel Pastrana bought the hacienda and rancho for a combined total of 2,000 pesos, which, after liquidating back debts on the properties, left the Maya communities with 1,600 pesos. On July 14, 1818, the *repúblicas* of Peto, Tzucacab, and Chansikin all assembled in Mérida; proclaiming that there was simply not enough money to go around, they invested the principal back into the two properties at 5 percent, with the returns to be used to say thirty masses for the living and dead inhabitants of the villages! This had the effect of financing creole landholding and of providing for the church as well, a clear instance of collusion between creoles and Maya elites.[32]

These acts of largesse became less common as the years wore on. With more people competing for limited land and opportunity, and with secular creoles increasingly jealous of the church, it seemed more prudent to conserve wealth. José Vidal Gil, priest of Abalá, typified the new trend by demanding in his will that all back obventions be collected after his death. Another modification was to route the money directly to the rural churches and not to the peasants, a strategy employed by José María Marin in designating legacies for the parishes of Tahdziú, Sacalum, Palizada, and Usumacinta, instead of to the peasants therein.[33]

Between 1823 and 1847, a space of twenty-four years, we find only four legacies for the rural peasantry. Of these, three existed only on paper, since the priests in question did not die until after the onset of the war. One case—that of Manuel Antonio López Constante—was particularly ironic. Few family networks better symbolized the linkages between secular creole elites and the clergy than the López Constante family. José Tiburcio López Constante served as governor in the "golden age" of the mid-1820s, while his brother Manuel Antonio was the *cura* and ecclesiastical judge of Valladolid, the principal church office of the entire eastern section. With the rural peasants of his territory López Constante was, to say the least, generous. He stipulated that all his goods be distributed among the poor of Valladolid, Tixhualahtún, Kanxoc, and Yalcon. But if his sense of noblesse oblige was keen, his timing was poor. López Constante lived on for another twelve years. Rather than being mollified by the articles of his will (of which they were undoubtedly ignorant), the local Mayas hated the church authorities in Valladolid, whom they blamed for thwarting their lawsuits against *curas* and ministers in the nearby villages of Chichimilá and Xoccén. When the war reached Valladolid, the rebels seized López Constante and executed him.[34]

The issue of debt therefore involved more than simple peonage. There had also been a larger "culture of debt" which to some degree mitigated the pressures which debt and taxes imposed upon the peasantry, even if its effects were more symbolic than real. Rebel demands during the Caste War rejected what seemed to the peasants as new and more rapacious practices and insisted on a return, now on a scale that was truly significant, to the practices of a past century.

LABOR

Labor was as complex an issue as land or taxes. The gradual expansion of commercial agriculture, particularly sugar, altered the fundamental labor conditions of rural Yucatán, creating both opportunities and tensions for peasants of all economic levels. Sugar fields required roughly the same preparation as *milpa*. The somewhat longer growing season of sugarcane, however, placed a second agricultural cycle over that associated with corn. During the dry season of March through May, workers slashed away the undergrowth which had taken hold in the prospective sugar field. Workers selected out larger pieces of wood to serve as fencing, then set fire to the unwanted bramble that remained. Unlike the peasant *milpero,* field hands worked the ashes into the soil with iron tools. Planting took place at the beginning of the rainy season of June–August. Workers laid sections of the cane seed at intervals along shallow trenches, then covered them with soil. All of this work, together with the periodic weedings, was done by *luneros.* Because the cane required fifteen–eighteen months to mature, any given field would not require intensive labor for a year and a half. However, the *zafra,* or harvest, which ran from December to May, was a period of intense activity, in which haciendas hired out local peasants to work as cutters and haulers.[35] These overlaid work rhythms—the *milpa* and the sugar field—were to have an impact on the timing of the Caste War. In July 1847 the hardest work of the both *milpa* and hacienda was over. More Maya peasants found time to gather and discuss events.

To some extent peasants worked through the lure of wages, a practice they had come to know and accept. By the 1820s all but the remotest peasants had been touched by the money economy; if anything, opportunities for wage labor increased after the break from Spain. *Luneros, kocheros,* and *vaqueros* were common. Maya peasants laid bricks, dug wells, and carried goods for competitive wages. Paid Maya workers also included those who received a government paycheck for carrying mail between cities, such as the route between Mérida and the port of Sisal.[36] But those who purchased or compelled Maya labor nonetheless found that peasants continued to exert a powerful control over the pace and method of labor. "The Indians, as usual, worked as if they had their lifetime for the job," observed John Lloyd Stephens, perplexed that his archaeological hobbies failed to interest the average peasant.[37] Priests and estate owners extracted only faintly better performance.

One of the more revealing legal disputes of the 1820s involved a Maya road-building crew who worked on contract. Erimiro Uicab and Juan Cob, both of the village of Ekmul, contracted to build a road for Joaquín Antonio Dondé, brother to the priest who was then spearheading sugar development in the Tekax area. The two Mayas promised a lime-surfaced and stone-edged road, six *varas* wide, which was to pass from Dondé's hacienda to the hacienda Kanyuyum of Juan Ignacio Langores and from there to the road leading to Tixcocob. In exchange, Dondé agreed to pay a daily bottle of *aguardiente* and a ration of corn and, upon completion, "a barrel of the same liquor."[38] In addition to maintaining pre-Columbian styles of road construction (the contract is a perfect description of the *sacbé,* or "white road"), the Maya workmen were able to insist upon payment in the preferred forms of commodities.

Mayas also worked in positions of managerial responsibility on the haciendas, positions commonly supposed to have been the exclusive property of mixed bloods. Their most logical calling was to serve as *mayorcol,* or superintendent of the estate's *milpa* planting, since the Maya was above all a specialist in cultivating corn. Despite their positions of responsibility, these employees did not need to be literate; the lengthy legal proceeding over the estates of Juan García Fernando of Becal reveal that none of his managers was literate and that all of them were Maya. Despite their obvious regard for García Fernando's authority, they appear to have lived on fairly good terms with him; Maya staff and peons handily managed the properties themselves in García Fernando's absence.[39]

This is not to suggest, however, that the familiar dynamics between lord and peasant did not apply. The *hacendado* retained his social and legal prerogatives, often leaving Maya workers to rely upon daily resistance and traditional mores in order to protect their interests. One of the more interesting episodes of Maya estate management involves conflicts of power and culture on a property near Tsemul. Santiago Chuc, whom the documents specifically identify as an "*indígena,*" contracted to take a position as *mayorcol* on the estate of *alcalde* Juan Nepomuceno Ortega. In the spring of 1840 Chuc oversaw the slashing and burning of Ortega's fields. But disaster struck at planting time, for Chuc discovered that rats had eaten the seed. Ortega held his Indian *mayorcol* directly responsible for this debacle. He proceeded to beat Chuc before the other workers, jailed him, confiscated his thirty *mecates* of *milpa,* and readjusted his bill, leaving him fully responsible for the lost seed. The real issue between the *mayorcol* and his master was one of responsibility. Was Chuc responsible for safeguarding the seed? Or were the rats, as Chuc himself described them, a "plague," a natural disaster which he could not control? After all, a lowly peasant could not be held accountable for acts of God. On this point the issue turned, each side interpreting events according to his own interests.[40]

For estate owners, the problem lay in disciplining the workforce according to their own needs and expectations. Maya peasants lived with one foot in a subsistence economy; many performed wage labor but cushioned themselves against wage incentives by maintaining ancient subsistence practices. Those who did engage in wage labor had long-standing expectations of what they were to be paid; any attempts to alter wages met with resistance, and a landowner who reduced his pay to field workers was apt to face strikes or migrations. Moreover, the peasants expected a wide variety of privileges which made labor discipline all the more difficult. Peasants who did not live on the estate demanded to return to their own fields at certain times of the year, times which coincided with periods of peak labor intensity on the estates. Peasant labor also protested the wide variety of coercive tactics such as beatings and debt peonage and often succeeded in making their protests heard. In sum, despite the need for labor, Maya peasants could to some extent evade coercion as well as wage incentives.

To maintain some degree of control over the labor process, creoles employed a device left over from colonial times. Since the peasants owed church taxes which they frequently would not or could not pay, the landowner retained a convenient method of labor discipline. He had only to pay the obventions in advance to the *cura*. At this juncture the local judge interceded by ordering that peasants work off their debt in coerced labor to the estate owner, normally in such labor-intensive projects as weeding or cane cutting. Thus the *cura* functioned as a banker in more ways than one, for he loaned human labor as well as money. The town magistrate served as a labor clearinghouse, usually directing some portion of the labor to his own projects as well. The *hacendados* received labor at below the standard rate—a 50 percent discount, according to some of the surviving complaints filed by peasant workers—and the *cura* received the steady flow of income. His revenues funded not only the institution of the church, but the entire economic life of the peninsula.

Initially the tax-debt system had several advantages over conventional debt peonage. It allowed a consortium of prominent creoles to control and direct the labor at hand; rather than striking a contractual agreement with individual workers, the *hacendado* merely had to come to an understanding with the local judge. Peasants could at no time demand their account and place themselves on the market; their labor was assigned. Moreover, the system provided a justification for strongarm tactics, since by this point the peasants were already debt-dodgers and thus under a form of legal coercion. Incidentally, *subdelegados* also used these same strongarm tactics on creoles from time to time, as when the *subdelegado* of Oxkutzcab sold off local sugarcane to pay a rancher's creditors. The difference in this case was that coercion was limited to control of property, not of person.[41] The most important point is that, unlike the peon labor described for porfirian Yucatán, the system allowed commercial estates to operate in tandem with still-autonomous villages.[42]

We find several examples of this labor system in the 1830s. In Chicxulub, north of Mérida, the local peasants owed the priest a long-standing debt of some 139 pesos on back obventions. A local landowner, José Mesquite, paid the money and used the magistrate to direct Indian labor to his hacienda to do weeding. The plan was to provide token payment at half the standard rate. In this case, however, the *república* refused to cooperate, and the *batab* organized a meeting of "some eighty Indians" in the public house to resist Mesquite's demands. This action, smacking as it did of Indian rebellion, caused the judge to throw the *batab* and two *alcaldes* in jail.[43]

For officials who oversaw this system, the line between public works and private enrichment often grew hazy. One common abuse was to penalize the peasant for breaking one of the multitudinous restrictions and as punishment assign him to labor detail on one's own property. When this pretext was lacking, officials simply assigned them to private projects as part of their *fagina* duty. Ironically, the man appointed to investigate the Chicxulub incident— Enrique González, magistrate of Conkal—was himself operating a labor clearing-house involving many of these same abuses. At planting time González impressed peasants of nearby Cholul to work his fields as well as those of his son, the *subdelegado,* and of the local *cura,* a certain Father Córdoba. This took place in spite of the fact that peasants were paid up and current on all taxes. González demanded that each week two laborers provide him with seven sacks of henequen fiber apiece. His modus operandi was to work through the *batab,* having him distribute ½ real per *mecate* cleared and jail those who refused this below-market wage, a type of carrot-and-stick approach.[44] When peasants complained to outside authorities, the irate González threw them in jail, on charges of shirking their duty of killing locusts, "and of the bad example they were giving to the others." In this case, at least, the corvée operation of the local officials had become too patent, and while not reprimanding them, the executive office ordered the arrests suspended and the peasants released.[45]

The same methods turned up in the southern sugar region. In Quelel (near Peto), José Leandro Chan, Francisco Pool, and Gregorio Pool complained that the local magistrate was making them harvest and break sugarcane on estates as far as ten leagues from their village. Refusal to cooperate had already landed several members of the *república* in jail. Peasants argued that the sugar ranchos were health hazards, although we cannot say whether they were referring to the prevalence of disease in these areas or to the hazards of the sugar work: "evil winds," a malevolent supernatural force associated with (among other things) machinery, may have symbolized both.[46] Of greater significance, they argued that the labor machinations had generated a factional war within the *república.* The *teniente* and the second *regidor* defended local peasant laborers; but the *batab* and senior *alcalde* cooperated, as did the two junior *regidores,* both of whom owed their position to the magistrate's influence.[47] Commercial growth thus allowed ambitious Maya elites to manipulate labor-related issues to their own advantage.

The obvention-labor system also seems to have operated in the sugar country of Hopelchén, where "the collectors of the *señor cura* have moved against certain individuals remiss in paying obventions, to the point of giving work to those who have no other recourse, to earn money with which to pay." The tidiness of this system notwithstanding, the *cura* and subprefect of Hopelchén fell to chronic quarreling over who was in charge and filled the archives with their letters of mutual recrimination.[48]

As these anecdotes suggest, executive responses to local corruption depended on several circumstances. Higher-ups tended to overlook the small abuses of lone officials unless they resulted in public complaints and thus merited discipline—not so much a reprimand for their immorality as for their clumsy execution. With large systems of corruption like the one described, little action was possible. An understanding between the local judge, *cura*, *subdelegado*, and *batab* was in fact a political base which one did not jeopardize. Instead, the governor restricted himself to trimming minor grievances without cutting at their root.

Legally sanctioned labor drafts for various public works (the practice known as *fagina*) also continued after the separation from Spain. Peasant labor was the only means available for such projects as road construction. Maya peasants might well have participated, however irregularly, if the economic incentives had been adequate. But the Yucatecan state had no money with which to pay them and so had to resort to corvée. Among the various tasks for which the state found the peasants so convenient, few raised as much protest as cemetery construction. Exactly why this was is not clear. We have no written accounts of such construction for the early nineteenth century, but presumably it involved not merely the clearing of land but also the arduous work of removing rocks from the ground, an odious process since Yucatecan soil was nothing but a limestone substrata under a thin covering of dust.[49]

Whatever the causes of their discontent, peasants regularly sought to excuse themselves from the graveyard shift. The ever-quarrelsome natives of Nohcacab came up with one of the best excuses, namely, that the cemetery completed there in 1779 was still perfectly serviceable. However, the Nohcacab peasants had the disastrous habit of pushing their luck, for they registered this petition on the same day that they asked to be exempted from paying the contribution. The state threw out all of these petitions in a body.

Finally, in addition to the better-known *fagina* labors there were other occasional chores which the peasants found bothersome and generally best avoided. Thus in Tsitya, the *alcalde* impressed José Bruno Chi for the irksome business of killing locusts. Chi protested but was informed that the matter admitted no excuses. In a similar vein we find José Benito Be of Tepich petitioning to be relieved of public guard duty in the town square. The authorities energetically denied his request.[50]

Finally, there was one other form of peasant corvée: military service. This new obligation distinguished independent Mexico from the colonial years, for the process of statebuilding and national defense sharply increased the demand for soldiers. In theory, military service was reserved for urban riffraff, since virtually everyone else—including Indians, students, children, and so forth—was exempt. But the demand for riffraff far exceeded the supply, and Mayas often found themselves pressed into service to fill out the rosters. This was particularly true from 1836 onward (see chapter 5). Compulsory service always provoked resentment, and desertion by people of all races and creeds remained endemic throughout Yucatán's turbulent nineteenth century.[51]

MOBILITY

Another issue related to the complex of land, labor, and taxes was mobility. Though Yucatán was somehow failing to grow rich, the new emphasis on economic liberalism and commercial agriculture had resulted in some pronounced demographic shifts. Growth slowed in the older and more established areas of Yucatán while accelerating in newer territories (see table 3). Of the eight *partidos* which manifested growth rates higher than the national average, we may discount two as unrepresentative: Carmen's growth took place in a largely deserted outpost, far removed from the areas experiencing pre–Caste War tension; and despite Bacalar's tripling in size, the overall number restricted it to a Spanish outpost in a thinly occupied wilderness. This leaves two areas of real growth. The first was a metropolitan region composed of Mérida and Camino Real Alto, Campeche's immediate economic extension. Second, we find strong growth in the sugar-producing areas of Valladolid and Beneficios Altos. Tizimín, which lay immediately to the north of Valladolid, also experienced a population boom; the attraction was not sugar, which was scarcely cultivated here, but rather the expansion of cattle, henequen, and logging, as well as subsistence farming, into a relatively unoccupied region. The Caste War would materialize in a string of communities extending southward from Valladolid into Tihosuco and Ichmul, the principal towns of Beneficios Altos, and would find additional support among impoverished workers and small freeholders in Tizimín. Towns of Beneficios Bajos, where growth was less pronounced, would follow their lead but would not initiate conflict. Elsewhere, however, the changing economy exerted an opposite

TABLE 3   *Yucatecan Demographic Changes, 1821–1835*

PARTIDO	POPULATION, 1821*	POPULATION, 1835**	AMOUNT OF CHANGE	PERCENTAGE OF CHANGE
Bacalar	2,863	3,986	+ 1,123	+39.2
Tizimín	29,480	37,168	+ 7,688	+26.1
Mérida	30,803	37,801	+ 6,998	+22.7
Beneficios Altos	54,713	66,680	+ 11,967	+21.9
Camino Real Alto	45,753	54,447	+ 8,694	+19.0
Valladolid	55,199	63,164	+ 7,965	+14.4
Beneficios Bajos	45,199	49,433	+ 4,244	+ 9.2
Carmen	4,009	4,364	+ 355	+ 8.9
Costa	76,501	78,846	+ 2,345	+ 3.1
Campeche	29,401	30,167	+ 766	+ 2.6
Camino Real Bajo	42,870	41,726	− 1,144	− 2.7
Champotón	8,712	8,183	− 529	− 6.1
Sierras	113,322	102,964	− 10,358	− 9.1
TOTAL	538,970	578,939	+39,969	+ 7.4

*Adapted from "Cuadro IX: Población de Yucatán, (Censos)," in Salvador Rodríguez Losa, *Geografía política de Yucatán,* vol. 1, *Censo inédito de 1821, año de la independencia* (Mérida: Universidad Autónoma de Yucatán, 1985), appendix, no page numbers.
**Adapted from "Cuadro estadístico de la provincia de Yucatán, según los informes que me fueron dados por Sres. Espinosa, Rejón, Hernández, y según mis propias observaciones," in Federico de Waldeck, *Viaje pintoresco y arqueológico a la provincia de Yucatán (América central) durante los años 1834 y 1836,* trans. Manuel Mestre Ghigliazza (Mérida: Compañía Tipográfica Yucateca, 1930, orig. 1837), no page numbers.

effect. Growth slowed in Costa, where cattle and corn haciendas had reached saturation. It also slowed and even reversed itself in Campeche and its surroundings, a subregion that had entered a prolonged economic decline. The Sierras were highly developed prior to independence; their rather striking population loss was in part a dispersal of their inhabitants to less developed (or less regulated) areas and in part a relocation to untabulated ranchos and hamlets in the region's southern interior. The war would find a second home among the inhabitants of these outlying hamlets and mushroom communities.[52]

These macromigrations had their counterpart at the individual and family level. By the beginning of the nineteenth century, internal migration to and from all points of Yucatán was pronounced. Doubtless much of this reflected the influence of the great provincial capitals like Mérida, which drew in rural migrants who subsequently relocated to other towns.[53] However, the far greater area of transfer was in the countryside. One of the most elemental of rural conflicts was the struggle between the peasant's tendency toward migration and the priest's efforts to force the population into stable settlements. From the peasant's point of view, there were ample reasons to relocate from time to time. Packing up and moving offered a convenient escape from hassles with local political authorities, as well as from taxes and forced labor obligations. But the most fundamental reason for migration was the search for new cultivating lands. *Milpa* farming eventually exhausted local lands; at such times the *milpero* would set out with his machete in hand and his paltry goods slung in a sack over his shoulders, searching for new terrains where he might begin once more the process of slash and burn. These movements were not all flights to the hinterland. In most cases they simply rearranged themselves in the same or nearby parishes. Departures were not necessarily permanent; on the contrary, many continued to identify a given village as home. Only in those exceptional cases in which the migrants stumbled upon some gem of a property—usually with a water source—did they settle down for good and formally declare themselves a rancho.[54]

It was always possible that migrations could result in new villages. Although the majority of Yucatecan pueblos enjoyed an ancient history, others had grown by coral-like accretion and had assumed the status of "pueblo" only recently. One example of this was the rancho Cholul. In August of 1844 the two magistrates of this rancho—Juan de Dios Díaz and José Lino Can—prepared a brief history of their community. They described in the most idyllic terms how people in their little stretch of earth had raised bumper crops from time beyond memory; how its reputation had drawn more and more citizens, carrying with them their beasts and goods; how it had become a Yucatecan land of milk and honey. In Cholul everyone farmed corn except the women and children. Even the old folks worked. Peace and tranquility prevailed. The only disquieting feature in this new Canaan was the pernicious influence from other towns. Cholul lay midway between Tabi and Yaxcabá, and the *alcaldes,* tax collectors, and *fagina* bosses were prone to imposing their demands upon the rancho. As a matter of preserving their earthly paradise, Cholulans now sought township status. Its citizens even offered to raise a church through their own resources. The request was granted, and in honor of its voluntary act of association, Cholul became Libre Unión, now an unassuming highway town which vacationers pass on their way from Mérida to Chichén Itzá.[55]

The quest for township was a drama which played itself repeatedly in the decade before 1847. Small ranchos and settlements, hoping to liberate themselves from the domination of their neighbors, sought to establish their own judicial and executive bodies that would keep decisions and resources within the little community. In April 1840, for example, Ylario Tus, who would later serve as a rebel Caste War chief, led the *república* of Pisté in breaking from Dzitás.[56] Five years later, with the coordinated participation of both the local creoles and the Maya *república,* Uaymax split from tax-hungry Sabán; both "new" villages would later serve as points for Caste War mobilization.[57] At times, however, the careful plans backfired, and the rancho ended up reaffirming its status as a satellite. Such was the case when the rancho Telé tried to break from Chikindzonot. Local magistrate Julián Pech, writing for himself, the *república,* and "other principal *vecinos*" of the rancho, argued that Telé already possessed more than the necessary two hundred inhabitants, as well as an *audiencia* and plaza. But subsequent investigation revealed a less glimmering picture. Pech himself proved to be the only literate individual, while the vaunted *audiencia* house was nothing more than the remains of the *casa principal* from when Telé had been an hacienda and *cofradía.* The petition failed, and Telé remained merely another hamlet on the tax and *fagina* rosters of Chikindzonot.[58]

These initiatives were anathema to the clergy. Their own economic livelihood depended on access to as many parishioners as possible. In a larger sense, the clergy's mission remained the rationalization of the rural peoples, a duty to identify and tabulate which maintained direct continuity with the days of spiritual conquest. Throughout the first decades of independence, then, a single issue was to surface repeatedly: to whom did the wandering peasants belong? To the *cura* who presided over their traditional home? Or to the *cura* whose territory they had recently entered? Yucatán's ever-conservative church tended to favor home parishes; nevertheless, the conflict was never resolved with any finality, and the resulting confusion offered advantages to the peasants themselves.

One revealing case study comes from the parish of Hoctún in 1829. A group of Maya living on the hacienda San Lorenzo Tak became disenchanted with their situation and sent out reconnaissance in search of better pastures. The scouts returned with news of a promising site called Ch'ich' ("bird"). The only problem lay in claiming this terrestrial paradise, for Ch'ich' lay outside the confines of Hoctún, in the adjacent parish of Cacalchén, and was considered part of that parish's common land. Desiring to proceed as legally as possible, the would-be immigrants applied to the *república* of Cacalchén; this body informed them that these were indeed Cacalchén lands but nonetheless granted them permission to relocate. The peasants also received the permission of the *subdelegado.* The immigrants immediately transferred their *fagina* labor obligations to the new parish and for all intents and purposes became Cacalchén peasants.[59]

Trouble arose when Raymundo Pérez, *cura* of Hoctún, got wind of the situation. In January of 1832 Pérez dispatched a letter to the bishop demanding that the "ill-advised" peasants be restored to his own jurisdiction and his own tax rolls. But the peasants could now count on the other *cura* to take them into his own tax rosters and declare them citizens of Cacalchén. In his arguments Pérez cut to the heart of the matter. It was true that Ch'ich' lay closer to Cacalchén; but if peasants could move to wherever they pleased, and in so doing transfer their church tax obligations, then would this not amount to peasant autonomy over church authority? To accept this meant removing creole restrictions on the peasant society, a step which few creoles and fewer clerics were willing to accept. Peasant autonomy would throw church funding into havoc, since no *cura* would know from one minute to the next what his projected revenues would be, who were his debtors, or where he could find them. His arguments proved persuasive. The bishop's investigator recommended ceding Ch'ich' to Pérez "until further analogous circumstances permit a ruling of the best possible means, over the respective parish territories."[60]

The story of Ch'ich' contained most of the features associated with the peasant migration controversy: rival creoles, the peasant quest for better lands, and the effort on the part of all to maximize their control over their own autonomy and resources. Shortly after the church imposed its ad hoc solution to Ch'ich', the entire conflict over migration and church taxes erupted again in the district of Tekax, where peasant migration fit into an even clearer story of subregional development. The problem here was that, as vacant lands north of Tekax began to fill with commercial estates, peasants from the smaller communities began to migrate further southward in search of new *baldío* lands. Doubtless many intended to maintain connection with older communities which they regarded as home. But there remained the possibility that these migrants would pull up stakes altogether and found permanent rancho communities. Who then owned the rights to their obventions: the pastor of their ancestral home or the pastor in whose territory they now worked?

Tekax, one center of such controversy, was also a leader in the new sugar industry and provincial capital of the south. As *cura* of Tekax, Silvestre Antonio Dondé stood over an expanse of some twelve thousand souls, yielding annual revenues of as many pesos. As a man of the world, Dondé was part of one of the most respected families in Yucatán. Though a rock-ribbed centralist, he was a liberal in his economic beliefs and came to assume a leading role in the local oligarchy, another example of the church-liberal fusion which characterized this period of Yucatecan history. In 1842 Dondé had joined a "patriotic society" of Tekax whose purpose was to promote smooth economic growth by forcing members to accept arbitration of a society commission should disputes arise; members had to possess capital, a farm, or "an honest trade." No mere fellow traveler, Dondé was in fact the society's president.[61]

The *cura* owned extensive sugar properties in the area and in May 1846 filed a *denuncia* adding 1.25 square leagues to his estate in Tzucacab, thirty kilometers southeast of Tekax.

Dondé's efficient practices tended to stir up discord among his ministers in outlying auxiliaries. In earlier times the money from the ministers of the parish had split revenues from local fiestas such as the annual celebration of San Diego held in Becanchén. Ministers also took in pittances from the services to peasants, irregular revenues which trickled in like the sales of so many raffle tickets. Dondé centralized all revenues and put the ministers on steady salaries. But the ministers saw their comparative earnings decline as the sugar boom transformed Becanchén and elsewhere. Through no choice of their own, they had traded opportunity for petty security.

Dondé's success also threatened the *curas* of smaller parishes in the district, particularly Pencuyut. Tekax's economy exerted a strong pull on those seeking work, while Fr. Dondé exercised a strict watch for new taxpayers entering his territory. Between the two towns lay bad blood of long standing. Pencuyut was a small parish, only separated from its parent community Teabo in 1821. For these reasons Fr. José Mugártegui of Pencuyut protested when Dondé demanded church taxes from a number of Pencuyut peasants who had cultivated temporary *milpas* in the Tekax area. Fr. Dondé, he charged, "has in fact despoiled me of a considerable part of them, under frivolous pretexts, and exaggerated my miserable ability to compete with his influence."

> It is the custom in all the villages which lack sufficient lands for farming, that the inhabitants go out in search of them, and where they find them they set up temporary quarters while they harvest, returning later to their neighborhood. Those of this [parish] do likewise, and go out to work the lands around Becanchén, but they do this without dissociating themselves from the parish where they are administered, and after the harvests they return to their homes, which they do not move, and there pay their contributions, civil as well as religious.[62]

Mugártegui went on to argue that the custom had always been to respect the *matrículas* of the other pastors; otherwise, he himself could demand taxes from the migrants in his own parish. Custom and usage had merely entitled the host-pastor to collect funeral expenses from the migrants who died within his territory. Dondé responded with the argument of de facto residence. Who knew whether these Indians intended to remain permanently or not?[63] Both sides then proceeded to their respective magistrates, whom they induced to swear out statements to the effect that the peasants belonged within their parish jurisdiction.

The church's decision once more favored the home parish. Under the arbitration of a third party—the *cura* of Ticul—the two pastors drew up a list of the temporary migrants, whose obventions would then go to Pencuyut. Predictably, this satisfied no one, for the whole issue rose up again in the following year.[64] The clerical fights over migrant church taxes thus had two related motives: payment and principle. Obventions and incidental fees could form as much as 10 percent of annual parish revenues. In regard to principle, the matter of precedent in determining who claimed whom, five peasants were as worthy of a fight as five hundred. If the *cura* wished to maintain stable financial control over his parish, he could afford neither to lose its inhabitants, nor to let wandering farmers reside untaxed within his jurisdiction. It was a problem that the church failed to solve definitively at this critical juncture and a loophole of which the peasants took full advantage.

Although none realized it at the time, the conflicts of Cholul, Ch'ich', and Tekax bore the embryos of civil war. As the Yucatecan economy expanded, new growth areas came to resent the continued social and economic power of the old towns. The desire for decentralized power, for autonomy at the most local level, was ultimately a force that could unite Maya peasants and creole elites throughout the frontier. Less labor, more land, an end to taxes: these could serve political discontents as cries that would rally the indigenous masses behind them. Doubtless such options never occurred to the upright and principled ministers of Tekax parish. But time had a way of eroding principles. In the future, other Yucatecans would prove less obtuse, less circumspect, and a great deal more opportunistic.

MULTITUDES OF GRIEVANCES, DECADES OF QUIET

Land, labor, taxes, and migration were the promontories of the historical landscape. But the other side of the golden age often consisted of far more miniscule controversies. Difficult to reconstruct, still more difficult to weave into generalized patterns, these low-level quarrels and tensions were often uppermost in the peasant's mind. For this reason it is worth a moment to consider some of the dramas of daily life which made their way to the historical record.

Among the knottier problems of rural life was custody, the matter of who should live with whom. This was particularly an issue in a society of high death rates and often bewildering networks of kinship, *compadrazgo,* and master-servant relationships. Some accounts have asserted that small-town officials were in the habit of selling orphans as servants, even when uncles, aunts, and godparents were perfectly capable of supporting them.[65] We find occasional episodes of this, as when the son of Alejandra Ek of Sotuta was taken from her and delivered to a house in Mérida.[66] In February of 1821 Josefa Zulú moved to reclaim custody of her two granddaughters, Francisca and Rafaela, who were then in the power of a certain Simón Manzanilla. The court reviewed the case and one month later ordered Manzanilla to restore the girls to their grandmother.[67] Similar claims surfaced in small towns throughout Yucatán.[68]

As with the Sotuta example, Maya women seem to have initiated the majority of custody suits. The care of Maya children was almost entirely within their responsibility, and they assumed leadership in addressing cases in which local authorities had interfered in Maya family matters. But peasants angered by wrongful separation could raise unpleasant legal battles, and for this reason it is difficult to believe that the practice was chronic.

In a more figurative sense, Maya women struggled for legal custody of their husbands as well. Marital grievances about their personal lives found their way into the courts, usually to be dismissed out of hand. At times it is hard to blame the authorities for their exasperation. What was the governor to do with the wayward husband of María Chan, who was routinely sneaking off his work in Tecoh to go to Mérida, the home of his "other woman"?[69] But neither the rules of community nor Spanish law served as absolute preventives to the quest for polymorphous pleasure which to some degree had characterized pre-Columbian life, particularly for the nobility.[70] In certain ways, the emerging plantation society encouraged moral laxity. To retain their resident work force, estate owners would do almost anything, including keeping away angry relatives. Local officials who drew their support from these planters abetted them in this by stonewalling officials sent from other towns to retrieve illicit runaway couples.[71] Moreover, seasonal labor on haciendas encouraged "secondary" marriages at the workers' temporary homes, a pattern found today in such places as Peru and El Salvador, where migratory labor is common.[72]

As the story of María Chan suggests, Maya women did not necessarily have the same perspective as their peasant husbands. Maya peasant society was strongly paternalistic, and the main business which drew Maya women to court was not land or taxes but rather bailing their husbands out of jail. On these occasions the women had to be defenders, prosecutors, and bonding agents all at the same time. These episodes undoubtedly reflect the importance of the dyadic household as the undergirding of the peasant economy. They also reveal the determination of these peasant women of audacity to act upon their own interests when necessary. One case of this was Mónica Puc of Na-balam, who argued against both the *alcalde* and the *batab* to get her husband out of jail after one of his drunken sprees.[73]

Explicit racial tension flared only infrequently in the documents. This was not so much because the races were treated equally, but because Spanish colonial corporatism had made separate rights and privileges the norm. But ethnic identities were not as clearcut as the modern scholar might imagine. Mayas seldom called themselves "Mayas" or "peasants," but rather *"indios,"* (less frequently) *"macehuales,"* or the fashionably republican *"ciudadanos."* But occasionally complaints regarding double standards did surface. Thus we find Sipriano Balam and others of Temosón complaining "that only the *naturales* and much less the hidalgos and whites do all the labor of the patrols and deliveries."[74] Relations between Mayas and mixed races were not always harmonious, either. While the former tended to fall within the governing influence of their community's traditions and social mores, the latter were more typically people adrift, the artful dodgers of the 1820s, for whom the proprieties of peasant culture meant little. Matters became particularly touchy when pure Mayas were called upon to enforce authority over citizens with some Spanish blood. In Tinum, 1821, a Maya peasant named Tomás Canul was serving guard duty when a public brawl erupted among a certain Gregorio Gil "and other *vecinos* of color." Canul's sergeant ordered him to break up the rumpus; Canul obeyed, but the mestizos immediately lay aside their differences and began pelting Canul with rocks. The case ended with Canul appealing to the *alcalde* to arrest Gil and others *"de pelo"* (that is, "of the lower class").[75] Still and all, racial conflict was not the overt basis of quarrels for most of the surviving documents.

Harsh physical punishment remained a Maya grievance throughout this time. Though it was outlawed in theory, virtually everyone who dealt with peasants resorted to whipping at some point: priests, *alcaldes, hacendados,* and *batabs* all wielded the lash, and many asserted frankly that it was the only way they could find to bring discipline to bear. However, the inclusion of reports of whippings became so automatic in peasant grievances that it is now difficult to separate fact from rhetorical embroidery. Peasants counted whiplashes not individually but by the tens and even hundreds. When whippings indisputably did occur—as, for example, the blows which Raymundo Pérez admitted directing against wayward peasants in Macuspana, Tabasco—the aggrieved peasants invented elaborate stories, in this case to the effect that Pérez kept a mulatto manservant whom he used for the specific purpose of thrashing peasants in the plaza. This sort of bombast proved an effective device for calling attention to their grievances.

In other circumstances, the matter of whippings could involve unusual questions of calculus which peasants attempted to turn to their advantage. When Manuel Cocob decided to leave his old master Manuel Correa, he asked for his account; instead he received a thrashing. Cocob convinced a local judge to absolve him of any debt: the whiplashes, he argued, had taken the place of debt payment. But the governor's office, finding that "it being a bad example, attending the character of the Indians, to receive monetary indemnification for the outrageous and prohibited practice of whipping," reversed the decision. Cocob had to pay, and only then could the *subdelegado* punish Correa.[76]

Depredations by estate cattle were yet another peasant grievance and one which they often solved by their own initiatives. We have known for some time that Maya peasants engaged in cattle theft.[77] (And in the watery country around Bacalar they stole boats instead of cattle.[78]) This sort of low-level resistance later prompted one creole to reflect that the Maya peasant lacked the constitutional vigor needed for violent crime: "Above all he is a petty thief . . . But by their pettiness these thefts escape the actions of justice."[79] Just as often, the peasantry simply killed cows and horses that were causing predations. These "bovicides" were a far less celebrated group. Their method was to kill their enemies not in their *milpa* but rather at some slight distance, then leave the carcass to the buzzards. How they killed them is unclear, but if the body were discovered the peasant would solemnly protest his innocence. We should not take these protests too seriously: if all were true, then Yucatecan *milpas* would have been something like the legendary elephants' graveyard, a place to where the animals instinctively wandered when their hours were drawing to a close.[80]

Of course, the most common (and successful) peasant strategies were simply passivity and inertia. The slavish obedience which superficially characterized their attitude toward elites was usually hollow ritual, and peasants ignored their obsequious duties as much as circumstances allowed. Creoles understood this. It accounted for their constant suspicion toward and vigilance over the rural Maya. But travelers were apt to mistake pretense for reality, a tendency which more than once set them up for rude surprises. The foreign traveler Norman discovered this when he arrived in Yaxcabá:

> *By five o'clock the inhabitants began to leave their hammocks and made their way to the Casa-real, knowing, apparently, by instinct, or some faculty peculiar to the inhabitants of small towns, that*

> *strangers had arrived. In this instance, we were glad to see them; for*
> *we were sadly in want of a dry place to rest in. They offered to do*
> *everything for me. We told them our wants, by showing them the*
> *rooms of the Casa-real. They promised to get others, appeared glad*
> *to serve us, and treated us with great politeness. Off they started, as*
> *we supposed, to fit us out for the night, and that is the last we ever*
> *saw of them. This is mentioned merely to show a marked characteris-*
> *tic of the people. A stranger, with a sanguine temperament, in this*
> *province, must suffer!*[81]

Peasant grievances in the years 1820–1839 were widespread and varied. But rarely in those years did aggrieved peasants actively revolt and never in systematic fashion. Defense of peasant interests continued through lawsuits, daily resistance, and nothing more. The reasons for this are not mysterious. Peasants confined themselves to minor acts of resistance first and foremost because these acts still answered their needs. There was also the problem of leadership. The class of Maya elites who might be expected to lead such a revolt were still participating in the larger political and economic system, still working their old familiar roles as rural brokers. The Maya elites were suffering their own headaches (see chapter 4) but so far had managed to adapt themselves to the changing times. Finally, peasants still had no reason to believe that revolt was possible; there had been no massive political convulsion such as the civil wars which would strike in the 1840s. State and agrarian crises had yet to coincide.[82] These factors combined to perpetuate the *paz colonial* for nearly two decades after the lowering of the Spanish flag.

In concluding this discussion of the lesser-known conflicts of the golden age, it is worth a moment to examine in detail an obscure lawsuit which nicely captured many peasant concerns and attitudes. The story revolved around water-well duties in the village of Nohcacab. It was, in fact, the same *noria,* or mule-operated water pump, which the traveler John Lloyd Stephens had witnessed and described during his second trip to the peninsula.[83] Local peasants did compulsory service by taking turns walking behind the animals. Locals who stopped for water paid for the service by donating a handful of corn, which was used to feed the animals. The system served as a source of water in a region with few accessible wells or *cenotes.*

In March of 1832 nine local peasants[84] launched a suit against *alcalde* Luciano Negrón. On the previous Saturday morning Negrón had come to the *noria* and asked for the first Maya *alcalde.* Juan Anastacio Keb, who was second of that office, replied that the first *alcalde* had gone out to eat, where-upon Negrón struck Keb and others with a stick, accused them of being drunk and of not giving the beasts adequate rations, and ended by jailing Keb, Juan Kuyoc, and an unspecified number of their fellow *norieros*.[85]

On the surface, the incident seemed to invoke the traditional conflicts of rural Latin American history: forced labor, abuse of the peasantry, and so forth. But in the subsequent inquiry issues emerged which at once showed unexpected consensus among peasant and creole, as well as some subtle but essential differences. Under orders from the government, Manuel Freyre, *sub-delegado* of Sierra Alta, investigated the matter. He interviewed five peasants and five creoles. Regarding the mere bones of the account, the peasants unani-mously upheld the particulars given by Keb: the inquiry regarding the first *al-calde,* the beatings, the accusations, the imprisonment, and so forth. Creoles, to the contrary, stated that Negrón had merely knocked off Keb's hat with a "baton," that the Mayas had answered him with insolence, and that he had consequently jailed them.

Only when witnesses began discussing the justice of the event did the real issues emerge. At no time did the peasants protest their obligatory labor at the *noria;* nor did they necessarily condemn the fact that Negrón super-vised them. Rather, the issue was the matter of surplus corn. Because Nohca-cab's water wheel had done such an outstanding business, it routinely brought in more corn than the mules could eat, at least at one time. Prior to 1832, the peasant *norieros* had fed the mules their two daily meals and at the end of their weekly stint had divided up the surplus grain among themselves. (Peas-ants also charged that Negrón was closing access to the water after 8:00 A.M., too early for their tastes.) Negrón, however, had decided to stockpile the surplus grain to feed the animals during the rainy season, when no one came to the well and when the grain contributions consequently ceased. It was a conflict of control over surpluses: peasant vs. organized state. Negrón, as representative of the Yucatecan state, tried to maintain steady control over revenues at the cost of liquidating traditional peasant "privileges." Poor peasants, to the contrary, tried to maintain a traditional "right" to surplus returned to them via redistribution. Peasants consequently accused Negrón of stealing the corn for his own profits; creoles accused the peasants of using the corn to barter for *aguardiente.* The issue was not so much the forced labor, by now largely a given and perhaps even accepted by the peasants as a remedy for the town's chronic lack of water. Instead, conflict revolved around whether peasants should enjoy traditional access to relatively small amounts of surplus.

CONCLUSIONS

Yucatán's development after 1821 continued many of the processes which had been underway since the Bourbon reforms. With the lifting of protectionist barriers, Yucatecan entrepreneurs expanded their investments in commercial agriculture. However, the result was a blend of old and new. Sugar cultivation increased, and the less-developed southern and eastern frontiers became the new areas of demographic growth. Economic returns failed to fulfill expectations, so that the government maintained many of the old tributary features of the colonial state.

For poorer peasants, the situation posed a varied combination of stresses and opportunities. As land alienation remained piecemeal, peasant villages were able to slow the commercialization of land use; others took advantage of the situation to establish private properties of their own. Peasant workers continued to oppose compulsory labor practices and also resisted taxes, cattle depredations, harsh physical punishment, interference in their domestic affairs, and restraints on their geographic mobility. For the time being, however, resistance did not move to open rebellion. The state which had governed and helped to define them since the mid-1500s still gave no sign of weakness or collapse. Like the *norieros* of Nohcacab, they seemed prepared to accept a large amount of exploitation provided that certain traditional rights remained intact.

Four # DILEMMAS OF THE MAYA ELITE

He governs us at this village, and he teaches us the royal law of Lord God.
—The *república* of Xcupilcacab regarding the expected role of their *batab*[1]

We live under the despotic yoke of a cacique named Damaso Yc, who daily attempts to put an end to our existence.
—THE PEASANTS OF CHICHANHÁ regarding their *batab*[2]

Not every Maya was a simple *campesino* tilling his fields and toiling at the behest of the many authorities. While the relative weakness of poor peasants made them vulnerable to a wide range of abuses, the situation of the Maya elite—and above all, the *batabs*—differed in many ways. Though we have seen something of this figure in the late colonial period, the *batab's* social position becomes clearer in the years 1821–1847. We are able to learn more about the methods of election, the career track of its occupants, and the specific duties which were expected. As suggested by the contrasting comments above, tensions were building which would contribute to the formation of a class willing and able to provide revolutionary leadership.

HIDALGOS AND *REPÚBLICAS*

After 1821 the Maya communities continued to play home to a variety of elites, some important, some fairly trivial. Before turning to the more essential of these, it is worth a moment to consider that class of faded aristocrats known as the *indios hidalgos*. These were the Mayas upon whom the Montejos themselves had bestowed hereditary titles and privileges in reward for their collaboration during the conquest.[3] But to what extent had the hidalgos remained a real and distinguishable class? It would be questionable to still regard them as some wealthy and privileged upper tier of society. On one hand, there are few reliable markers of their status within existing documents. Usage of honorific titles such as "hidalgo" and even "don" was erratic in the chaos of the early national period, when every man became his own scribe. Yucatecans tended to apply them in cavalier fashion, as in the 1842 *matrícula* (church tax roster) of Homún, in which all male Mayas were lumped together under the generic title of "hidalgo."[4] The traditional tax exemptions of the hidalgo were also uncertain. As late as 1844 Yucatecans were still debating whether the remaining hidalgos were to pay taxes like creoles, but for the most part the exemption continued.[5]

Even laying aside linguistic vagaries, and despite references to a hereditary hidalgo class as late as 1849, there is little concrete evidence to suggest that the hidalgos of 1821 constituted an upper crust of rich peasantry.[6] The most powerful and influential peasants in any community were those made so by material wealth and family connections, and it was those who entered *república* service. "Hidalgo" was by now a hereditary title which carried a slight emotional uplift for its owner, but not much else. We do find occasional mention of hidalgos carrying on minor land transactions in the area north of Mérida.[7] Similarly, a Maya document from Nohcacab briefly describes the well-digging service operated by an hidalgo named Cecilio Kuyoc, in this case an affidavit verifying work done for a local priest and providing the names of workers and their collective salaries.[8] But as an indicator of real wealth, it was probably less accurate than the titles of nobility found in nineteenth-century England and France.

Scattered examples fail to offset the general absence of the hidalgo from key political and economic processes after 1821. Commercial changes had devalued the political currency of this group by the end of the colonial era. Moreover, those who did claim to be hidalgos were apparently concentrated in the older colonial centers, not in the south or east. The 1826 *matrícula* of Peto, for example, contains a grand total of one, a woman of Spanish maiden name; extant documents from other frontier towns make no mention of them whatsoever.[9] By all evidence, hidalgos had no hand in fomenting the revolutionary movements of 1847.

Finally, we must reject the argument that promises of hidalgo prestige drew Maya recruits for the government during the Caste War. In 1847–1848, this recycled form of *hidalguía*—even when voluntary—involved ad hoc material and political privileges, not the emotional resonance of some long-empty title. The one feature which gave *hidalguía* significance was its tax-exempt status, and it would be that privilege which formed the continuity with the resurrected *hidalguía* of Caste War military recruitment. Doubtless this interpretation will not satisfy those eager to see the perpetuation of pre-Columbian structures in Maya society. But the fact is that the hidalgos were déclassé.

Far more significant as a political force were the Maya *repúblicas*. These survived, officially or otherwise, through all the byzantine political shufflings of the early national period. They handily weathered the constitutional crisis of 1813–1814 and were operating in full force in the late 1810s. But the short-lived return of the Spanish liberal constitution in 1820 once more dictated their abolition. Interestingly enough, this official ban did not apply to the *batabs,* who were retained officially and exclusively as tax collectors. Peasant elites responded to the threat by simply disguising *república* operations, that is, by retitling themselves "assistants" to the *batab.* This altogether obvious strategy enraged those creole officials who opposed the whole notion of Maya self-government. As the *alcalde* of Maní observed:

> *The officeholders of the ancient* república de indios *have served up to now merely as tools for tyrants to oppress the others, and one cannot hear that they could be reconstituted under the name of assistants or anything else without believing that the true object is to continue the old operations.*[10]

The charges of tyranny amounted to little more than rhetorical tropes. But in other regards the *alcalde* spoke accurately. With or without a constitution, Maya elites continued to perform the role of leaders, tax collectors, and general community enforcers, the latter fact attested by their numerous reprimands for conducting illegal whippings.[11]

The old ways formally returned with independence. A congressional decree of July 26, 1824, reaffirmed the traditional role of the *batab* and *república* in Yucatán, thus maintaining continuity between the colonial and postcolonial orders.[12] Included in the decree was a list of duties for the newly reestablished bodies. First, the peasant governments were to oversee the continued reduction of Mayas living in remote territories. Second, they would also attend to their most important business, the collection of all manner of taxes. Included among these was a land rent of one real for every twenty *mecates* over one hundred. Third, the *batab* himself was to ensure that parents sent their children to *doctrina* classes and to see that village peasants attended church on Sundays (an obligation which they were presumably avoiding). Fourth and last, the *batab* and *república* were to observe the decorums of their office; although the specifics of these were left unstated, they presumably involved sobriety, promptitude, and a healthy respect for church and state.

Of course, the foregoing "clarifications" articulated an official version of the *república*'s role, a view of urban state-builders and one which lacked appreciation for the subtleties of rural society. Noticeable by their absence were references to providing local justice, village prestige, maintenance of land titles, or any of the other issues which undoubtedly concerned peasant leaders. The summary quality of the job description represented an intended trimming of roles and a retreat from the levels of Maya participation inspired by the Spanish constitution. The decree of 1824, along with its subsequent clarifications, was intended to guarantee that the *repúblicas* did not evolve into a form of peasant self-government at the municipal level. For all their ceremoniousness, these institutions lacked many of the powers of active governance.

But the Mayas involved saw other possibilities. Indeed, the *repúblicas* maintained the tradition of brokering, of mediating complaints—between peasant community and priest, between community and government or the church hierarchy, and so forth. Moreover, their influence and opinion came into play particularly in those moments when the parish's countervailing powers fell into dispute. This was the case in Cantamayec, 1826, when the *cura* called upon the local *república* to defend him in a feud against local creoles. Fr. Juan Manuel Manzanilla had fallen into a bitter public row with a certain Manuel Cetina. After a series of mutual recriminations, Manzanilla produced as validation an affidavit from the local peasant hierarchy stating, in suspiciously simple terms, that the *cura* was a faultless individual, whereas the entire Cetina family was corrupt.[13] Trivial in itself, the episode provides one of many examples of local elites seeking out the *república* as an ally.

The potential split between prescribed and actual powers rendered circumstances and personalities all the more important. Indeed, much of the tenor of peasant municipal bodies depended on the character of the individuals involved. Process of election was therefore important but, alas, not entirely clear to this historian. By the time of independence, creoles and Mayas had arrived at a system for selecting *batabs* which reserved final control for creoles but still accommodated the interests of the indigenous communities. When a *batab* died or resigned, the local *república* tendered a list of three choices for a replacement. Representative was this Maya-language petition from the *república* of Ekpetz, 1830:

> *We the* alcaldes, regidores *and* escribano *at this village carried out an election, as our esteemed* subdelegado *commands, to consider the three most respected and virtuous men. We the officials [present] below the names of the men, one of the three to be selected for* batab: *the esteemed Don Justo Yc, the esteemed Don Francisco Dzul, and Don Matías Kanil.*[14]

The *cura* and *subdelegado* reviewed the list, invariably choosing the first candidate. The *subdelegado* then forwarded the recommendation to the governor, who formally approved it. Such a system contained checks and balances. The *república* understood that their first candidate was the real candidate. Given the right of review by outsiders, they were less likely to advance the names of troublemakers (who did indeed exist). At the same time, in accepting the recommendation of local Maya of property and reputation, creole authorities recognized the advantage of working with the communities. This process also provided the *república* with opportunities for strategies of their own, since they could enhance the first candidate's viability by adding second and third choices that were unacceptable or at least less desirable. Whatever the opinion held by Maya or creole, the three-name system endured until well after the Caste War.

Creoles did not designate *batabs* or other *república* members, but they manifested great concern over their resignations. If a *batab* wished to leave his post, the matter demanded a formal request to the government; rather than giving the matter a mere cursory review, officials studied these requests with high seriousness, at times rejecting them on the basis of insufficient justification. The implication ran that the *batab* was somehow trying to shirk responsibility. In fact, this same suspicious concern was extended to any Maya official trying to leave his post. In February of 1844 the *república* of Tiholop explained that Antonio Noh found it necessary to retire because of ill health. Ever suspicious, the *subdelegado* of Yaxcabá sent Tiholop's *alcalde* to investigate. The diligent *alcalde* discovered that Noh had a severe case of hemorrhoids which prevented him from sitting down.[15]

With the exception of the *batab* and sometimes the *teniente,* all offices in the *república* changed annually. Participants alternated a year in office with a year out of office, so that each year witnessed a nearly complete turnover in personnel.[16] For example, the Homún *república de indígenas* varied as follows in December 1817 and August 1818:

	1817[17]	1818[18]
batab	José May	José May
teniente	Pedro Uicab	Andrés Dzul
alcaldes	Bernardo Chan	Apolonio P'ol
	Lucio Batab	Calsto Tutsim
	Lorenzo Pol	
regidores	Lorenzo Che	Juan Chan
	Santio Cutz	Luis Xece
	José Chable	Cesario Chim
escribano	Pedro Chan	Lorenzo Che

Here all offices but that of the *batab* had changed hands. The only other figure who remained on the *república* was Lorenzo Che, who passed from *regidor* to *escribano*. In all likelihood, his retention signaled the limited pool of literate individuals available for the latter position.

We find a similar rapid turnover in Hunucmá, 1826. Between February and July of that year the *república* changed as follows:

	FEBRUARY 1826[19]	JULY 1826[20]
batab	Rufino Matú	Rufino Matú
teniente	Luis Chay	Luis Chay
alcaldes	Juan Batista Ek	José María Matú
	José Antonio Chuc	Francisco Cahum
regidores	Ylario Cauich	Yldefonso Ek
	Enrique Puc	Bernardino Pot
escribano	Ysidro Matú	Sebastian Chay
	José Coronado Camal	José Coronado Camal

In this case, *batab* and *escribano* remained the same, but the body also maintained continuity with the office of *teniente*. Thus, high "executive" officers tended to conserve their positions, as these were positions involving technical skill, while the two bodies of representative or consultative positions witnessed regular turnover.

A somewhat later (1865) document from the town of Sitpach describes yet another system of office selection. Here peasants elected the lower-ranking *república* members for one-year terms. *Tenientes* served five-year terms, *batabs* ten. If the *batab* successfully completed his tenth year, he was allowed to remain in office until he chose to resign or until removed for misconduct. But given the problems of the job, together with the fact that most *batabs* assumed office at a mature age, it would have been unlikely that many reached the ten-year option. Within a decade of service the *batab* was likely to have alienated part of rural society.[21] Other variations of office progression may have occurred, but sparse documentation in the early national period makes this difficult to test.[22]

The office of *teniente* may have been a grooming station for future *batabs*. However, *tenientes* did not always rise to assume the higher office, a fact established by the nomination letters of the 1820s and 1830s. This phenomenon prevailed in 1829 in four towns of the Tihosuco region: Telá, Tiholop, Tepich, and Tihosuco itself. In each case, the *teniente* appears as part of the *república* nominating another party for the highest office. In the case of Telá, the *batab* nomination was of individuals who were not current members of the *república,* since all officers are accounted for in the signatures. There remains the possibility, then, that *tenientes,* like modern-day vice-presidents, were selected not for probable succession, but on the basis of more immediate political considerations.[23]

Not every peasant wished to assume the responsibilities of *república* office, which may have become more onerous and even at times disreputable as liberal advances began to erode the *repúblicas'* autonomy. In Yaxcabá, 1835, Bartolomé Yah applied for exemption from the position "for lack of ability" and on the grounds of having a family to support. Like the fiesta systems of highland Chiapas, the duties of the Maya officials involved an outlay of time which encroached upon one's normal economic activities.[24]

For all the chaos of the early national period, the *repúblicas* held their own. The governor and congress once more upheld the principle of collection through the indigenous *repúblicas* in a decree of November 1833. In addition to its usual percentage, the *república* received half the revenues from first-time Maya payers, that is, those who had reached their sixteenth birthday. One-quarter of this special cut went to the *batab,* one-quarter to the *escribano,* with the remaining one-half divided between *teniente, alcaldes,* and *regidores.* Despite official limits to their prerogatives, then, these bodies continued to be means through which peasant elites found both prestige and livelihood.[25]

THE BATAB

The most important officeholder was the *batab,* certain facets of whose role we have cursorily examined in previous chapters. Some have argued that after independence the cacique replaced the *batab* as part of a general weakening of the Maya elite.[26] But the continuities between the two offices are clear, while the disappearance of the term *batab* itself has been overestimated. For that reason I tend to group the two together under the original Maya term.

There were many factors which helped to place one at this pinnacle of peasant success. The most important assets for the would-be *batab* were property, family connections, a command of Spanish (and often of literacy), and the respect of both the Maya and Spanish communities. Above all, the office was supremely political. No *batab* could float on a pre-Hispanic reservoir of deference and good will, nor could he venture a single move without calculating its effect in both the Maya and creole worlds. It was a calling which only the most talented could master.

An essential to this high office was material wealth. Then as now, men with a vested interest in the status quo were less likely to cause trouble and more likely to rise in power. No master archive records the wealth of these native brokers, but some fragmentary evidence is available. One of the few known inventories of a *batab*'s property in the nineteenth century is that of Clemente Uc, who served in the community of Dzibalchén. Uc owned a riding horse and three mares; a masonry house with tile roof; a rancho named Chichmuc (with peons and salaried servants); a herd of thirty cattle; five hundred beehives, actively producing; and eight hundred *mecates* of *milpa*. He and the *república* produced the list as part of a petition to have him reinstated to his office. The material possessions of this *hijo de algo,* the inference ran, qualified him for public service.[27]

Elsewhere property and enterprise were associated with the position of *batab*. Vicente Pech, whose career will be discussed presently, owned the *sitio* Xcacalchén near Yaxcabá.[28] Santiago Chale, *batab* of Tecoh, was able to mortgage his hacienda Kukulá, for a goodly one thousand pesos; the money, ironically enough, came in part from the church's *fondo de cofradías,* a reservoir of loan capital created by liquidating the peasants' communal fiesta properties.[29] Similarly, a stray remark in an 1846 land *denuncia* reveals that Macedonio Dzul, longtime *batab* of Peto, owned an estate near Kancabchén, somewhat to the south of his hometown. This was almost certainly a sugar rancho or hacienda, given the nature of the adjoining properties and the general economic trend of the region.[30] The literate and worldly-wise Dzul was also active in corn production, possibly for commercial purposes, by the mid-1830s. In 1836 he fell into a dispute with the *subdelegado* of Peto, who seized his fields shortly before the harvest. However, the *subdelegado* selected the wrong victim in Dzul, who was on cordial terms with prominent individuals throughout Yucatán and who was accustomed to the intricacies of financial dealings and lawsuits.[31] Dzul hastily repaired to Mérida, where he swore out a series of affidavits against his enemy, all citing the appropriate supporting legislation and all graced with his peculiarly elegant signature.[32]

Batabs had also been among those most able to take advantage of the urban grain markets. Their expertise in gathering taxes and food surpluses, together with their knowledge of political and economic networks, naturally speeded them to the center of the trade. By 1818, a time of grain shortages throughout the east, the *batab* of Kauá was prosperous enough to donate one hundred *cargas* of corn for the benefit of Valladolid. In this case, however, he lacked his own mule drivers and had to request carriers from the local authorities. The donation may have reflected the *batab*'s political weakness more than generosity. At the same time that this remarkable largesse was underway, the *regidor* of Valladolid had to sue *vecinos* to get the corn they had contracted to deliver.[33]

If material wealth mattered, so did family connections. Members of certain prominent clans made likely candidates for *batab,* their family connections neatly dovetailing with advantages of property and prestige. The Pat patronymic had been important in Beneficios Altos at the time of the conquest, as evidenced by its prevalence in the *encomienda* rosters after 1540. Although it is doubtful that they constituted some sort of frontier dynasty, fragments of the Pat clan indeed dominated the position of *batab* of Tihosuco in the first half of the nineteenth century.[34] In Mopilá the Chan family regularly dominated elite positions and in 1842 occupied no fewer than four positions on the *república,* including *batab, teniente, regidor,* and *escribano.*[35] Here and elsewhere, nomination by family was a way of preserving social ranking in the face of cultural and economic change.

In several cases we know the public service record of individual *batabs.* There is, for example, the history of Tomás May, the *batab* of Huhí, near Sotuta. May was born in 1763, two years after Jacinto Canek's ill-fated rebellion. Perhaps the most striking feature of his public service was that he began late, for it was not until 1815, at the age of fifty-two, that he became *pocitario,* the official who oversaw peasant contributions to the local grain fund. May held the office for seven years, then spent a year as *procurador,* or village representative, "in the time when there were *ayuntamientos*" (1822–1823). He apparently discharged these positions with probity and afterward bypassed all other intermediary positions in the civil hierarchy to become *teniente.* Three years later, in 1826, came the title of *batab* itself. By this time May was already sixty-three. He found the job exhausting, and when he retired three years later, he included in his resignation a request to be exempted from personal contribution, even though he still had four years to pay. In view of his service and on the recommendation of several *vecinos* who vouched for his account, the government granted this request, and May retired, untaxed, to the autumn of his years.[36]

Consider also the service record of Gregorio Na, *batab* of Ticum. Na was born in 1776. His activities until 1831 are unknown, but he first assumed the role of *batab* that year at age fifty-five. Two years later he "was removed," to use his own words, but regained office in the following year and served until 1840. At that point he was once again "removed," this time to be replaced by a certain Manuel Dzul. But Dzul himself died three years later (1843), and Na returned, at an advanced age and in ill health. With prospects of revolution stirring, it seemed a propitious moment to call it quits.[37]

We also know something of the public career of Germán Chuc. In his resignation letter of February 1847, Chuc explained that he had been the *batab* of Espita for ten years and in the ten years before that had served as *escribano*. His failing eyesight now prevented him from fulfilling his duty as tax collector. And, he noted in a rather unusual turn of phrase, "I have served not only my village, but also my country ['*patria*']."[38]

Clemente Uc of Dzibalchén was yet another who came late in life to the ancient title. He resigned in 1838, at the age of seventy, having served as *batab* since 1828. This placed Uc's birth in 1768. His adulthood and years of public service had transpired during the late colonial period, and he had been forced to deal with the accelerating changes after 1821. By the time of the war, there remained very few who could remember those earlier times. The point was significant: for the *batabs* as a group, the possibility for returning to the paternalism and corporate protection of the late colonial era dwindled as the collective memory of those days faded. Increasingly, *batabs* found themselves caught between polarized interests without the old protective state mechanisms.[39]

What precisely did the *batab* do in the decades after independence? Part of his office involved setting an example of loyalty to other peasants. The *batab* was always to appear in public sporting his ceremonial hat and baton (we know nothing of their exact appearance) and was expected to encourage peasant participation in the church sacraments. This special dress advertised the *batab*'s superior social position and visually linked him to the ruling regime. Above all the *batab* was a tax collector. True, creole entrepreneurs procured contracts to bring in tithes, obventions, and the personal contribution; true also that the government regulated the business, imposing a bewildering series of requirements and restrictions upon would-be collectors. But once the collector received his contract and mounted his horse for the interior, he found himself in the exclusive company of Mayas. His only means of collecting from them was to solicit the aid of the *batab*. Even the priests, who knew their rural parishioners on a fairly intimate basis, applied to this same recourse. In the case of the Homún tax rebels, for example, the minister, who himself expected to receive 5 percent, nonetheless relied on the *batab* to deliver the goods and only canvassed the peasants in person when the *batab* failed him.

A letter from Peto (1840) testifies to the persistence of Maya involvement despite "official" collectors. José Sotero Brito had recently replaced the late *cura* José María Lanuza. As he explained to the bishop, his greatest difficulty was with a truculent minister who was, in theory, to have busied himself with collecting back obventions owed to Lanuza. But the minister spent all of his time lounging about in haunts of the village. The true collectors were "the same Indians who collected in the time of Fr. Lanuza." The new *cura* suspended the collector and worked directly through the Mayas.[40] The numerous middlemen, consistent arrears, and susceptibility to peasant resistance made rural tax collection inefficient, but creoles continued to work through traditional tributary systems, doubtless for lack of any real alternative.

THE POWER OF THE PEN

One of the *batab*'s trump cards was literacy, or at least access to those who had it. Lines of written words were among the arteries linking Maya elites to the creole world. And yet this was hardly a simple matter of domination through paperwork. In the final analysis, literacy gave the *batab* advantages in dealing with both the elite and peasant worlds and so simply reinforced the ambiguities—social and political—of his position.

Maya literacy took place within certain broad historical traditions.[41] The more visible of these was the practice of writing brought by the Spanish and maintained under independent creoles. Unfortunately, we know comparatively little regarding the creole literacy in this rural world. Even among those of Spanish ancestry, literacy was not universal, a fact which provided creole elites with the means for excluding the hoi poloi from office. Certainly local powers such as officials, merchants, estate owners, and above all priests were literate. But neither the pre-Columbian past nor the centuries of colonialism had served to make the written word more accessible to the average peasant. Literacy remained a power largely reserved for elites.

Indeed, in many ways writing was a means for constraining and restricting peasants. The most obvious example was the land title. But in addition the *recibo,* or receipt, was necessary to prove that he had paid taxes; the *nohoch cuenta,* or "big bill," was the passbook which recorded his hacienda debt and hence determined whether or not he was free to move at will. The surviving

matrículas of Tzucacab and Peto (1826) both contain Maya marginalia indicating which taxpayers had fled (*putsul*) and which had died (*kimen*).[42] Of
course, literacy and reliance on written words carried an unintended danger.
In the larger sense, it objectified states of knowledge and states of affairs and
hence carried a potential threat for a world based on deference and inherent
inequality. It also rendered legal affairs subject to counterfeiting and falsifica-
tion. Along with land titles, the *recibo,* and the *nohoch cuenta* came forgeries,
presumably obtained through corruptible *escribanos* or unscrupulous non-
Mayas who trafficked among the villages.[43]

Though statistics are lacking, it is clear that the *batab* and fellow *república*
members were more likely to be literate than was the average peasant. And
when the *batab* himself was illiterate, he received assistance, as did for example
the *batab* of Sacalum, who collected the contributions "accompanied by an
individual who is able to read."[44] Most often such help came from the *república's* scribe, or *escribano*. Usually, though not always, requiring basic writing
skills in one or both of the peninsula's languages, the position of *escribano*
was one of the few which demanded technical expertise outside an artisan
or shamanic capacity, and it often served as an entrée to the position of *batab*.
Their documents bear the stiff and ungainly orthography of those little accustomed to writing. Ylario Tus, who later served as *batab*—*and* as a Caste War
military leader—was the *escribano* in Pisté in April 1831.[45] In the case of Germán Chuc, the *batab* had also served a long apprenticeship as *escribano*. The
mere practice of filling out receipts and tallying contributions gave the *batab*
an exposure he would otherwise have lacked.

In addition there were activities of the *república* which offered more experience with writing and composition. It is clear that these local juntas
produced a large quantity of documents, of which only a small fraction sur-
vives.[46] Extant papers in the Yucatecan archives make frequent reference to
letters, complaints, and petitions from the village *repúblicas*. Even when the
batab did not actually write them, he participated in their composition, listened as they were read, and scrutinized them as did the other peasant officials, critiqued them and redrafted, learning all the while the elements of
phrasing and diction and the subtleties of written communication. His position, then, involved written as well as spoken language.

In rural Yucatán it was easy for literate peasants to divert their talents to
unscrupulous ends. When the Maya *ayuntamiento* of Nunkiní drew up their
arbitrios in 1813, they knew well the value of written documentation, for they
advanced a scheme whereby acquitted taxpayers received a certificate from
the *batab;* those lacking this certificate would be liable to double payment.[47]

Or: when the *batab* of Tixmucuy collected personal contributions from Santiago Pech and his sons, he gave the illiterate peasants what turned out to be
a receipt for two months, then attempted to re-collect for ten months.
More than one *batab* worked some sort of receipt trick to make up for sagging
revenues.[48]

At times the *batab* could also make use of more literate allies. The hostility
which some creoles felt toward the rural clergy provided leverage for peasant
elites who independently lacked the connections or technical expertise to advance their own interests. The best example of this is the story of Gregorio
Apán, *batab* of Nohcacab. In 1820 Apán was serving as *teniente* when the restored constitution temporarily relieved him from this duty. "From that moment," he reminisced, "I began to enjoy a profound peace of mind among
the joys of the laborer, who without anxiety shares the fruit of his labor with
his family." But the eventual restoration of the *repúblicas* recalled him to
office. Unfortunately, this restoration coincided with the arrival of Peto's new
coadjutor, a certain Pablo Villafania. The new priest, to whom Apán applied
the common but slightly sardonic Maya epithet *chichan cura* (the "little pastor," that is, the minister), had decided to use outlying ranchos like Nohcacab
as his private sinecure. Villafania thus came "to squeeze out the mellow liquor
of obventions and maintenances from the collectors." Apán was to serve as
personal collector and provisioner for the new priest and his "retinue." When
Apán protested, Villafania responded with rage and physical abuse. Apán,
who was illiterate and spoke only Maya, took his complaints to the liberal
newspaper *El yucateco.* The anticlerical editors then ghosted the story, couch-
ing it in the purple passages seen above.[49]

Literacy was thus an administrative technique, a means to personal gain,
and a weapon in the ongoing politics of rural life. But when larger issues were
at stake, the *batab* could turn this same literary skill to more sophisticated purposes: communications with distant allies and secret messages, perhaps in the
service of some conspiratorial murmuring against the status quo. In this light,
literacy suddenly appeared as a powerful and dangerous force. The Caste War
leaders had all acquired the basic skills of writing. Writing has long been associated with social domination. The establishment of written words relates,
however obscurely, to the fixing of behavior and identity and to the domination of a larger field of social discourse. In the case of the Caste War the original leaders were village elites who enjoyed this skill. After their elimination
(most of the original *batab*-caudillos were dead by 1850), power devolved to
mestizos and secondary peasant figures, some of whom also understood the
secrets of the written word.[50]

CONSTITUENCIES

The dual identities of enforcer and protector, writer and translator, patron and scoundrel, all made the office of *batab* supremely political.
The history of this elusive but pivotal class of Mayas therefore involved a succession of shifts and manipulations which served to keep the *batab* in his special situation.

The *batab*'s first pressure came from above. Performance expectations depended in no small part on decisions and personalities that lay above him in
the chain of government. Above all, that meant bringing in government revenues; and if the *batab* succeeded in that, creole authorities were often content to ignore the rest of his activities.

One example will suffice to show the pressure of tax collection on the
Maya elite. In the 1830s, in the hinterlands around Chichanhá, the *batab*
(name unknown) formed an understanding with minister Juan Nepomuceno
Trujillo to go easy on tax collections. The far-flung quality of settlements and
the low level of political control over forest Mayas made rigorous enforcement difficult. In exchange, the local Mayas ignored Trujillo's own lax life-
style. The understanding was apparently satisfactory from the *batab*'s point of
view.[51] But local arrangements could end abruptly when new pressure came
to bear from above. In April 1841 the *cura* Antonio Glory visited his minister
in Chichanhá to collect on back taxes. Afflicted "with an insatiable thirst for
money," Fr. Glory demanded immediate payment of all back funds. This included 528 pesos in silver, 20 in corn, 3.3 in beans, and "7.6 of the first
trimester of the current year which the cacique had already collected." The
abrupt collection of 528 pesos bit into Trujillo's own fees from minor obventions. By demanding full and immediate payment, Glory put the *batab* in the
position of having to renew tax pressure on the local peasants. The situation
eventually forced Trujillo's resignation and departure. In July of 1841, Glory
accused Trujillo of neglecting the mass, embezzling parish records, plotting
to burn down local houses, living on his *milpa* with a concubine, and many
other crimes that "would proceed to infinity if I were to recite all the corruption and laxness of this priest." As usual, the sudden concern with morality
related to fiscal disputes.[52] For the moment the *cura*'s hard-line policies prevailed. During the Caste War, however, peasant hostility to Glory was so extreme that officials found it necessary to reassign him to Camino Real in order to continue with peace negotiations.

While *batabs* struggled to accommodate elite interests, they also faced pressure from below. Peasants expected ombudsmanship and representation from
their *batab*. But the unwavering demands for taxes in a fluctuating economy

proved a source of popular resentment; attempts to maintain fixed tax revenues in the face of declining safeguards exasperated the peasant masses, who had by now gone through a millenialist episode believing that taxes had ended forever. Taxes had returned, and with them had come a renewed interest in commercializing the land, all placing the lower peasantry in greater pressure than ever. For all these reasons tax collecting was unpopular business.

Thus, while communities put up with a great deal from the *batab,* they also paid him back with endless tax resistance. Often this took the form of legal protest.[53] But peasants employed more than lawsuits in their war against the contribution and the obvention. The over-zealous collector risked not only loss of standing in the peasant community, but even personal violence.[54] The *batabs'* collection responsibilities also made them unwelcome figures on the haciendas, where *hacendados* and peons occasionally united in the common cause of tax resistance. Manuel José Mugártegui, who owned the hacienda Yaxcopoil outside Umán, resented the intrusions of Gregorio May and ran him off with threats of a whipping. Brought to court by the affronted *batab,* Mugártegui defended his actions with countercharges that May was overcharging the peons. Both complaints were conceivably true; but tax resistance was the overriding theme of the episode.[55]

Whether free villagers or estate peons, Mayas could seize the initiative against their *batab* even when creoles remained silent. The minister of Samahil, Julián Acevedo, discovered this fact when he used the *batab* to extort local peasants, many of whom were now living on estates. He directed the *batab* to collect not only the rents for the current year, but also receipts previously given out for the previous two years. These papers constituted the peasant's only record of payment, and without them he could have no protection against extortions. Peasants who protested—such as Julián Tun of Tanchén and Pedro Canul of Kuchel—suffered whippings when they refused to hand over their receipts. While creoles refused to implicate a local priest in wrongdoing, peasants spoke out immediately. Numerous local Mayas, including members of the *repúblicas* of Samahil and Bolon, all denounced not only the minister but the *batab* as well: this, from the very men who served with the *batab* in the village hierarchy![56]

Still other subtleties colored the situation. The *batab* needed tax collection monies but could not afford to appear too rapacious. A reputation for greed would not only jeopardize his social status, but also threaten his ability to collect taxes as well. At times the *batabs* were therefore reluctant to do their appointed work, as one official complaint testifies: "This *cabildo* has noted the scant effort which the said cacique makes in this collection, and [it is] only by this collection being urged on that any part of the money has come in."[57]

Furthermore, there was no reason why peasants who held out on creole authorities would not hold out on their *batab* as well. And there was greater physical risk for the Maya collector since if anything peasants were far more likely to kill one of their own than to risk the penalties of murdering a creole. For example, the mystic bond between Maya commoner and noble did little to shield *teniente* José Cauich and *alcalde* Lucas May, stabbed to death by angry villagers in Chichanhá.[58] Similarly, in 1818 the inhabitants of Chikindzonot became so indignant with their *batab* (José María Yamé) that they burned his house down.[59] The periodic reluctance of *batabs* to collect money may have owed partially to some ethnocultural solidarity of the Maya peoples;[60] but it also reflected a realistic assessment of the hostility *batabs* would suffer at the hands of irate peasants who formed one of their two crucial constituencies.

Still, it is worth noting that accounts of *batabs* who were "soft on taxes" are easily counterbalanced by evidence of tax-collection hardliners and, correlatively, that peasants maintained a popular awareness of these too-avid collectors. Among the hardliners was the man who served as *batab* during the sugar boom of Hopelchén in the 1840s. "[W]e can no longer look with indifference on the violence, outrages, and arbitrary acts of the cacique Don Juan P. Chan," the local *república* complained. In addition to tax extortions, Chan drew forced labor from surrounding ranchos for projects primarily of benefit to the creole-dominated *cabecera*.[61]

Another tax zealot was Felipe Cauich of Sabán. Like Bolonchenticul, Sabán lay in the deep south and witnessed no real growth until the nineteenth century. Cauich's extant Maya-language reports (1844) on tax collection document this *batab*'s scrupulous work and his willingness to imprison non-payers.[62] He had apparently been drawn away from the old patron-client relationship between local priest and *batab,* for in the following year he joined several creoles in a trumped-up attack on the resident minister.[63] In 1847 Cauich barely escaped execution at the hands of irate peasant insurgents; he remained loyal to his creole patrons, consequently earning the sonorous if empty title of "hidalgo" from the Yucatecan congress.[64]

Additional cases from the remote southern interior suggest grass-roots resistance to manipulations from the *batab*. In January 1831, for example, the *república* and peasants of a village (name unknown) somewhere to the southeast of Tekax began a legal war with *batab* Dionicio Yi for malfeasance, labor extortions, and physical brutality. They accused Yi of sacrificing their interests to the service of *cura* José Casimiro Carrillo, "since he owes his elevation to him." The *república* implicitly recognized that the *batab* stood between them and creole authorities like the *cura*. They acknowledged the immense

political debt the *batab* owed to his pastor; yet at the same time they understood that power was to flow in both directions, that theirs was a position
of rights as well as duties, and that the *batab,* while acting to enforce the
cura's rights, was also to defend in some measure the interests of the peasant
community.[65]

The later inconsistency of revolutionary initiative in frontier communities
like Bolonchén, Hopelchén, Chichanhá, Sabán, and Chunhuhub probably
related to the fact that the *batabs* of these towns were often at war with their
own constituencies throughout the late colonial and early national periods.[66]
Why the instability? The answer lay not in Spanish subversion, but in the relative absence of Spanish authority. These *batabs* lacked political strength and
moral suasion precisely because colonial rule had been weak here. The Spanish presence had been sufficient to coopt the native elite but inadequate to
make him an unequivocal authority among his Maya peers. Without clearcut
support from authorities outside the village the *batab* remained like certain
African chieftains prior to the arrival of European allies: weak, lacking definitive powers of sanction, and fair game for disaffected parties. The situation
was reversed in the old northwest, where creole elites could enforce hegemony but where economic opportunities for Maya elites were fast disappearing. Instead, the Caste War would emerge in the middle area of Valladolid
and the northern Beneficios Altos, lacking the creole hegemony of Mérida
but nevertheless hardly the cutting edge of the frontier.

PEASANT ELITES
AND PARISH POLITICS

The office of *batab* held real possibilities for wealth, prestige,
and upward mobility. At the same time, not everyone wanted the job, for it
also entailed risks. If the local Spanish officials turned against him, if the *cura*
wanted to collect back taxes, if famine or pestilence struck, or if for any reason the peasants simply would not pay their taxes, then the position of *batab*
became a liability which could lead to quarrels, loss of community standing,
lawsuits, or even jailings. The *batab* remained a man poised between two
worlds. As long as he could negotiate between them, he would enjoy the
fruits of his office.

Several cases from the Yucatecan interior illustrate the delicate equilibrium of parish politics in the early national period. We examine four villages:
Tixcocob, Yotholim, Yaxcabá, and Tixcacaltuyú. These local minihistories

document not only the balancing act which the *batab* had to perform, but also the way in which different personalities and situations affected overall relations between peasants and creole elites.

Tixcocob

Few case histories illustrate the complexity of the *batab*'s social position, or the extraordinary dexterity of these peasant politicians, as the story of Pablo Cauich of Tixcocob. Cauich's problem was his inability to determine where public coffers ended and his own pockets began. Local officials first caught him embezzling in 1835. They were about to prosecute him, "but a misplaced compassion paralyzed the business"—that is, the *cura* (José Ramón de Cepeda) stepped forward to cover the missing pesos. Cauich narrowly escaped justice, but far from inspiring remorse, the episode taught him that crime did indeed pay, for he persisted with his improprieties over the next four years. Not content with dipping into church monies, Cauich also embezzled the percentage that should have accrued to the *república*. In 1837 the *alcalde* had covered a shortfall on Cauich's solemn promise to resign his office once the taxes for that year were collected. But 1837 came and went and Cauich quietly forgot his promise. In 1839 the local *junta municipal,* though lacking authority to unseat Cauich, formally stripped him of his duties as tax collector, and the *subdelegado* assigned the job to a local creole. But Cauich was resilient. He set out for the remoter *sitios* and ranchos of the parish where he began making impromptu collections of his own. His strategy was to demand four reales apiece from the local widows, on the grounds that he was setting up a legal fund to defend them against "secret attacks."[67] At this point the new *cura,* José Clemente Romero, succeeded in having Cauich removed from office in August 1840.

What is noteworthy is not that the creoles dismissed Cauich, but rather that they put up with him for so long. Cauich's appointment as *batab* must have rested on political skill, for he was able to persuade two of the town's prominent citizens to cover his shortfalls. He also enjoyed some measure of confidence among the rural Maya peasants, since some were willing to use his protection against "secret attacks."[68] Perhaps they thought these attacks were a real possibility and considered it the *batab*'s role to defend against them. After all, confidence rackets do operate upon real levels of fear and expectation. It is also arguable that Cauich's actions did not significantly differ from political behavior in other places and times and that he simply saw taking advantage of tax collections as a way of competing in the rural milieu. His story thus exposes the many interpretive threads woven into the office of *batab:* roué, scoundrel, politician, collaborator, protector of the people, victim of creole exclusionism, and competitor in an open market. The most skillful *batabs* knew how to maneuver among the conflicting identities.

Yotholim

Another *batab* who navigated between the fragmented local powers was Paulino Uicab of Yotholim. In the time of Uicab's father, Yotholim had been part of the curacy of Oxkutzcab. But as the southern hinterland grew in population, the curacy became too large, so that the authorities detached Yotholim and Xul in 1821. In the newly autonomous municipality Uicab bore the grandiose title of "first *alcalde,* cacique, and extractor of patriotic personal contributions of this village of Yotholim and its comprehension." Yotholim had the same multilayered collection system as elsewhere. Despite the presence of two creole tax collectors (José Ignacio Bonilla and Lucas Mena), Uicab actually performed the collections and handled much of the paperwork.[69]

In June of 1824 some of the local *vecinos,* together with Uicab, launched an attack on priest José Leocadio Espinosa of nearby Oxkutzcab. They had discovered that, even though Espinosa's nephews Miguel and Santiago lived in Yotholim, the *cura* had kept them off the tax rosters. Espinosa argued that the two were actually residents of Oxkutzcab, and when his nephews had presented documentation to that effect, the city officials had harassed them by throwing them in jail. The attack succeeded, and the nephews had to pay back taxes to the municipality. In a curious turn of events, then, the *batab* was accusing the priest of obstructing tax collection.[70]

The case posed dilemmas for Uicab. On one hand, he would hardly have been likely to press for payment against the wishes of the *cura* who, until the rumpus of 1846, clearly did not believe his nephews should be on the village tax roles. On the other hand, reduced tax rolls meant less money for a collector, who operated on commissions, while pressure to make up the difference would have fallen upon the majority of payers, namely, the peasants. In this case, support of jealous *vecinos* governed Uicab's interests, for the *batab* would hardly have operated without support; with it, the complaint reached the governor's office. The case involved a collaboration of *vecinos* and *batab.* In later years, the difficulties of navigating between these elite interests disenchanted Uicab, who came to serve as captain to a local militia of 780 peasant insurgents during the Caste War. Of his eventual fate we know nothing, but he was still an active rebel caudillo as of 1850.[71]

Yaxcabá

The first story from Beneficios Bajos involves Yaxcabá, the "green land beside the water." In one sense, Yaxcabá enjoyed extraordinary continuity. Fr. Bartolomé José del Granado Baeza, a member of an elite Valladolid family, served as *cura* from 1780 to his death on February 13, 1830. Though a secular priest, his relationship with the peasantry was a throwback to the early days of the Franciscan missions, a combination of paternalism, self-denial, and an absolute faith in the prerogatives of the church. Granado Baeza's extant writings, notably the often-quoted ethnography (1813) he composed for the benefit of ecclesiastical representatives in Spain, repeatedly equate harsh, physical beatings with "charity" and divine love, the same identification of punishment and spiritual improvement which characterized Landa's quest for heretics in the 1560s. Granado Baeza also spent considerable energy tracking down non-Maya offenders, such as an assistant minister who molested local girls or atheists who stirred up trouble among the villagers. At the same time, however, Granado Baeza's tenure held positive aspects for both peasants and *vecinos*. He virtually never left the parish, a point which appealed to the peasants' preference for stability. He also restricted his earnings to church rents and *capellanías*. For peasants this meant that he did not combine his religious duties with the demands of estate ownership. *Vecinos* appreciated the fact that Granado Baeza did not compete with them economically.[72]

Given Granado Baeza's reluctance to intrude in secular affairs, political power in Yaxcabá devolved to Claudio Padilla, the town's *alcalde*. This included supervisory power over the *batabs* of the parish: without the *alcalde*'s approval, one's career as *batab* was likely to suffer. In 1827, for example, Padilla became disenchanted with the *batab* Lázaro Camal for failing to proceed actively enough in tax collection and produced documents signed by the *batab* of nearby Cancabdzonot, testifying that peasants "who came to pay their obventions could not find the cacique or the *escribano* in the *audiencia* building, or in their homes."[73] Camal was subsequently dismissed, in essence, for failing to align himself with the local creole power base.

Power shifted dramatically after Granado Baeza's death in 1830. His successor, Fr. Eusebio Villamil, was a strange man indeed. In business and politics he was one of the most successful of the Yucatecan clergy, in time rising to become dean of the cathedral while his brother acted as president of the Yucatecan congress. Yet to the people of his parish he was an object of contempt, a source of rancor, and a target for personal attacks. The formative moment in Villamil's life came during his apprenticeship in the missions of the Petén. Spanish colonialism had arrived late to this region. Its principal import was ill-will, while the main feature of the Petén Maya was an undisguised paganism still evident among rainforest peoples such as the Lacandons.[74] After one hundred years of titular Spanish occupation it remained one of the remotest territories of the western hemisphere. The experience of living through a smallpox epidemic here (Villamil's duty had been to abort the fetuses of dead mothers in order to baptise them) left him with a condition similar to the post-traumatic stress suffered by combat soldiers. For years afterward he wandered from job to job and from town to town, unable to settle into any position for too long. Above all, the days of the Petén converted him into a thorough hypochondriac.

Chronic obsession with politics and his own health turned Villamil into an absentee *cura*. He inherited the parish of Yaxcabá after the death of Fr. Granado Baeza, but Villamil rarely left Mérida in the entire thirteen years that he held the post. While farming out the actual management to a long string of assistants, whose tenures were usually brief and unhappy, Villamil remained in the city, nursing what one detractor sarcastically termed his "habitual morbidity." Faced with imminent death and an unruly people, Villamil's only solace lay in constantly rewriting his will—at least five different versions exist—and in carrying out his master study on the temperature fluctuations of Mérida, "taken with a Fahrenheit thermometer at six in the morning, midday, and six in the evening . . . in an apartment well ventilated." (Villamil concluded that Mérida's evening temperature varied by no more than fourteen degrees annually.) Like many hypochondriacs, Villamil lived to a ripe age, either because his fears were imaginary or else because the obsessive attention to health managed to blunt the ravages of serious illness. He died in 1857, in his eighty-first year.[75]

In the meantime, the *batab* had also changed. Camal's replacement died in 1832 and was succeeded by Juan Ceh. At some point Ceh's administration gave way to that of Carlos Chan, who then resigned in February 1841. Next came Vicente Pech, an aspiring peasant entrepreneur who later joined in the 1840s rush to claim public lands. Pech resigned in April 1844, possibly as a political maneuver to keep from being caught in the growing conflict between Villamil and his disgruntled parishioners. The office of *batab* now went to Baltazar Cob, who had been *teniente* in 1832. But his reign was brief. Within the year, Cob lent his name to a petition attacking Villamil. Hostility against the *cura* centered on two points: his political and economic success and his practice of absentee pastorship, which petty elites such as Claudio Padilla saw as detrimental to local interests. The decision was ill-advised. Even though Claudio Padilla had led the revolt, Villamil was too well connected to be challenged by a rustic band of petitioners. When questioned about the complaints, he replied that parishioners were simply jealous of his success. And of that he had no reason to apologize: "I did not take a vow of poverty," Villamil retorted. Within three weeks Baltazar Cob was thrown out and replaced by Carlos Chan, the man who had stood as third choice in 1832. Chan himself joined another anti-Villamil petition, although the conclusion of the episode is unknown. Villamil himself remained in power to the time of the Caste War.[76]

Batabs like Baltazar Cob fell from grace when a shift in power away from the parish undercut their alliances with local elites. In this case, at least, Maya attempts to maintain stable power through the traditional means of office-holding failed due to political realignments beyond their control. The instability of Maya officeholding in Yaxcabá had the effect of further weakening the office. The upshot was the town's failure to provide leadership or initiative in the early months of the Caste War.

Tixcacaltuyú

The parish of Tixcacaltuyú offers a final example of how Maya elites maneuvered among the fragmented powers of rural society in Beneficios Bajos. The story is noteworthy as well because it offers a hitherto unknown sequel to the famous uprising of Jacinto Canek.

In the 1820s the main political authority of the region was the powerful *subdelegado* José Francisco de Castro, stationed in Motul. The Castros were to remain a force for many years; a carved stone on the outskirts of modern-day Sotuta memorializes the completion of the road to Hocabá, by Gov. Miguel Castro y Arroz and *subdelegado* José María de Castro, in October of 1856. The other authority was the clergy and its network of friends and supporters. This rival network centered around the person of long-time *cura* José Manuel Berzunza and included his ministers, together with the town officials and big-men who were not part of the Castro group. Finally, a few key Maya families dominated these parts: the Abán, the Chable, and the Chi. In the 1820s Urbán Abán ruled as *batab;* Pedro Chable was his *teniente,* the man groomed to receive power, provided that he conduct himself with shrewdness and circumspection; waiting as *alcaldes* were Aparecio and Teodoro Chi. Like all successful village leaders, Pedro Chable enjoyed the support of kinsmen, chief among them being his brother Juan Esteban Chable and Pedro's two sons, Bacilio and Manuel.

In the mid-1820s a series of Maya grievances emerged, apparently related to jockeying for power in the new society. The peasants of this town began the 1820s in a dispute with Fr. Berzunza. The specifics are unknown, but their quarrel apparently related to issues of the peasants' freedom to settle in areas lying outside the parish, something that Berzunza opposed.[77]

It is worth noting how quickly the Maya communities learned to adapt themselves to the accustomed rhetorics of liberal society.[78] Whereas peasants would have once prostrated themselves as humble servants of the monarch, they now complained of "oppression" and "the unhappy Indian immolated for the sake of the most heinous despotism."

> *Never, your excellency, has anyone seen the wretched of our class more destitute of recourse, nor more persecuted by the perverse men who are filled with malice and the means to expropriate for themselves the authority over all the pueblos and to inflict upon them all acts indignant to the spirit, and much more with the benefit of impunity.*

The injured human spirit, the cry against despotism, the violation of justice, the manipulation of the masses: these could have come straight from the philosophes, and Lorenzo de Zavala himself could hardly have faulted the diction. However, peasants were peasants, and elites were still elites. For good measure, then, petitioners of Tixcacaltuyú also reminded their audience of the immense gulf between power and weakness and of the obligation which the former held to the latter. "The poor of our class," "the abandoned," await "the paternal zeal of Your Excellency" and "the providence of the government." These protections were in fact owed to the petitioners because of "the profound respect" they felt toward the new system; they knew that it would protect them "with the consideration owed to our ignorance and total lack of reason and understanding." What stone-hearted magistrate could resist these claims?

But on June 26, 1826, the Tixcacaltuyú *república* abruptly reversed strategies by mending fences with Berzunza. They wrote out a document not merely importing powers of attorney to him, but lavishly apologizing for their earlier attack. In fact, they claimed, the fault was not so much theirs, but rather of the person who wrote it, for this unnamed individual had filled it with all sorts of exaggerations which the Indians had never intended. They hereby declared the previous accusations null and void.

Behind this reversal of tactics lay the issue of control over the hacienda Huntulchac, near Quisteil, the town where Jacinto Canek had staged his disastrous uprising. The razing of the buildings and the salting of the earth had extended not only to Quisteil, but to the hacienda as well, the place cited in the colonial manuscripts as the place where Canek's band had made its final stand.[79] Although abandoned for those many years, perhaps because of the stigma of the rebellion and the fear it engendered regarding the local Indians, the corral and the house still remained. Now, sixty-five years later, Maya farmers had regathered on this same property and were using it for *milpa*.[80] As the peasants pointed out, its long vacancy and their equally long squatting meant that the original owner—whoever he may have been—forfeited all previous rights to the land. Above all, the peasants pleaded with Berzunza to prevent Huntulchac from falling into the hands of cattle ranchers, "because it would be harmful to us."

In their appeal to Berzunza, the Mayas harkened once more to the moral economy, to recall the great deeds of Berzunza and his fatherly role over the little people of Tixcacaltuyú. He had done them precisely such favors in the past; he had freed them from *lunero* service under *subdelegado* Castro, who had once demanded one hundred workers each Monday; he had liberated them from similar service at Bacalar "along with our beasts"; he had been a loving and devoted father, generous of purse, and had himself renovated the village church. Never at a loss for strategies, the peasants appended the testimony of seven local witnesses, all Spanish, who not only shared concerns about the fate of Huntulchac, but also bore witness to the Mayas' deep spirit of "humiliation."

The fact was that the peasants had good reason to believe that Berzunza would come to their aid. The new owner of the hacienda Huntulchac was *subdelegado* Castro himself, and a feud between Castro and Berzunza had been smoldering for some time; Castro accused the priest of laxity in clerical responsibilities, Berzunza countering with charges of malice and personal greed. Now, fulfilling all of the Mayas' worst fears, Castro had turned Huntulchac into a cattle hacienda. In 1831 Castro launched a campaign to transfer the hacienda out of Tixcacaltuyú and into Tixmeuac; the motive was to remove Maya laborers out from Berzunza's aegis and to avoid paying obventions to this hated rival. The purchase of Huntulchac hurt Berzunza in other ways as well, because a large number of Mayas had already left the parish to escape problems associated with cattle ranching.

Peasant elites like Urbano Abán and Pedro Chable performed highly political roles within their parishes. They led peasant bodies which shifted allegiances according to which *patrón* happened to best serve their interests. They employed contrived rhetorical devices calculated to exercise the greatest effect over their audience. Although the audacious men of Tixcacaltuyú seem to have lost their battle for the hacienda, they showed themselves able enough to take up the political war.

THE BATABS AFTER 1840

The indigenous act of balance could not go on forever. As the years of independence wore on, as prosperity continued to elude the peninsula and Yucatecan liberals grew more determined in their bid for control, rapid and erratic changes in land tenure and tax policy undermined the position of the *batabs*. As church rents grew more precarious, and as collection became more difficult, indigenous office became more complicated, and more hazardous. Simultaneously, the gradual expansion of non-Maya elites in rural areas tended to crowd the *batab* out of available opportunities and qualify the prestige he had once enjoyed. The indigenous elite's standing within the community, as well as their economic footing, fell deeper and deeper in jeopardy. Unable to continue at their old politics, the *batabs* in time found themselves forced to choose between the erratic patronage of officialdom and a peasant support base which was at once popular and radical. Only a small minority chose the latter option, but it was enough to engender an enormously effective revolutionary alliance between peasant elite and poor masses: hence the Caste War.

The security—or better said, the desirability—of peasant office declined markedly in the wake of Yucatán's political and economic upheavals. Indeed, although records of *batab* office tenures are fragmentary, there is evidence to support that turnover increased in the 1830s and 1840s. The available documents indicate the following number of departures from office:[81]

REASON FOR DEPARTURE	1818–1827	1828–1837	1838–1847
Resigned	2	16	23
Dismissed	3	4	3
Died in office	0	7	6
Reason unknown	3	12	6
TOTAL	**8**	**39**	**38**

The relative stability of the colonial period was giving way to difficult times in which many preferred to excuse themselves from public office.

At least up to the mid-1840s, though, the system held. The absence of revolutionary initiatives related to the fact that Maya elites—the *batabs*—still remained actively engaged with the non-Maya polity. As in colonial days, the *batab*'s role was to mediate between the many competing forces of the countryside. *Batabs* continued to collect taxes, maintain parish rosters, assist in village petitions, and so forth. Despite deepening stresses, the situation endured at least through the 1820s for the simple fact that rapid, radical change had yet to occur, and because state structures, long hegemonic, still gave no sign of their impending collapse.

Five   # THE IMÁN REVOLT

The chord touched by Imán has vibrated, the way has been shown to designing and unprincipled men, of causing an excitement and making themselves fearful.
—A FOREIGN TRAVELER on Yucatán's civil wars[1]

There arose a tolle, tolle *against the* curas, *supposing them to be enemies of the new system because it lowered the rent.*
—SILVESTRE ANTONIO DONDÉ, *cura* of Tekax, on the rising anticlericism of the 1840s[2]

In 1839 Yucatecan elites launched a revolt which overthrew the centralist regime and severed political ties with Mexico. Commanded by a Tizimín estate owner and military officer named Santiago Imán, the uprising gave poor peasants new hope for tax relief. As in 1813, popular expectations quickly passed beyond the control of church, rural officials, and traditional peasant elites. At the same time, the revolt sparked a new period of commercial transformation, particularly in respect to land tenure, as some 460,000 hectares of *terrenos baldíos* became private property. Thus, while Imán heralded the beginning of Yucatán's brief existence as an independent nation, he also shattered the already fragile stability of rural society.

SEPARATION AND RETURN

The Imán revolt had multiple origins. Since the second half of the 1830s, the Mexican markets for Yucatán's sugar and sugar products had reached saturation, in part the effect of strong competition from Cuban and Tabascan rum. Falling prices resulted in economic hardship for Yucatecan producers and for merchants formerly loyal to Mexico.[3] Moreover, Mexico's own instabilities in the 1830s carried adverse effects for the Yucatán peninsula. Mexican elites found economic development restricted by such factors as peasant autonomy, church control over much of the national wealth, and the difficulty of competing with cheap foreign imports. The general impoverishment of the treasury hampered centralized state-building and encouraged the nation's far-flung provinces to break away from Mexican control.[4] In an effort to suppress separatist movements in Zacatecas and Texas, the Mexican state made use of soldiers conscripted from the rural Yucatecan masses, thus resulting in peasant outmigrations and antagonizing provincial elites who found themselves inconvenienced by disruptions in the labor force; orders to return the runaways to their homes were fruitless.[5] Mexico's contradictory strategy— exploiting one province to pacify another—contributed to the formation of revolutionary leadership in the late 1830s. Provincial resentment naturally focused on the Yucatán's centralist allies: Santa Anna himself had appointed state governor Pedro Marial Guerra, brother of Bishop José María Guerra.[6]

On May 5, 1839, a clique of disaffected Yucatecan soldiers pronounced against Mexico and the centralist government. The man who was to lead this revolt, Santiago Imán, was born in 1800 to a relatively well-to-do family of the Oriente. His father, Faustino Imán, came from the patriarchal class; he occupied numerous political offices and also dealt in real estate.[7] By the 1840s the son Santiago emerged as a property-owner and merchant in his own right.[8] His surname was an ancient Arabic term meaning "priest."[9]

More portentous, however, was his military career. Santiago Imán held the rank of captain in a unit known as the Seventh Active Battalion. Despite their dynamic name, the battalions were actually a sort of national reserve designed to keep would-be caudillos on the payroll and out of trouble.[10] Imán had served as an officer since age twenty-five and had over a decade of experience in recruiting soldiers from among the riffraff and peasantry of the Tizimín region.[11] All might have gone smoothly, except for the disastrous Texas wars. Imán's military rank, previously a sinecure, now made him the villain in a recruiting drive that was antagonizing virtually every sector of Tizimín society. Imán thus entered into a conspiracy against the centralist government. The authorities learned of these activities almost immediately (1836) and threw him into an Izamal jail. Pleading hemorrhoids, Imán procured his release into the custody of an herb doctor the following year, then set about fomenting a full-scale rebellion.[12]

Imán's initial skirmishes were inauspicious. The early history of his revolt largely consisted of retreats in the face of superior centralist forces. The greatest fighting of the revolt took place in the *partido* of Tizimín, not only in the *cabecera,* but also in the surrounding settlements of Calotmul and Sucopó, towns "fortified with various lines of parapets and tenaciously defended." Separatist troops entered these towns by force and subjected them to sacks and pillages, actions which their commanders later tried strenuously—and unconvincingly—to deny. In most cases the prizes were the gold and jewels which ornamented the churches—poor booty in the long run, but virtually the only glittering objects to catch a soldier's eye. Typical in this regard was the silver crown seized from the church of Sucopó, crushed in the mêlée but eventually retrieved by the *cura* of Calotmul. Churches had long been the physical symbols of wealth and authority in this rural world, and they now became the chief target of social discontent.[13]

Initially Imán occupied Tizimín with a force of some five to seven hundred men. Already the movement revealed the type of proto-class tendencies that were to characterize the later Caste War. His soldiers were a rowdy bunch drawn from all parts of the rural poor: mestizos, deserting soldiers, sympathetic *vecinos,* and above all Maya peasants, all of whom tore through the streets of town whooping and firing their guns in the air to intimidate the local gentry. With the local monied elements at his mercy, Imán imposed a "voluntary" property tax. He also threatened to shoot anyone who refused to sign his federalist pronouncement—or so later signators claimed. Finally, Imán requisitioned corn and cattle from the surrounding estates, threw up a series of fortifications along roads leading into Tizimín, then dug in his heels to await the coming centralist forces.[14]

But fighting against soldiers proved more difficult than intimidating priests. Centralists routed the Imán forces in Espita, Chancenote, and San Fernando Aké and finally succeeded in dislodging the caudillo himself from Tizimín on December 12. Imán's fortunes sagged even further when attempts to raise a corresponding revolt in Tekax failed: the young rebels descended into brigandage and were put down with popular support.[15]

Imán retreated eastward to Chemax. Lacking real alternatives, he expanded his practice of mobilizing peasants by promising, among other things, to eliminate all church taxes. His motive was not philosophical opposition to the church but simple opportunism; indeed, like many rural patricians Imán himself worked closely with priest-relatives to build up the family fortune, in this case managing the investment of his young nephew's *capellanía* in a Tabascan cacao hacienda.[16] Nevertheless, his decision was a fateful one. Hostility to church obligations had been a constant factor in rural affairs, an issue which rural elites knew would mobilize peasants. Less certain was their ability to deliver on their promises, or to control peasant activism once it began.

It should be pointed out that in demagoguing the peasants Imán was no great innovator. Rather, he built on a decades-old tradition of appealing to Maya support. As early as 1821, a certain Antonio Güémez, municipal secretary of Calotmul, had placed himself at the head of a peasant mob in order to settle scores with a local enemy. This particular incident had arisen during the annual fiesta; a local official had caught Maya *vaqueros* pelting a bull with stones, apparently in preparation for the bullfight. Ordered to stop, the *vaqueros,* made bold by *aguardiente,* had responded with insults and blows, even to the point of forcing the official to the ground and riding him like a horse. General pandemonium had followed, and soon Güémez was leading an angry band of peasants in an attempt to storm the house of the *ayuntamiento* representative. Only the intervention of cooler heads had prevented the affair from turning into a lynching.[17]

But the Calotmul episode was only a beginning. In the following year, six "malcontents" managed to raise a mob of some fifty Mayas in the town of Maní. In this case the specific grievance was the taxes which the new government expected the citizens to pay. Local authorities managed to put down the revolt with a squadron of soldiers.[18] Similar episodes would occur in the following decades, particularly during the federalist-centralist conflicts of the 1830s. In 1836, for example, a disgruntled soldier named Felipe Medina tried to whip up anticentralist sentiment in Kanxoc, outside Valladolid. Medina paved the way for Imán by appealing to popular anticlerical sentiments, presumably with relation to church taxes. By the mid-1830s the Campeche militia supplemented its forces with a contingency of Maya peasants armed with machetes. Indeed, the patron-client relationships which prevailed in the countryside made the peasants particularly susceptible to military service. Suffice it to say, then, that Yucatán enjoyed a precedent for elites mobilizing peasants around the issue of taxes. It needed only the right circumstances to tempt men like Imán, made desperate through their own weakness, into arming the indigenous masses on a grander scale.[19]

The recruiting of Maya peasants borrowed heavily on rural tax collection systems: local elites enlisted Maya *batabs,* who in turn worked the masses. Here and in subsequent campaigns, the chief organizers were Imán's lieutenants. One was Pastor Gamboa, a deserter from the Tizimín regiment. Another was Vito Pacheco, a man who had smuggled goods throughout the Oriente and was widely believed to be responsible for a sensational murder a few years earlier; Pacheco now joined the Imán revolt, his political opponents charged, to escape punishment for "his horrendous crimes."[20] The lieutenants in turn utilized the talents of local *batabs* and other influential Maya peasants. In Imán's 1842–1843 campaign, for example, the outgoing *batab* of Espita, Germán Chi, did much of the recruiting of soldiers to repel the Mexican invaders, explaining the situation in Maya to the local peasants and forwarding lists of Maya volunteers. In Chichimilá, Imán's lieutenants utilized the services of Manuel Antonio Ay, future *batab* and Caste War conspirator. The process was the same elsewhere along the frontier towns: *batabs* and their fellow Maya elites received first-hand experience in raising supplies and weapons and in mobilizing peasant soldiers.[21] In addition, Imán and his officers practiced rural terrorism, assassinating creole officials known or suspected to be loyal to the centralist regime. This last policy was effective at the time but would later yield bitter fruit when these same terroristic pressures were brought to bear against Maya elites.[22]

The implications of Imán's activities did not escape local elites who stood to lose by the sudden mobilization of the peasants. Santiago de la Cruz Relase, a prominent man from Sucilá, outside Tizimín, moved his entire family to Izamal for protection. But after centralist officials, the people most worried were the rural *curas,* who saw their privileges being traded away as bargaining chips in the federalist strategy. In Espita the *cura* allowed the local centralist commander to turn his church into a fortress to defend against the federalist raiding parties which were becoming a common affair. Rather than risk everything on the defense of the centralist garrisons, he prudently withdrew all jewels and decorations "in precaution against the accidents which might occur."[23]

Valladolid, the largest town of the region and the key to military victory, was a rustic and retrograde preserve of the old colonial elites. The 1835 cholera epidemic seems to have struck hard at the scant prosperity that had existed there. The Indian church staff had largely abandoned their offices. Far from revering official cult properties, the local Mayas used the grounds near the church doors for a latrine under the cover of night, "so that the baptismal chamber is always filled with a foul odor." Weeds choked the atriums of the smaller barrio churches, and locals had stripped the interiors of candles, mantlecloths, icons, and anything else they could carry.[24] The surrounding communities, places like Xoccén, Kauá, and Chichimilá, swarmed with lawsuits involving peasants, priests, and rival creole elites.[25] Legal decisions handed down from the vicar's office in Valladolid satisfied no one and merely served to unite the warring parties in their hostility to this frontier capital.

The cumulative moment of Imán's revolt and populist strategy came here on February 8, 1840. There is little detailed information on Imán's attack on

Valladolid, but fleeting references suggest that both the conflict and its aftermath were harsh. It began as a raid on the barrio of Sisal, with thousands of
Maya recruits filtering into the streets and plazas. The centralist commandant,
Carlos María Aroas, took little notice of the gathering hordes until it was too
late; in fact, he ignored reports and postponed any immediate action until he
had completed his dinner. Only when Aroas went to confront the mob did
he realize its true proportions. The two sides exchanged shots, and within
minutes the skirmish degenerated into a lopsided rout and general sacking,
the first of several which the city was to suffer during the decade which followed. Three days after the battle Imán himself entered the city in regal fashion, carried by Maya *koché* bearers, and the victory was complete. Within
days, all cities but Campeche had seconded Imán's pronouncement, and after
a brief siege, that too fell in line with the new republic.[26]

Fêtes and honors now descended upon Imán like summer rain. The new
regime proclaimed July 25 a special day celebrating "the caudillo of the Lib-
erating Army of the East." Displays and festoons in Mérida's citadel of San
Benito and the government palace; a round of artillery fire; the coordinated
ringing of Mérida's church bells: all these commemorated the Liberator and
his deeds.[27] Exactly how enthusiastic the clergy felt about ringing their bells is
debatable. Because of Imán's revolt, many rural parishes now lay in ruins, either
bankrupted by forced requisitions or devastated by actual fighting. Priests in
Valladolid continued to keep their families in outlying communities.[28] Moreover, an edge of coercion lay behind the festivities. A few months earlier,
when the *cura* of Muna had failed to ring the bells of the town's massive
church in support of the revolt, the *alcalde* halted the collection of all obventions, even in their reduced form:

> *They have reduced me to the* derechos de estola, *which means only
> baptismal fees, because the people are no longer bothering to marry or
> to pay for burial, and . . . because my health is severely broken, I
> never go on horseback because of my illnesses, and I have instructed
> those on the haciendas that when they become ill, they should come
> to this village for me to assist them, since I no longer have money to
> pay for* kochés.[29]

Indeed, the memory of Imán's revolt would linger in the minds of Yucatán's more peaceful and established citizens, the first glimpse of a time of
troubles which threatened to erupt again at any moment. In Tixkokob, the
mere prospect of renewed conflict sent the *cura* (José Francisco Sabido) flying
to his hacienda Hunpicdziú for safety. "After such destruction as we have suf-

fered," he wrote to a friend, "I assure you that people are afraid even to be in the same village, and for that reason I have kept myself in the backlands in fear of a thousand and thousand evils."[30]

In November 1842 Mexico's president, General Antonio López de Santa Anna, sent a punitive force to reclaim the peninsula. But this time Yucatecans were ready. Under the command of General Sebastián López de Llergo, they again resorted to peasant recruitment. Gamboa, Pacheco, and other Imán officers assembled an army of some two thousand Mayas, a force which included the Maya commander Cecilio Chi, *batab* of Tepich and later one of the two principal caudillos in the Caste War. In one extant letter exchanged between Maya commanders at this time, Captain Miguel Canul briefly discussed the enemy advance and reported that "all my men have gone in search of their food."[31] The grass-roots militias of Chi, Canul, and others had little difficulty in repelling the invaders, and Yucatán remained independent, again through the arms of the Maya peasant soldier.[32]

Ironically, Yucatecans would surrender their independence. For while emotionally gratifying, peninsular separation from Mexico soon led to economic hardship, since Yucatecan sugar planters and merchants found themselves cut off from their principal market. After a year of declining revenues, the peninsula agreed once more to reunite. However, the reunion was largely a matter of tariff agreements, for Mexico exercised virtually no control over Yucatán's internal affairs for the remainder of the decade.

Yucatecans ratified the reunion with Mexico through a massive plebiscite in which the prominent Mayas of most towns (109 of 159) participated. Signators included some of the most politically active batabs: Jacinto Pat of Tihosuco, Macedonio Dzul of Peto, Vicente Pech of Yaxcabá, Ylario Tus of Pisté, and many others. Most towns had more than one Maya signator; a few had fifteen or more. Nor did all vote for approval. In Tixcacaltuyú, for example, two creoles and two Mayas outvoted the three Mayas who voted for rejection. Finally, two villages (Tesocó and Tekom) had *only* Maya signators. In larger interior communities such as Peto, Yaxcabá, Tekax, and Tihosuco, the broad mixture of Spanish and Maya names suggests the degree to which Maya elites had become accustomed to political participation.[33]

LIBERALISM RENEWED

Imán's revolt brought more than a change of flags. Liberated from the constraints of Mexico, and with federalists safely in control, Yucatán now launched into a program of social and economic change that anticipated

by fifteen years the more famous reform under Benito Juárez. The new Yucatán separated the formal bonds of church and state, attempted to culturally
integrate the peasantry, and lifted the old colonial constraints which had
served to prevent the emergence of agrarian capitalism. The peninsula's advance over central Mexican developments stemmed from the fact that independence wars had not wrecked devastation here. Yucatecans had entered the
1820s with a sense of optimism and purpose, and this same optimism persisted
into the 1840s.

The first project of the new liberal regime was to reorganize Yucatán into
a more manageable state. Jettisoning the old *partidos* of colonial times, the
congress set up five departments, each known by its capital: Mérida, Campeche, Izamal, Valladolid, and Tekax. These divisions amounted to a concession to changing demographic and political influence. The areas of growth—
the southern and eastern sugar territories—now commanded greater political
autonomy, with Espita, Tekax, and Peto now enjoying more influence. De-
population had been particularly intense along the Camino Real, a region
whose economic vitality had attracted so many Mayas in the late colonial
period but which had proved unable to compete with the new sugar lands.
Thus, in April 1846 the *cura* of Calkiní found himself unable to collect his
back debts, for the simple fact that the peasant rate-payers had all fled.[34]

The realignment carved up much of the *partidos* which had once been centers of prosperity. The two halves of the Camino Real were no longer autonomous but divided between the metropoles of Mérida and Campeche. So
too, the Sierras Baja and Alta now aligned themselves with Mérida and Tekax
respectively. Tekax absorbed both Beneficios, confirming that their corn-
producing powers were now more at the service of sugar planters than of the
old urban markets.[35]

More to the point, however, was the issue of land. Imán's revolt precipitated one of the most audacious land grabs in Mexico's history, one which
succeeded in wresting several hundreds of thousands of acres from peasant
production, all in the space of seven years. The privatization of the *terrenos
baldíos* would form a central event in the emerging rural conflict.

Previous land alienation laws had failed to radically alter patterns of legal
ownership. But the new legislation set two qualifications that weighted the
balance in favor of prospective landowners. The first came on April 5, 1841,
shortly after a peasant army had served to keep the provincial liberals in
power. It limited the size of community *ejidos* to one square league centered
around the village church. In one stroke, the liberals eliminated whatever legal basis the peasant farmers might claim for maintaining *milpa* outside a limited confine.[36]

The real watershed, however, came in the following year. Unable to pay back-wages to the soldiers who had fought in the last campaign, President Miguel Barbachano offered *baldíos* in lieu of money. The concession extended not only to soldiers, but to anyone who had served Yucatán during the recent war. This included a number of wealthy individuals, priests and landowners chief among them, who had loaned money which the state could not repay.[37]

The new laws established affordably low prices. For properties between Seibaplaya and Tabasco, the prospective owner paid eight hundred pesos per league; from Capo Catoche to Belize, six hundred; best of all, along the sugar belt from Champotón to Bacalar, five hundred. Island property ran at a stiff one thousand pesos, and "any other point on the continent," four hundred pesos. Properties in this last category enjoyed such a discount because "any other point" primarily referred to the northern zone, where *hacendados* had long since snatched up the choicer lands. Five percent remained the necessary downpayment.

The results of the new enabling legislation failed to follow the path set forth in the public rhetoric. True, many soldiers did file *denuncias*. But much land, in fact the majority, went to direct purchasers, to capitalists and estate owners who possessed the wherewithal to make the most of this opportunity. Of the 459,923 hectares alienated from the public domain, only 129,594 went to soldiers, against 330,330 to outright purchasers.[38] Looking at the matter another way, of the seventeen individuals who received the maximum *baldío* awards (two square leagues), three were *curas*, four military officers, and ten private landowners.

Who profited from the privatization of land? Naturally, those who had led the fighting in the early 1840s filed and won substantial claims (see table 4). Santiago Imán, now sporting the title "brigadier general," acquired two square leagues outside of Sucopó. Also filing large claims were Imán's officers: Antonio Trujeque, Vito Pacheco, Pastor Gamboa, José Cosgaya, and José Dolores Cetina.[39] But it is doubtful that many of the military officers intended to retire to a life of husbandry. Of the six who received more than a league of land, three immediately sold their property to land developers, often at a fairly modest price.[40]

A second group of individuals acquiring larger properties were affluent priests. Here the *denuncias* reflected the economic stratifications within the church, for while priests of all rank sought property, three out of every four were *curas*. Moreover, larger claims went to *curas* whose considerable tenure had allowed them to establish themselves among the local polity. Few events symbolized the fusion of Yucatán's clergy into the rural bourgeoisie like the partnership for property development between José Calisto González, the

TABLE 4   *Largest* Denuncias: *Claimants of Two Square Leagues of* Terrenos Baldíos

DATE	PLACE	INDIVIDUAL	OCCUPATION
1844			
July 26	Bacalar	Alonso Peón	entrepreneur
Sept. 13	Dzoncauich	Jacinto Guerrero	entrepreneur
Sept. 13	Dzoncauich	José Esteban Guerrero	entrepreneur
Oct. 8	Sucopó	Santiago Imán	military officer
Dec. 7	Becal	Juan García Fernández	entrepreneur
1845			
Jan. 3	unspecified	Manuel Peón	entrepreneur
Jan. 10	Samahil	Eduardo Padillo	military officer
Jan. 28	Telá	Antonio Mais	priest
Mar. 9	Xul	José Dolores Cetina	military officer
Mar. 15	Maxcanú	Joaquína Cano	entrepreneur
Mar. 17	Tihosuco	Antonio Trujeque	military officer
Apr. 3	Dzilán	Domingo Escalante	priest
June 11	Kikil	Manuel Ponce	entrepreneur
1846			
Jan. 12	Tzucacab	Felipe Peón	entrepreneur
Mar. 13	Tixcacalcupul	Eusebio García Rejón	priest
Apr. 24	Espita	María Ana Domínguez	entrepreneur
Sept. 17	Becanchén	José Felipe Capetillo	entrepreneur
1847			
Jan. 13	Muna	José Cosgaya	military officer

Source: ANEY, misc. dates.

elderly *cura* of remote Chunhuhub, and Don Yndalecio Montforte, a creole elite of Ichmul. In this case the new land was an addition to the estate Nocac, outside Tituc, which González had brought to the deal.[41] The most prominent of these individuals was Antonio Mais of Tihosuco.[42] But the list also included *curas* of Homún, Teabo, Ichmul, Chunhuhub, Xul, Espita, Becal, Sacalaca, Chemax, Tixcacaltuyú, Peto, Temax, Maxcanú, Tunkás, and Sacalum. The new clerical holdings were geographically diversified, falling both within and without their individual parishes. Various ministers and Mérida-based cathedral functionaries also claimed properties. Manuel Antonio Sierra O'Reilly, minister of Bolonchenticul and brother of liberal ideologist Justo Sierra O'Reilly, acquired 1.5 square leagues in nearby Sahcabchén. His brother, the man who as president of congress had signed the alienation laws, acted as his agent in the matter.[43] The last *denuncia* awarded prior to the catastrophe was in fact to a priest, *cura* Domingo Silvos Escalante of Espita, acting as an agent for his brother Vicente; the property in question lay outside Sucilá.[44]

We should also note that there were numerous *denuncias* both secular and clerical which failed to appear in the notarial records, apparently because peasant-initiated lawsuits delayed or altogether prevented their approval. These are now known only by fleeting references to the lawsuits involved.[45]

A third identifiable group consisted of well-established secular landowners like Felipe Peón, owner of a vast tract which included the ruins of Uxmal. In addition to making his own *denuncias,* Peón bought up properties which soldiers had received as pay, offering them hard cash in place of undeveloped property. Under the *denuncia* program, Yucatecan entrepreneurs accelerated their plans for developing sugar, whose need for regular water and large labor forces antagonized the Maya communities of the southern and eastern interior.[46] Given the oligarchic tendencies left from the colonial era, it was hardly surprising to see property expansion proceeding along family lines, with names such as Peón, Navarrete, and Escalante taking the lead.

Occupation of political office was by no means the key to claiming land, but its usefulness should not be underestimated. Claudio Padilla, long-time *alcalde* of Yaxcabá, obtained three separate awards totaling nearly two square leagues. Present too was Juan Pio Pérez, now remembered as a Maya linguist and scholar but then a *jefe político* in Peto; Pio Pérez expanded his Maxcanú estate with 1⅛ leagues of *terreno baldío* in October 1846.[47]

No fewer than twenty-six of the *denuncias* were awarded to women. Three of these were acting on behalf of husbands or grandchildren; the remainder were private entrepreneurs, the majority of whom (fourteen) had claimed the properties as additions to their existing estates. One woman, Joaquina Cano, claimed no fewer than three *baldíos,* totaling three square leagues and making her one of the largest acquisitors in the entire peninsula.[48] Two half-league *denuncias* were additions, while the two leagues carved out of the region of Maxcanú appear to have constituted a new development. Manuela Chacón, a creole widow-entrepreneur, took control of one league near Muna only after a legal battle with the people of that town.[49]

Along with land came monopolization of water as well. In a terrain characterized by aridity and drought, this was perhaps even more important than mere possession of the earth. Some 127 of the *denuncia* awards specifically mention either a *cenote* or a well. Typical in this regard was the *denuncia* by Agustín Badillo, petitioning for the lands "which include the *cenote* Ach'unch'en of the jurisdiction of Río Lagartos." At least half of the *denuncias* of water sources were located in the arid north, in the *partidos* of Izamal, Espita, or Tizimín, and in terrain lying just to the north of Valladolid. The importance of the watering sites to the masses is evidenced by the fact that many possessed popular names which were used to identify not only the water source but also the surrounding lands.[50]

In many cases occupation and exploitation of land preceded the request for legal title. Thus, Matías Estévez had occupied the two leagues of land along the Río Hondo before bothering to formalize the arrangement. The property, already known as "Estévez del Río Hondo," provided work for some sixty people from surrounding villages, "sons of the land" who came to cut mahogany and logwood when the rhythms of *milpa* farming permitted.[51] This process would be repeated numerous times throughout the great land rush, as commercial farmers sought to legitimize their claims. In fact, one of the largest and most strategically important of the clerical *denuncias,* that of Antonio Mais of Tihosuco, was simply to formalize his pre-existing operations over two square leagues, complete with well, near Telá.[52]

But numerous Mayas also took advantage of the situation. No fewer than forty-two claims went to individuals with Maya surnames. Most of these were soldiers receiving the designated one-quarter league. But ambitious individuals claimed more. Vicente Pech, former *batab* of Yaxcabá, obtained two claims totaling 1.2 square leagues, and Luciano Puc obtained a square league outside of Peto.[53] Nor were these the only such cases. *Batabs* relied on the patronage and assistance of local creole elites to help them access the *denuncia* process.[54] At times the quest for land caused the *batabs* to play the role of acquisitive Spaniard. One such aspiring Maya elite was José María Tus, *batab* of Kauá in the mid-1840s. His attempt to absorb land from the properties of the Camal brothers of Ebtún provoked bitter complaints. José Poot was another, occupying the land which had been commonly worked by members of the Uitzil family of Peto.[55] But other Mayas lost, such as the Maya who, in trying to claim *terrenos baldíos* in Izamal, lost out to the rival claim of two soldiers. Maya peasants thus competed on the new terms for control of resources.

In addition to land acquired through *denuncia,* of course, innumerable Maya continued to own private property at this time, property of which little is known but whose peasant ownership cannot be doubted. At Tibolón, Pascuala Chi and Manuel Aké owned haciendas of name and value now lost to history.[56] As late as 1846, Maya properties could to some degree still be identified with specific families, as, for instance, certain tracts of land near Mamá, some linked to the May clan, others to the Che.[57] If the patterns of late colonial peasant properties held true, much of this amounted to little more than small farms, fallow lands, or even property that was largely useless.

These facts notwithstanding, it is clear that aspiring Maya remained junior partners in the operation, for the majority of public lands passed, at least on paper, into the hands of whites. It served as a frustrating lesson that the Maya elite could not expect to gain equal access to the new wealth. They usually lacked the capital for outright purchases, while filing for a soldier's pay had the effect of ranking them beside poor whites and Maya peasants, an exercise in downward mobility.

What is most noteworthy about the *denuncias* is not that they helped provoke the Caste War, but that they took so long to do so. One factor which may help explain this is that to Yucatecans of the 1840s the privatizations did not appear as precipitous as the rather tightly clustered documents of the notarial archives make them appear to historians. Wording of many of these *denuncias* suggests that much of the 1840s' legal process simply ratified titles to land which growers had already occupied and brought into cultivation.[58] To the historical actors, then, the process may have appeared as far more gradual.

It is also important to note that peasants first spent considerable time and labor combating the *denuncia* process through legal channels.[59] The most popular and immediate strategy was simply to demand the rejection of a specific *denuncia;* at least twenty-eight villages used this ploy, apparently to good effect in some instances, for the disputed claims fail to appear among the finalized awards found in the notarial archives. Peasants of Yalkuk (in Sierra Baja), Dzonotchel (near Peto), and Chancenote all succeeded in halting property development plans by entrepreneurial priests, for example.[60]

The second most common strategy was to legally protect what little remained in the way of village lands. Peasants could accomplish this by having their *ejidos* measured and certified; or, if the settlement was not officially a village, to apply for incorporation and, hence, village status and protection. A corollary measure to these was to petition to have violated *ejido* property restored. Of course, the strategy of using the new legislation to obtain legally sanctioned village lands was by no means new. The peasants of Champotón had already adopted this tack as early as 1813, when they sought common lands under the decree of the Spanish Cortes of November 9, 1812.[61]

Measuring the role of peasant elites in these complaints is a difficult matter. Of the fifty-two communities with documented legal actions, only twenty specifically mention either the *batab* or *república de indígenas* as plaintiffs; interestingly enough, none come from Beneficios Altos, source-point of the rebellion. (It is at least conceivable that Maya elites were involved in complaints from Ekpetz, Dzonotchel, and Ekbalam, all of Beneficios Altos, but we have nothing to document this.) However, five come from the region of Valladolid.

These included the town of Xoccén, which filed an anti-*denuncia* suit no fewer than four times and whose elites were closely allied to those of nearby Chichimilá, a leading Caste War community. At the opposite end of the spectrum, one complaint opposed a questionable lot sale by the *batab* of Izamal. Still another suit revolved around an intra-Maya dispute among the peasants of Peto.

Peasants also sought to halt or retard the land alienation process by still other legal maneuvers. *Milpa* farmers in Ticul petitioned to prevent creoles from stocking land with cattle, in hopes of mitigating one of the worst effects of commercial land use. Upon occasion the tables were reversed, with a creole as the farmer and Mayas as the would-be ranchers.[62] Finally, peasants sought to negotiate borders with the existing properties in hopes of reaching some accommodation.

These ill-documented legal battles constituted an important but long-neglected aspect of rural destabilization. They refute notions of peasant passivity and peasant dissociation from the creole legal and political apparatus. The Maya towns of Timucuy, Xcan, Yaxcabá, Tixhualahtún, and Xoccén advanced their suits not once but three, four, and even five times. The variety of legal strategies is also noteworthy. The peasant litigants squared off against all the important figures of the society: *curas,* military officers, *latifundistas,* and so forth, the people whose hands Stephens saw the peasants kiss in apparent subjugation. But in the larger reading, these suits are perhaps best seen as delayers. They retarded the commercialization process, a struggle which the peasants were losing; and they delayed the radicalization of the Mayas themselves, who would not rise up until a full two years from the date of the last recorded lawsuit.

Patch (1992) has correctly observed that the amount of land alienation was an imperfect predictor of peasant insurgency.[63] It is true that the Caste War had its genesis among villages of the political jurisdiction of Peto, the scene of the highest percentage of alienated *baldíos;* moreover, it enjoyed a somewhat later reinvigoration near Hopelchen, another scene of much land alienation. But the insurgency also found strong support around Valladolid, Tekax, and Bacalar, places where comparatively little property was awarded. As I shall argue in chapter 6, I believe that the villages most likely to rebel were those which had experienced military mobilizations between 1839 and 1847 *and* also lay along smuggling routes between Valladolid and Belize. Towns such as Tihosuco and Tixcacalcupul had histories of prolonged intraelite conflict which taught the local Mayas valuable lessons concerning ambition and opportunity. These factors, coupled with the massive land alienations, provided them with both motive and means.

Finally, it is important to note that peasant insurgency in these villages mobilized around the immediate promise of tax reduction. No mentions are made of land claims until caudillo Jacinto Pat began to negotiate with the government in 1848, and even then the majority of the articles in the treaty (which Pat soon repudiated) dealt with tax issues. The explanation, I think, is that both tax grievances and land alienation constituted the immediate symptoms of a larger process which had commercial transformation as its motor. Peasants contented themselves to petition for tax relief as long as they still enjoyed recourse to land and only took up active rebellion when tax burdens coincided with loss of that recourse. Peasants mobilized themselves in 1847 around tax issues precisely because they had learned to do so, beginning with the constitutional crisis of 1813 and continuing through various episodes of daily resistance in the 1820s and 1830s; the Imán mobilizations had merely expanded and perfected the technique. Thus, tax relief, while a major goal in itself, also served as a code language that came to encompass the totality of popular discontent.

While the restructuring of land tenure proceeded, the Yucatecan congress issued a new law codifying labor practices and reaffirming the nation's reliance on the old practice of labor debt. This reissuing largely restated practices which had existed since the 1700s, making estate peons strictly accountable for their debts while simultaneously providing the mechanisms for relocating from one estate to another. Peasants could separate themselves if a new owner assumed their debt, but also if they could prove bad treatment on the part of their old master. Incidentally, heredity debt was not legal, but specifically prohibited.[64]

Another cornerstone of this new liberal edifice was the Vagrancy Law of 1842, a decree mandating the seizure and forced service of transients, troublemakers, and social undesirables. This new law was a model of thoroughness. It defined as vagrants an enormous number of people, including those lacking visible means of support; habitual drunks and gamblers; those who had jobs but failed to work at them most of the year; those of good health who nonetheless begged from door to door; illegitimate orphans; children not native to their village of residence; children from families which operated gaming houses, kept bad company, frequented "suspicious places," or lacked the inclination to learn a useful trade; incorrigible and disobedient children abandoned by their parents; and finally, those who jeopardized their families' good reputations by ridiculing the authorities and singing satirical songs and rounds. Those convicted faced harsh penalties. Vagabonds of good health, ages seventeen to forty, could expect eight years in the military. Transgressors over forty would "be assigned to whatever establishment in which they can work," presumably the estates. A second offense would mean double-time, resulting in a potential stint of twenty-four years forced labor. Children would be assigned guardians as the local magistrates saw fit. This measure was clearly an attempt to provide labor for the estates, but it served the dual purpose of helping settle a countryside now reeling from coups and revolts. Shortly after its passage we find it invoked in several arrest warrants, for the most part involving peasants fleeing the northeast for the southern interior.[65]

Still another subdrama to the *denuncias* was the issue of *baldío* rents. The lands belonging to peasant villages were protected, at least in theory, by a grant of one league in all four directions from the village church. (In reality, this would not have allowed sufficient land to continue cultivation using *milpa* farming techniques, the only method possible.) Moreover, the law required that in order to pay for the surveying of village properties, the peasants would be responsible for a new tax of one-half real for every *mecate* of first-year *milpa* farmed on public lands.[66]

This policy quickly gave way to abuses, the simplest of which was overcharging. When the *alcalde* of Izamal collected rents from the *milperos* of nearby Huhi, he charged one real per four *mecates,* as opposed to the official rate of one per ten, thus drawing off a 150-percent illegal profit for himself.[67]

But even if it had been administered with complete circumspection, the cultivation tax would have proved unpopular. In Ichmul, Tiholop, and Tacchibichén, *milperos* refused to pay the new land tax; the wording of the law designated lands worked in 1845, but the peasants charged that they had planted their fields in the previous year. In fact, they succeeded in obtaining an exemption for this. (The unusual planting schedule suggests that they may have been growing sugar, since corn planting and harvesting would last from spring to fall of a single year.) The rent issue also raised complaints in Tacchibichén, where the *batab* and *república* framed legal petitions against the practice and its abuses, only to see them dismissed.[68] But the tax was internally divisive as well. In Temosón, where the peasants had successfully pooled their resources to purchase surrounding *ejidos,* those who had not participated in the original purchase argued that they were not liable for such taxes. This transparent attempt to foist community expenses onto fellow villagers forced the *batab* and *república* into costly legal proceedings, exhausting time and resources which would have been better spent in expanding or protecting village properties.[69]

Like so many other tax programs, the *baldío* rents failed to generate the revenues for which so many had hoped, largely because of grass-roots resistance. Where the rents did succeed was in contributing to long-term destabilization on a variety of fronts. Once the Caste War began, the government

hastily abolished *baldío* rents in a vain effort to placate the rebels, a belated re-
pentance of the national folly.

In addition to privatizing communal lands, the liberal agenda also included
a cultural strategy of Hispanicizing the Maya through education. On October 31, 1840, the new government reissued the 1784 decree of the long-dead
bishop Piña y Mazo, commanding each *cura* to take into his house two Maya
boys whom he was to train in spoken and written Spanish. Now, fifty-six
years after its original publication, the decree once more proved impracti-
cable. Bishop Guerra's office flooded with distraught letters of the rural clergy,
whose search for cooperative and interested Maya was as futile as Lot's quest
for good men in the land of Sodom. The *cura* of Cenotillo explained that
Mayas found Spanish too difficult to pronounce.[70] From Cansahcab, there
could be no talk of expanding clerical responsibilities without increasing their
already decimated revenues. In Carmen there simply were no Indians, save for
"the very few . . . who are on the *rancherías*." But others identified the problem as a general weakening of clerical control over the natives, a problem
which had only worsened since the eighteenth century. Indeed, for many the
cumulative effect of political events in the last thirty years proved a source of
rueful speculation. The *cura* of Motul summed up the matter nicely:

> *I have inquired among various knowledgeable people. And they as-
> sure me they are of the opinion that, since the transition from the
> Spanish government, the Indians believe themselves free to dispose of
> their own affairs, without anyone being able to oblige them to the
> contrary. They no longer wish to hand their children over to the
> curas to serve as domestics and household members, in order to be
> educated or instructed.*

The *cura* went on to provide an anecdote drawn from his own experience to
illustrate this:

> *I asked the alcalde of this village to provide me with two children.
> And he did so, but it was only to attend school at the accustomed
> hours; they in no way left the power of their parents or entered mine
> as domestics. This arrangement presented a decided obstacle to learn-
> ing the Castilian tongue, since upon leaving school they spoke
> nothing but their own language. Although they were brought to me,
> within three days one of their fathers came and reclaimed his son,
> stating that he wanted the boy to devote himself to agriculture. I
> knew that I lacked sufficient power to compel him—my advice and*

persuasion being in vain—so I thought it best to let him take the
boy away.[71]

The drive for Spanish literacy thus foundered on obstacles which had characterized the peninsula since the days of Landa. Peasant intransigence, together
with sheer superiority of numbers, were still forces beyond the power of the
decrees and constitutions which streamed out of Mérida. This was to be the last
attempt to radically modify peasant culture in the old Yucatán, until the explosion of peasant revolt, itself a force beyond the control of its generals and
caudillos, took matters from human hands.

THE MELLOW LIQUOR RUNS DRY

Such were the broad contours issuing from the revolt of 1839.
But what of Imán's original promise, the abolition of church taxes? Had this,
the most ancient of peasant grievances, been lost in the confusion of wars
and *denuncias?* Hardly. Events soon proved that the general's words had fallen
upon eager ears and that the spirit of tax resistance was stronger than ever.
The revolt set into motion a complex tax struggle which touched all sectors
of the society and which, in the final analysis, proved as divisive as the question of land tenure.

The revolt produced numerous consequences for the peninsula's churches,
most of them regrettable. The first was economic devastation in towns where
the fighting was most intense. José Otorio, one of Valladolid's *curas,* wrote:

> *I cannot find expression appropriate to convey to Your Holiness the*
> *ruin which my parish has suffered . . . experiencing already the*
> *shortage of resources necessary for survival, I have decided it best to*
> *depart together with my family on the 11th of this month, just like*
> *[teniente Ylario] Medina, while the storm which threatens us close*
> *at hand subsides.*[72]

Marauders also sacked Tizimín, carrying off lamps, icons, silver accoutre-
ments, and the stores of dried corn. In addition, they made off with the
church decorations from nearby Sucopó. Back in Mérida, politicians received
news of the sack with anxiety but believed that by effecting a few compro-
mises, such as reduction (*not* the promised abolition) of the church tax, together with a vigorous plan for liberal control, they could ensure that the in-

cident at Valladolid would remain an isolated aberration. It was, in fact, a shadow of things to come.[73]

Beyond initial damages, the overall political and popular climates grew colder toward the church, forcing it to assume a lower profile. Tekax offers an interesting study in this regard. Prior to the Imán revolt, *cura* Silvestre Antonio Dondé had been able to coordinate the expansion of his local empire alongside of overall regional growth. In 1838 he secured the bishop's approval to begin an auxiliary church in Becanchén, the parish *auxiliar* to which so many workers had been migrating in the 1830s. To this effect he secured an 825-peso loan from Tekax's *cofradía* of San Diego, a substantial portion of the projected total cost of 1,723 pesos. But the federalist revolt dashed this magnificent project. Dondé now found it advisable to shelve the project and retire to his rectory until the political winds shifted back in his favor.[74]

But to the peasants these problems scarcely mattered. On the contrary: the church's weakness was their own advantage. Once the new government was in place, then, the Mayas moved expeditiously to collect on their political debt. By April 1840 peasant communities such as Muxupip were demanding the exemptions which the general had so freely promised. When *cura* Antonio Avila continued to demand annual obventions in the form of thread, honey, or wax, the *batab* of Muxupip wrote to the governor to complain. "We are asking Your Excellency," he said, "to prohibit for us this payment of twelve reales a year as General Santiago Imán has communicated to us." In many villages, peasants declined to wait on government decrees and simply quit paying taxes by their own initiative. In the case of San Antonio Xul, a rancho community deep in Sierra Alta, peasant refusal to pay obventions resulted directly from Pastor Gamboa's promise of exemption when he had recruited them for temporary military service in Tenabo.[75]

At the same time, these problems counterpointed against all the traditional difficulties of maintaining revenues in rural Yucatán. Disease remained an active trouble for most rural Mayas, recurring again and again in small but lethal outbreaks throughout the 1840s and throwing the collection of rents and fees into confusion. Typhus and smallpox were particularly troubling.[76] These outbreaks lacked the devastating scope of the 1825–1826 and 1833–1835 disasters, but they nonetheless made it difficult to maintain orderly and productive lives. Moreover, grain shortages in 1843 and 1844 made peasants reluctant to share their remaining stores.[77]

Yucatecan politicians were uncertain how to treat the demands for church tax reductions. Despite an overall policy of removing the vestiges of colonialism, many still rejected the notion of church disestablishment. Most elites had linkages—familial, economic, or ideological—with Yucatecan priests. Others warned against the danger of letting the Indians think that they could bargain with the government.[78] As early as 1840, then, the new federalist regime thus found itself caught between popular expectations and the need to maintain old lines of exploitation and privilege.

The controversy fell squarely on the lap of the new governor, Santiago Méndez of Campeche, "a successful merchant, a plain, unassuming, practical man; apparently, however, not much versed in political intrigues."[79] Faced with the problems of separatism and the growing political demands of the peasantry, Méndez proved "vacillating, undecided, and unequal to the emergency."[80] He initially agreed to a plan that would retain a monthly one-real tax for Indian men but eliminate them altogether for women.[81] In the revised state of affairs the collection of church rents and the personal contribution were now under the power of the *subdelegados*.[82] This is not to say that *batabs* ceased to collect taxes. Nothing of the sort took place: rather, the same patch-work mechanism of collection remained, with *batabs*, now under new supervision, shouldering most of the actual burden. But this change in itself was significant. It helped weaken one of the oldest ties of rural society—between priest and Maya elite—and placed *batabs* in the hands of a domineering group of men less skillful in negotiating peasant interests.

In the long run the policy was a disaster. The peasantry was embittered over failing to shake off religious taxes altogether. The single-tax system also had the unintended effect of linking the peasantry's ancient grudges against the church with the new independent state. Now more than ever, noncompliance and debt-dodging had become civil offenses, while overthrow of the civil regime came to be seen as integral to the resolution of the church-tax grievance.

But the tax situation was still in flux. The 1842 defense against the Mexican invasion constituted another drain on Yucatán's already precarious finances, necessitating new and ever more onerous war taxes. Formal demand for money first appeared in June of 1842. The government raised a special tax of four reales on all men over the age of sixteen; property owners and capitalists of both sexes were to pay an additional two reales for every one hundred pesos of their actual wealth. But the need for resources continued undiminished throughout the year. In November the governor "invited" the citizens of all villages to give to the patriotic cause "with cash, grain, or whatever other type of food they can contribute."[83]

Next came the "integration" policy. After the 1842–1843 mobilization, the government again faced pressure for tax relief. In May of 1843 the government instituted a policy of "integrating" obventions back into its own collecting process. But what was given with one hand was taken away with the other. To compensate the church, the government increased the civil contribution to 1.5 reales monthly and agreed to give the church half the total proceeds.[84] Rural priests were to receive a centrally allocated stipend, a budget item which in all likelihood would have been the first sacrificed when finances ran scarce, as they so often did.

Not surprisingly, the integration policy resulted in hardship for many rural parishes, particularly those where the *cura* lacked the familial and economic connections to exert pressure for his own defense.[85] Rural priests complained to the bishop, who in turn complained to the governor in a series of letters throughout the summer of 1843.[86] By the middle of July this campaign seems to have borne fruit, since Méndez did away with the policy and ordered the confiscated money returned to the *cura* with no deductions whatsoever.[87] The law seems to have remained on the books, but its enforcement was stayed, or at least moderated, by the governor's July 13 order. Protests concerning lost obvention money continued through August, but by September the priests— who were not reluctant to complain—had ceased to complain.[88]

If tax collection policy remained troublesome and confusing, all the more so were its social consequences. The slashing of church obvention money, coming hard upon the abolition of tithes in 1833, reduced the rural church to a desperate position. With many of the church's ancient sources of revenue gone, the simultaneous powers of coercion and patronage sharply reduced its sway in rural affairs. As in 1813, the *curas* watched their peasant staffs desert. Certainly the most extreme case occurred in Ichmul, where the sacristans and *maestros cantores* went on strike: with obventions now abolished, nothing separated them from the mass of poor peasants, and they consequently demanded a regular salary for their services.[89]

By 1843 rural priests were paying for *koché* service out of their own pockets.[90] *Curas* published manifestos and open letters urging the reinstitution of the tithe, or the old obvention rates, or both. But try as they might, the effect of recent events was devastating. By March 1841 Izamal, which was a much larger religious organization than most rural parishes and required considerable overhead, was teetering on the brink of insolvency.[91] But even the smallest parish felt the effects of the crunch.

At the height of the summer obvention crisis, the church responded by instituting a strict rationing of government-allocated monies. A committee composed of four prominent clerics was appointed to establish a quota system for determining how much each individual curacy should receive. The composition of this committee is worth noting as a study in clerical power. It included José María Meneses, the political liberal and former interim bishop who had now retired to tend his haciendas; Tomás Domingo Quintana, brother of Mexican state-builder Andrés Quintana Roo; the dyspeptic Eusebio Villamil, powerful in both church and state; and the influential Raymundo Pérez, politician, developer, estate owner, and *cura* of Hoctún. In sum, it was a "wise-man" committee assembled for dealing with the most severe church crisis in three decades. The factors used in determining the allocation were tenure of the *cura,* number of ministers, and monthly expenditures necessary to maintain the individual cult. All three of these variables related in some way to the size of the peasant population. Large flocks meant large, lavish churches with higher overhead; collecting from and tending to these obligations required more clerical help; and *curas* were likely to remain longer in lucrative and powerful positions. The curacies of Mérida and Campeche naturally ranked high, the cathedral being the largest at 205 pesos, principally because of a double *cura* salary. These apart, however, the largest curacies all lay in the populous sugar-producing arch which swung from Valladolid southeastward to Bolonchén: Ichmul, Tekax, Ticul, Tihosuco, Tsitnup, Valladolid, Yaxcabá, Peto, and Holpechén. The list of affluent parishes formed a virtual map of future peasant insurgency. Only two other formations gained high ranking. The first included certain northern-central communities which had grown up around Mérida and the cattle industry, chiefly Izamal, Temax, Mamá, and Raymundo Pérez' own community of Hoctún. The second was the trade route between Mérida and Campeche, which included the historically prosperous communities of Calkiní, Hecelchakán, and Hocabá.[92] The more powerful branches of the church were saving themselves at the expense of weaker parishes.

In reaction to the loss of funds, some *curas* resorted to inflating the fees charged for religious services, the so-called minor obventions. It is impossible to say how inflated prices became, since price manipulations were by their very nature illicit and unrecorded. In the parish of Sotuta prices for weddings and burials reached such heights that angered estate owners filed suit on behalf of their workers.[93] The issue of exorbitant minor obventions remained a sore spot in church-state revenue negotiations throughout the 1840s. Needless to say, it was the peasantry more than anyone who resented the practice. Maya villagers saw the reward for their wartime service eaten away by tactics which violated ancient price structures. One fact illustrates how deeply the issue burned among the indigenous masses. In 1850, when Caste War caudillos were negotiating with Yucatán's ecclesiastical peace commission, their chief demand was a ceiling of ten reals per marriage—this, after three years of relentless warfare.[94]

Other strategies surfaced for tiding over church operations. Some revenue-starved *curas* reinstated old colonial taxes, such as the demand that *doctrina* children provide an egg every Thursday. This raised protests from peasants who believed that the colonial tax methods were finally behind them.[95] José Antonio Acosta of Conkal circumvented the ban on burial fees by charging a two-real coffin fee, technically not part of the religious service.[96] Some *curas* adapted to the hard times by pooling the reduced church revenues with their own private resources, a policy which was doubtless appreciated by their ministers and assistants. In Chemax, the *cura* was able to retire to his rancho Kantunil, ceding the paltry returns of the parish to his two ministers.[97] The *cura* of Tizimín, Fr. Buenaventura Pérez, found himself in such financial difficulties that he discharged his ministers, instructing them "to dedicate themselves to other occupations in which they can make enough to eat." But there were other casualties as well. In the sudden budget crunch, Pérez also had to quit paying his Maya sacristans and *maestros cantores*. Their reaction to this is unknown but was presumably no more favorable than that of the ministers themselves.[98]

The events of 1839–1843 rekindled the spirit of tax resistance which had flared in the constitutional years. Peasants in the ranchos which lay between towns, for example, proved formidable cases for the would-be tax collector and grew all the bolder with the expectations raised by Imán. Collectors who entered the ranchos found themselves attacked by Mayas wielding stones and clubs, Mayas led in some cases by the *mayordomo* himself.[99] The same held true for isolated settlers, as indicated by a report on recalcitrants living in the backlands between Xcan and Labcah:

> *So it is that in the wilderness between said ranchos there can be found many individuals living in secret in order to obstruct collections or demands that should present themselves, pretending to be* vecinos *of some different and faraway town or jurisdiction. And if they are made to labor, some withdraw themselves under pretext of going to fetch their receipts, while others carry forged receipts.*[100]

Nor was state tax collection of the 1840s any easier than the church collections of the 1810s. Juan Pio Pérez, best remembered today as a Maya linguist, had ample occasion to study the language of peasant tax-dodging when he served as *jefe político* of Peto. In 1844 Pio Pérez reported that current plans to collect from the dispersed rural population of Peto were infeasible. So many had been hiding in remote settlements for so long and with no receipts whatsoever that no one could hope to tabulate their back debts. If money were demanded of them, they would simply flee once more. Finally, estate owners themselves had no wish to pay the taxes of their residents and would go so far as to hide them from the collectors.[101]

Collection problems related directly to another important dynamic of rural society: the declining position of peasant elites. Not only did the *batabs* and their fellow elites find it more difficult to squeeze money from taxpayers; they also found themselves legally harassed for collection shortfalls, as was the case with Patricio Pat of Valladolid.[102] To avoid having these penalties fall back upon them, some *batabs* employed strong-arm tactics. Complaints against such methods surfaced against the *batab* of Mamá, who confiscated pigs to cover deficits. Complaints also surfaced against the unpopular *batab* José María Chan of Bolonchenticul, but the local judge, who valued his services in this regard, came to his defense.[103]

Given the difficulties of collection, some tried to escape the duty of *batab* altogether. The available evidence, though fragmentary, suggests that turnover in the position of *batab* accelerated throughout the early national period, reaching its height in the post-Imán years (see chapter 4). But not all succeeded. In San Marcos, a barrio of Valladolid, authorities flatly rejected the resignation of José Nieves Canul.[104]

These problems were compounded by blatant political intrusions, as local elites manipulated peasant offices to suit their own political interests. In Dzitbalché federalists forced out *batab* Luciano Mis by threatening to shoot him. Mis feigned illness in his letter of resignation, but the truth emerged in subsequent reports. But the new separatist government had little interest in restoring partisans of the centralists, and Mis was replaced.[105]

The matters of property and politics among peasant officeholders emerge even more clearly in the village of Dzibalchén, deep in the Campeche sugar district. Here the *batab* and *república* were federalist partisans, the *cura* and *subdelegado* centralists. After the beginning of the Imán revolt, the *cura* forced out *batab* Clemente Uc, who had served since 1823, and replaced him with the more pliant Juan de la Cruz Huchim. But when the centralist regime collapsed, the *república* seized the initiative by demanding that Uc be reinstated. Interestingly enough, they defended him not only on the basis of probity, but also on his *"fincas suficientes,"* his credentials as a rural bourgeois (see chapter 4).[106]

But Maya collectors were not the only ones to feel the pressure. The ministers whom *curas* used to oversee collections also struggled with the new difficulties. Thus in Peto the *cura* was forced to dismiss his minister, Francisco María Carrillo, for failing as a collector. Though officially charged with the responsibility, Carrillo let the local Maya church staff perform the collections and suffer the resistance.[107]

All in all, the separation from Mexico spelled hard times for the Yucatecan church and, by extension, for rural society. Peasant-based revenues suffered, while attempts to recoup lost income merely served to further alienate the church from Maya elites and commoners alike. In this spiral of delegitimization, it became all the easier for peasants to imagine direct action against the institutions which had governed them for three centuries.

"MURDER AND OTHER EXCESSES"

The final legacy of Imán's revolt was a heightened climate of political violence which penetrated into all corners of the countryside. The successes against Mexico had taught disgruntled factions that the shortest way of effecting their aims was to raise an armed mob. The authorities suppressed most of these teapot revolutions, but nevertheless there were hints that Yucatán, long habituated to colonial stability, was unprepared for the coming of true unrest. Jails failed to confine their occupants, who all too frequently escaped, sparking new revolts and forcing costly and cumbersome manhunts.[108] Also noteworthy was the growing level of Maya participation. In 1812 it had taken royal proclamations to bestir the peasantry, but now virtually anybody could do it, quickly and with the slightest of pretexts. By the mid-1840s politically related violence had become a common feature of rural communities.

A key factor here was the political composition of the larger and older rural communities. More than ever non-Mayas were now making their homes in provincial towns and villages. In addition to whatever stresses this caused for the Maya population, the demographic shift also meant increased rivalries among local elites. In the eighteenth century, creole presence in most provincial towns had been limited to figures of clear authority, such as priests, royal officials, and the handful of local planters. All of these enjoyed well-understood privileges and social ascendancy. After independence, the factions which controlled the state enacted measures to maintain that ascendancy in the face of demographic increase. Access to office depended upon literacy and upon participation in local militia regiments. This tended to exclude poorer creoles, who were often illiterate. Moreover, elites had more incentive for militia service, since they occupied officer positions. The rank-and-file of the Yucatecan army, on the other hand, consisted of poor creoles, mestizos, mulattos, and a few impressed peasants. These tendencies combined to keep the traditional gentry at the top of supposedly democratic governments.

Representative of the problems created by this system was the conflict which erupted in Hoctún in 1840. The parish had long been dominated by *cura* Raymundo Pérez and a small network of other creoles who held land and occupied political office. Seeking to escape their domination, the mestizos of Hoctún migrated to the surrounding *auxiliares* of Tahmek and Xocchel, both of which were communities almost entirely Maya in composition. Here the disaffected newcomers set up municipal juntas with themselves in charge. In May Pérez countered with a lawsuit to have the two hamlets' elections annulled and their juntas disbanded; in this process he obtained supporting testimony from the *batabs* and ranking *alcaldes* of both Tahmek and Xocchel. In addition to pointing out the upstarts' illiteracy and lack of military service, Pérez made much of the fact that one of them, José de la Cruz Pinzón in Xocchel, was merely a tailor. It was typical of the slanted nature of Yucatán's rural power structure that Perez' suit succeeded on all points.[109]

Growing rural instability also involved the towns' loss of control over outlying estates, estates whose owners were able to reassign themselves to the jurisdictions of small communities whose populations had grown just enough to permit *ayuntamientos*.[110] The guiding issues were control of tax and labor drafts. Estate owners were loath to surrender these under any circumstances, but they stood a better chance of controlling the process in the nascent political structures of recently incorporated towns, since long-entrenched power monopolies continued to dominate the old towns.

Whatever the issue, not all towns were fortunate enough to resolve their disputes via the law courts. Examples of direct political action literally exploded on the scene after 1839, for in addition to encouraging violence, the separatist triumph had also raised questions of who was to rule at home. Former allies of Imán now bristled to see a pro-Méndez government imposed over their own local network. As elsewhere in nineteenth-century Latin America, political coercion was at its crudest and most naked in the small towns, where self-proclaimed allies of Mérida political factions used unscrupulous measures to control elections for the new *ayuntamientos*.[111]

One principal area of instability was the same string of coastal towns where Imán had raised troops and fought his insurrection. Of course, the northeast was no stranger to violence: well into the 1830s pirates operated between the islands and the coast, raiding and burning ranchos and making off with canoes.[112] But the post-Imán revolts were of greater portent for the new nation, for they brought violence deeper into the interior and mobilized men who would play seminal roles in the coming Caste War. First came Espita. Here in

1841 a discontented officer named José Dolores Cetina, later to play a leading role in the Caste War insurrection, joined with "certain individuals of restless and turbulent spirit" in an attempt to overthrow the new *ayuntamiento.* The episode grew so threatening that the governor sent Imán himself to restore order.[113]

But Espita was merely one example of a phenomenon that was sweeping the towns from the northeast coast down to the deep sugar plantations. Calotmul suffered an abortive revolt only a few months later.[114] Among those implicated in electoral fraud and coercion in Peto was Macedonio Dzul, the *batab*-entrepreneur-litigant encountered in chapter 4. Enemies accused Dzul of rousting out peasants from outlying estates and compelling them to vote for the town-dominated candidates under threat of whippings.[115] At this same time, Valladolid as well experienced corrupt elections which provoked massive disputes. Factional quarrels in this old frontier capital involved a certain Bonifacio Novelo, whose role in the Caste War was to be even greater than Cetina's.[116]

The revolts of Espita, Valladolid, and elsewhere drew life more from factional quarrels than ideology. Without exception they perished in their cradles, but they carried ominous overtones, not least of which was the increasing level of peasant participation. Mayas were now turning up in precisely the sort of public activity which had been prohibited to them under colonial rule. In this sense, the early national period merely seemed to the peasants to be fulfilling its rhetoric of democratic political participation. The community quarrels of the 1840s provided a training ground for future insurgents and a rehearsal for future revolt, all crafted in the rhetoric of the early liberal regimes. In sum, political violence had become multiethnic.

Peasant participation in political furors was now everywhere. In Beneficios Bajos factional tensions boiled over in March 1842, when Yaxcabá's recently elected *alcalde,* José Tiburcio Díaz, was removed from office for being under twenty-five years of age. *Diacistas* raised a mob of some two hundred men, primarily Maya, from the towns of Yaxcabá, Tabi, Mopilá, Kancabdzonot, and Tixcacaltuyú, to march into the *cabecera* and demand that Díaz be reinstated. In some places the rebels used the *batab* and *república* as recruiters. Peasants joined up primarily because of the promise of exemption from future *fagina* service. The relatively small number of peasants recruited, about 120, probably reflected the obvious unlikelihood of success. If that was the case, their apprehensions were all too quickly proven, when a force of ten soldiers broke up the movement.[117]

Political violence drew in peasants in other places as well. The election of municipal *alcaldes* in Pisté, 1844, occasioned new rounds of fraud and coercion, sparking legal protest from the *república* and allied creoles. Elections for municipal *alcalde* also raised firestorms in Xcan, to the east of Valladolid, but the election was ruled valid and the *batab* and *república* came away with a sense of frustration over the legal system.[118] In Tiholop, long a scene of discontent, a rowdy group of creoles and some forty Mayas gathered to denounce the federalist revolt. The mob proclaimed that Santiago Imán himself was prisoner in a Mérida jail and that his Tihosuco confederate Vito Pacheco languished in a jail in Sisal de Valladolid. In part the mob gathering appears to have been rooted in local grievances: Roque Torrens, one of the mob leaders, was demanding office and in the course of the evening actually made off with the *alcalde*'s baton, a symbolic expropriation of power. Although the crowd eventually dispersed, the incident showed that Imán's campaign and strategies were common knowledge in the deep interior and that rural peasants' capacity for mobilization was assuming new dimensions.[119]

Peasant discontent also manifested itself through isolated acts of mayhem. Clearly, nineteenth-century travelers' accounts of Maya passivity on such grand estates as Uxmal told only part of the story. Within a year of John Lloyd Stephens' visit, the peasants of this vast estate murdered the *mayordomo*, a certain Castillo. On October 20, 1844, the governmental assembly upheld the death penalty for five Maya peasants who had committed "murder and other excesses" on the haciendas Uxmal and Chetulix. A sixth defendant, Domingo Cen, received a pardon.[120] In Acanceh, the peasants had become so incensed over the hegemony of the estates that they "maimed" the *mayordomo* of the hacienda Tepich, who only escaped death by the timely intervention of the owner, who also happened to be the local magistrate. The level of peasant activism in these incidents of mayhem was necessarily significant. But it is also worth noting that Acanceh's proximity to Mérida did not imply political quiescence, nor was the Maya elite invariably more compromised by creole interests.[121]

There were other omens as well. In later years creoles would opine that Indians were too timid and cowardly to commit any but the more petty of crimes. Yet the surviving records flatly contradict this. By 1844 the deepening social unrest was manifesting itself in numerous peasant crimes, including brazen acts like arson, rape, rioting, murder, and one case of "plagiarism" (presumably a forged passbook, tax receipt, or land title). In the meantime the crimes traditionally associated with peasants—cattle rustling, tax dodging, and the ever-present "disrespect for authorities"—continued throughout the peninsula.[122]

One direct measure of the perceived threat posed by Maya discontent was the fact that by 1844 one of the highest priorities of the revolutionary government was to demobilize the peasantry. We know that one of the communities subjected to such pressure was Tepich, for the peasants there lodged a grievance against a certain José Carrillo for impounding their rifles (*fusiles,* not the rustic *escopetas,* or shotguns) with no indemnification whatsoever. In response the government directed the *jefe político* of Peto to see that the peasants received a just price for the weapons, but not the weapons themselves.[123] Attempts to disarm Tepich once again in 1847 would function as part of the trigger to the Caste War. Meanwhile, anxiety over the waves of violence in the early 1840s precipitated outright confiscation elsewhere as well. Juan García Fernando, a Becal creole who owned five estates in the Camino Real region, routinely furnished his workers with rifles for deer hunting and for exterminating the jaguars which preyed on livestock. In January of 1843 the *alcaldes* at Nunkiní confiscated the rifles in Fernando's absence and without prior consultation, citing emergency decrees aimed at keeping the peace. The rifles remained locked in the local *ayuntamiento* house for nearly three years; after Fernando successfully petitioned to have them returned, he discovered that they had deteriorated beyond use, and now he had to sue to recover damages to his property.[124]

The Imán revolt therefore left a troubled legacy for Yucatán's rural inhabitants: renewed peasant expectations and resistance, reinforcement for anticlericism as a means to political ends, difficult choices for peasant elites, and a climate of popular mobilizations and political violence. These dynamics would hardly have augured well for any new republic. But they were even more ominous for one teetering on bankruptcy and plagued with insoluble animosities of race and class.

TO THE FUTURE

In staging his revolt, Imán had acted as the midwife to chaos. He had aimed at prying loose the centralist control which had dominated since 1834, but the true casualty had been the chain of brokers who mediated between national political structures and the rural peasantry. The complex tax structure which acted as Yucatán's nervous system suffered as taxes fell. At the same time, the fewer taxes became more difficult to collect, as old expectations of a tax millennium returned. These changes seriously damaged the church, which had long depended on peasant obventions. But it was the *batabs* who faced these changes at the most elemental level. Now their work was rendered all the more difficult by the sudden onslaught of land privatization.

To those who pondered Yucatán's true state of affairs, it was obvious that the new separatist politics, couched in familiar rhetoric of the Enlightenment but concealing deep colonial divisions and racial hatreds, held the potential for disaster. For the time being many Yucatecans could continue to deceive themselves into believing that all was well. But the energizing effects of the 1838 revolt and its half-fulfilled promises did not escape the foreign travelers who visited Yucatán in the early 1840s. Norman, the New Orleans bookseller who toured the peninsula in 1843, was the most trenchant of all:

> The country is not destined ever to be of any considerable importance in the political scale. Its resources are very limited; its capital small; its soil by no means fertile; it possesses neither good roads to any extent, nor a single navigable river; manufacturers are almost unknown, and agriculture is in the most neglected state. How then can Yucatan sustain itself, or ever figure as an independent nation? The idea is absurd, and could only be entertained by an enthusiast, and one totally ignorant of the elements required to constitute national greatness and prosperity.[125]

Despite his distinctly American assumption that bigger was better, Norman was correct in identifying the lack of industry and infrastructure, the meager resources, and the prevailing underproductivity. More importantly, he pointed to a feature which elites themselves, caught up in their obstreperous politics, tended to forget:

> Another circumstance worthy of consideration is the existence of a large colored population, far outnumbering the whites. Should Yucatan be left to itself, an insurrection among the Indians would be productive of the most awful calamities; and in that case, being entirely isolated, no foreign aid could be looked for to subdue the danger. The glimpse the Indians have just caught of what they may do, and their exertions in the last revolution being rewarded by a diminution in the amount of their onerous religious contributions, may probably stimulate them to make an effort to free themselves from the bondage of the whites. Many intelligent and well-informed men, residents and natives of the country, fear this may ultimately be the result; and it is on this account chiefly they regret the employment of Indians in the late contest. The chord touched by Iman has vibrated, the way has been shown to designing and unprincipled men, of causing an excitement and making themselves fearful; they

have only to hold out promises, however fallacious, to this race, and ensure themselves a certain measure of importance and notoriety. Ere long some "Tecumseh" or "Blackhawk" may rise up, and the most disastrous, heart-rending, and bloody scenes will be re-enacted.[126]

These predictions, the offspring in whose birth the general had figured so prominently, would mature far more quickly than anyone could have anticipated. The heartrending and bloody scenes lay only a few years away.

Six

"THE DEVIL WILL
OVERTAKE US"

*Things are found here which probably have not taken place even
among the wild Indians of the Californias.*
—ANTONIO MAIS, *cura* of Tihosuco, February 1847[1]

*If we are going to observe the formulas of the law with conspirators,
then the devil will overtake us and them both, without remedy.*
—JOSÉ EULOGIO ROSADO, on peasant insurgents,
  July 22, 1847[2]

The uprising which travelers and apprehensive creoles prophe-
sied had its birth in a line of villages extending from Chichimilá, just south of
Valladolid, to the southeastern community of Tihosuco. Today these communities all display monuments to their heroes, *batabs* who conspired to launch the
Caste War. The statues of Jacinto Pat in Tihosuco and Cecilio Chi in Tepich
are largely identical except that the latter, perhaps owing to the incendiary
reputation which has attached itself to Chi's legend, carries a torch in his left
hand. In Tihosuco, however, the birthplace and nucleus of the war, the greatest monument of all is the village church. All revolutions have their Bastilles,
symbolic edifices of the old power which must be struck to the ground as
announcements of the sudden inversion of power. In Tihosuco the edifice
which played this role was the village's enormous church. Its front half remains utterly destroyed. The remnants of the south side of its front arch stand
alone, denuded of plaster and carved stone, like a lone tooth in the skull of
some perished animal. The building still serves its original function as a
church. Its altar and pews are huddled far to the inside, away from the elements. Its most impressive feature is the carved stone altarfront, displaying

three faces of a design that is distinctly non-European: idols before altars, to adapt an old phrase.[3]

Surprisingly, there has been little effort to reconstruct the history of the basic Caste War communities. The following reviews what is known of the four most essential of these: Tihosuco, Tepich, Tixcacalcupul, and Chichimilá. Though undoubtedly we would care to know more, the available evidence does offer some idea of the issues and complexities—and the personalities—which defined the insurrectionary towns.

TIHOSUCO

The first and most important of the radical communities, Tihosuco, had long held out the promise of riches. The conquistadors had hoped and consequently believed that gold and silver deposits lay hidden somewhere within Beneficios Altos. Such deposits failed to materialize, but this fact did little to dampen the colonial imagination, and from time to time fantastical reports surfaced regarding a "lost mine" somewhere between Tihosuco and Ekpetz. Legend held that a settler had once discovered a gold vein in the lot surrounding his rustic home but that record of the property's exact location had disappeared during the upheavals of 1813. Still, optimism persisted. One hopeful wrote, "Trustworthy reports have persuaded us, with justification, that those vast stretches conceal precious minerals."[4]

As time went by, Tihosucans simply transferred these dreams to the realm of agriculture. Initially it was a land of subsistence farmers; but by the 1840s Tihosuco witnessed diversification into livestock and sugar. Indeed, by the last decade of the colonial era, its inhabitants had begun setting up sugar ranchos, complete with crude sugar-refining equipment. With sugar came commerce and opportunity. Many of the peasants became part-time *arrieros,* using their time away from the *milpa* to transport crates of sugar to the great cities far away. The incentive for this was hard cash from local *rancheros*. By 1818 demand for transport of sugar had grown so great that the Maya *arrieros* now found themselves continually away from home and fields, a situation not entirely to their liking. Moreover, the *rancheros,* who lived in the same frontier hardscrabble as the peasants themselves, characteristically operated in debt and waited on the return from their sugar to pay off their carriers. *Arrieros* disliked the arrangement. But rather than renouncing the freight business altogether, they haggled for better deals and even sued for government help in collecting their fees from the *rancheros*.[5] In later years half-pay in advance became a common arrangement in many places.[6] Sugar carrying helped establish economic and political connections between Tihosuco and the peasant communities along the road to the north.

But Tihosuco's trade was not only with Mérida and Valladolid. By the end of the eighteenth century, the town had also begun to orient itself toward the markets of the southeast, to the military outpost at Bacalar. Mayas of that region lived in far-flung hamlets nestled within a tropical forest that defied unwanted scrutinies. These were remote and isolated Mayas unwilling to part with their pitiful surpluses; nor did the Spanish possess the manpower to track them down and coerce them. *Bacalareños* also found it more difficult to farm commercially, for given the shortage of labor, Maya workers commanded higher wages than their counterparts in other regions of Yucatán. This lowered the prospects for estate owning in the eyes of the cash-strapped creoles. With abundant farming opportunities near the fort, peasants of Tihosuco and other villages had developed the custom of migrating southward for temporary work, carrying with them certificates of permission from their local magistrates. The only stipulation was that the migrant workers who remained in Bacalar for more than a month had either to become permanent residents or return to their native villages, local taxes and labor needs being the critical issue. Bacalar's continued sparse population suggests that most chose the second option.[7]

Given the problems of labor, it became expedient for *bacalareños* to purchase corn from Tihosuco and other large towns of the southeast. In 1800, for example, Tihosucans sold 1,389 *cargas* of corn to Bacalar for 1,263 pesos. No documents survive to explain who arranged these sales and who received the profits, but such large quantities almost certainly involved some purchase from peasant producers, even if the peasants in question received below-market prices. Corn sales to Bacalar continued in the following years. For Tihosuco, the outpost remained a guaranteed market due to its constant problems with predatory insects, specifically "a moth which lives [in the grain], known vulgarly as *gorgojo*." In a sense Tihosucans were defense contractors. The money they paid to church and state, as well as the money they later used to invest in sugar production and refining, ultimately came from contracts to supply the Bacalar military outpost.[8]

Tihosuco had still another enterprise: smuggling. It is impossible to gauge the volume of contraband which passed through this frontier village, at least on the basis of existing documents. We know that in some cases the products reached Tihosuco from the northern coastal hamlet of Yalahán, where traders brought them up from Belize by *canoas,* large vessels of pre-Hispanic design. One of the few individuals arrested for this crime was José Antonio Carrillo in 1845. On his rancho Neuelá, not far from Tihosuco, authorities found a boatload of clothes, textiles, and utensils, candlesticks, English shoes, tobacco, china, thread, iron griddles, copper engravings, and other petty commodities. But the *contrabandistas* dealt in more than knickknacks: they also did a lively trade in arms and gunpowder, raw materials for a society bordering on civil war.[9]

Merchants operating out of Belize provided most of this contraband. The trade was reciprocal: as Belizeans concentrated on logging and contraband merchandising, they came to depend on the cultivators of southern Yucatán to supply them with the food they needed and the *aguardiente* they loved. North of the Río Hondo, individuals such as the priest Andrés Rubio acted as middlemen between rural Maya corn producers and the Belizean purchasing agents resident in Bacalar. Elites in Mérida and Campeche (some of whom were themselves complicit) complained endlessly about this ruinous and illegal competition, but they were powerless to solve the problem. The frontier was large, the capital far away, and what this underproductive and overtaxed society could not manufacture for itself, the British were only too happy to supply.[10] Rather than diminishing, the trade with Belize—legal or otherwise—expanded in the 1840s, the result of simultaneous booms in northern Belize logging and southern Yucatecan sugar.[11]

Smuggling was an extensive operation to some degree countenanced by local authorities throughout the frontier. Rancho Neuelá's clattering collection of pots, pans, and candlesticks could hardly have traveled in secret. The operation demanded mule teams, porters, and middlemen of precisely the sort that transported sugar. Places like Valladolid and Tihosuco were too far inland to be called entrepôts; rather, they were regional warehouses which distributed the contraband goods throughout surrounding villages and hamlets. The middlemen were the *tratantes,* rural peddlers with an intimate knowledge of the countryside. Fibers of the trade included the *ranchero* who wholesaled the goods and stowed them on his property, the Mayas who carried them, the many people who bought them in cities and pueblos, and finally the officials who countenanced the operation. In Tihosuco contraband trafficking was simply a part of life.

Tihosucans had an uneasy relationship with the government in Mérida. Trade constituted a powerful link. But like most rural communities, Tihosuco had periodically been forced to subsidize national efforts, usually to the benefit of the urban elites who formed the core of most postcolonial political movements. As late as 1834 Tihosucans were suing to recover the forced contributions they had paid in early 1822 to help defend against a Spanish invasion which never materialized.[12] At the same time, urban merchants and rural producers continued to squabble over which end of the sugar business was to bear the greater tax burden.[13] It was hardly surprising that the communities along the remote sugar frontier developed their own internal political loyalties, a paranoid provincialism which made them only too susceptible to plots of revolution.

Like many of the rural communities, Tihosuco accommodated diverse factions and authorities which worked in opposition as often as they did in concert. The first and perhaps greatest individual power in Tihosuco was the *cura,* Antonio Mais. A native of Málaga, Mais first came to Yucatán in 1803. He was well connected, for he had arrived with his patron and fellow *malagueño,* Bishop Estévez y Ugarte. Mais served as the bishop's secretary, then rose to become dean of the seminary. However, the time for high-handed peninsular rule was drawing to a close. Mais' downfall owed to his habit of putting troublesome students in stocks; during the brief ferment of the constitution, the students crept into the courtyard one evening and burned them. The humiliation and subsequent ridicule caused Mais to resign his post.[14]

Initially Mais chose Ichmul as his new curacy. In 1803–1804 he had served as administrative secretary for the pastoral visits and was aware that the six thousand pesos annual rent made Ichmul one of the most lucrative parishes in Yucatán. But a few years later Mais abandoned Ichmul for Tihosuco, a curacy of half the rent and almost as remote as Bacalar. His decision only makes sense when seen as entrepreneurial strategy: Tihosuco lay at the very edge of the nascent sugar industry. Moreover, Mais himself knew something of the area's smuggling activities and their secret pathways: it was through here that he fled to Belize in 1829 after an undisclosed legal dispute, only to suffer the humiliation of being returned in chains and stocks.[15] Though his enemies referred to him as "a man of bad faith, an impostor and a discontent," Mais was also a talented survivor who would soon be free and securely established in Tihosuco.

Tihosuco provided him with the entrepreneurial climate he needed. When the *denuncias* of *terrenos baldíos* reached their height, Mais himself made one of the largest claims on record. Eight leagues south of Telá, Mais had established a hacienda modestly named San Antonio, within which lay two square leagues of *baldío* land; the *denuncia* now legitimized this as his private property. The *cura* also owned a rancho near Tihosuco itself. Whatever the nature of his career at the cathedral, Mais lived a stormy existence at Tihosuco. He appears constantly in the notarial records naming powers of attorney to collect debts or to perform unspecified legal services.[16]

Although Tihosuco's church rents remained high, clerical control was a matter of some difficulty. Evidence of this problem surfaced in 1835, when the church roof collapsed, destroying the cornices, confessional, the pulpit, four altars, and part of the walls. Even though the authorities had offered to furnish Mais with the requisite materials, and even though he "did not doubt of the cooperation of my parishioners, who hear me with love," the problem was getting those loving parishioners within earshot. The church catastrophe came on the heels of the cholera epidemic, and most of the peasants had scattered to their *milpas* or to parts unknown.[17] In Tihosuco as elsewhere, church *faginas* were clearly more than a form of despotism, in which the director of work simply announced to the workers where they were to be on a certain day and what they were to do. By keeping out of sight, Maya peasants avoided a good deal of such demands, thereby limiting effective control.

Mais' rivals to local power were a handful of ambitious creoles. Certainly the region had its share of older stock, such as the Vásquez and Megía families. But in the decades since 1800 a new breed of settler had begun to appear in Tihosuco: ambitious, often unscrupulous men who saw the frontier as a means of advancing their careers. Indifferent to political and philosophical tenets, fleeting in personal loyalties, they would eventually embrace revolution as a means to that end. Principal among these were Antonio Trujeque and Vito Pacheco, previously encountered as associates of the more famous Santiago Imán. The caudillo's triumph provided both of them with local political offices, and using Imán's anticlerical methods, they soon challenged the traditional pecking order in Tihosuco.

As in so many places, rural powers fought out their quarrels through the issue of urban property. Real estate values in the southern towns continued to rise. Church reconstruction in Tihosuco was completed by 1841; masonry houses went up, and streets were smoothed and leveled. Indeed, virtually all of the towns of former Beneficios Altos witnessed construction of masonry jails, churches, and *ayuntamiento* houses, the trademarks of progress.[18] In this case quarrels erupted over a public school building which Mais had apparently neglected to utilize. Pacheco, in an effort to discredit and embarrass the *cura*, publicly offered to furnish the schoolhouse himself.[19] This petty quarrel over a schoolhouse underscored the factionalism in towns later to become centers of rebellion. In Tihosuco, men such as Trujeque and Pacheco showed what was necessary for insurgency. They were truculent toward clerics and other authorities; they rallied the masses to further their political designs; they offered demagogic promises to end taxes; they raised secret stockpiles of arms and supplies; and they were too well acquainted with smuggling and conspiracy. The *batabs* who rebelled in the summer of 1847 thus had intimate experience with the techniques of insurrection which would catapult them to fame.

A third and equally important force in local politics was the Maya elite. The indigenous community may well have enjoyed some political clout by the end of the colonial period. A Maya signator appeared on Tihosuco's application for town status in 1813. Significantly, Mérida officials who reviewed the proposal had to browbeat Tihosucans into raising taxes on Indians "to animate their industry, since without legal obligation, they will without remedy hand themselves over to the disorders of inaction."[20]

In Tihosuco the Maya elite meant, above all others, Jacinto Pat. The southern *jefe máximo* during the height of the Caste War, Pat was the peasant caudillo most accessible to history. In at least one other instance his contemporaries referred to him as "Francisco Pat," and it is possible that he was the same Francisco Pat appointed as *batab* in May 1829. But this seems unlikely, since the 1828 *matrícula* specifically identifies him under the name "Jacinto." It is also possible that he had kinship ties to Chichimilá parish, where the Puc family was both prevalent and politically active; his wife was Feliciana Puc, and that particular patronymic was rare in Tihosuco.[21]

One apocryphal story tells of how Jacinto Pat traveled to Mérida in 1844 to acquire a copy of the recently printed *Historia de Yucatán* by López de Cogolludo. He appeared at the printing press of Gerónimo Castillo and purchased a bound copy for eighteen pesos. Castillo's son, who worked in the shop and told the account, portrayed Pat as "an Indian bordering on forty-eight to fifty years; he was dressed in the custom of his race, but with much decency, [with] white pants, and a white shirt as well, with gold buttons; elegant sandals and a fine straw hat." What makes the story doubtful, however, is that it did not appear until 1899, by which time Pat, long dead, had ascended into the heaven of Yucatecan legend.[22]

Pat was a successful estate owner, sugar cultivator, and distiller. His hacienda Culumpich still exists about one mile to the east of town. In the same vicinity Pat also owned the rancho Panabá.[23] Moreover, in August 1846, Pat, now specifically identified as *batab,* filed to claim half a league of *baldío* within Tihosuco parish. But by this time political violence was slowing the *denuncia* process (see below), and there is no record in the notarial archives of this property being awarded. One possible reading of events, then, is that by mid-1847 Pat saw himself as being excluded from the economic opportunities which others had enjoyed.[24]

The Pat family had dominated the local *república* as early as twenty years before the war, when one Pat served as *teniente* and two others were nominated as *batab.* But the Pats were active in creole politics as well. For instance, when a group of Tihosuco *vecinos* petitioned to revoke the appointment of the new *alcalde* and replace him with their faction's favorite, two Mayas appear among the signators: cousin José María Pat and uncle Cecilio Pat. (The latter was himself an entrepreneur who had filed for *baldío* lands, only to die shortly thereafter; his son eventually claimed the properties.) Economic interests and family ties naturally drew Jacinto Pat into political affairs. He first appeared as *batab* in a Maya document of February 1841, certifying the sale of an urban property (along with "its well, its walls, and its patio") to a local creole.[25] His ungainly signature also appeared on the list of prominent citizens approving the proposed reunion with Mexico in 1843. José María Pat also voted for approval, as did Cecilio Pat, who was by now a member of the municipal junta. Vito Pacheco signed as well. The document placed the Pats in close association with the town's creole elites.[26] In March 1847 Pat's name appeared on a list of the 237 Tihosucans eligible to vote in the elections for a deputy to the Yucatecan national congress, one of ninety Mayas who participated.[27] All in all, Pat gave every indication of being politically active and on good terms with the local intelligencia.

But if Pat chose to associate himself with non-Mayas, he also maintained good contact with the average peasant. Pat demonstrated his power to assist lowly *milperos* in 1843 when cultivators of the rancho Hunukú, three leagues from Tihosuco, sought incorporation and half a league of surrounding *baldío* land. They had been driven from their own properties some time previous when a local entrepreneur bought up the land and founded the hacienda Nocac. When the *alcalde* of Tihosuco received their petition, he asked Pat and the *república* for clarification; Pat subsequently informed him that the *milperos* of Hunukú (which included several of Pat's relatives) were hardworking and peace-abiding. In fact, the village lacked the requisite population for incorporation, but on the basis of Pat's strong recommendation the *jefe político* of Peto conceded Hunukú the land anyway. The *batab* had the power to dominate, but he also had the power to reward as well.[28] Doubtless ranchos like Hunukú were little more than "barracks communities," encouraged by estate owners to provide convenient labor supplies; in time, its insufficient land would have produced deep tensions. But for the moment, Pat's assistance was a godsend to the *rancheros*.[29]

Details of estate formation are unclear, but some of the larger contours are evident. Certainly Tihosuco began the century with few great properties: in 1802 there was only one hacienda within the community's jurisdiction, a certain Xcabil. But commercial properties multiplied in the years after 1821. As of 1845 there were only six haciendas, but the smaller ranchos remained numerically superior (ten). Land alienation made some headway at first, with eight *denuncias* awarded, most notably to the heirs of Cecilio Pat, to Antonio Mais, or to local adherents of Santiago Imán. But the process stumbled thereafter: of the twenty-nine applications filed in 1845 and 1846, a mere five were actually awarded (see below for a discussion of delays in the *denuncia* process).

Land alienation in Tihosuco actually lagged behind that either of Peto to the west or of the admittedly more barren lands of the central coast (between Motul and Tizimín). The gulf between local ambitions and Mérida's centralized control was widening.[30]

Changes in land tenure complicated relations among peasants, churchmen, and planters prior to 1847. For one thing, expansion of the sugar frontier strained the parish tax system. As sugar estates formed, many of the village peasants migrated outward in search of *milpa* land; small-scale sugar planters did likewise, moving in tandem with their intended workforce. This diaspora of taxpayers further strained the already weakening church revenue system. As sugar estates had first sprung up around settled communities, the planters attacked church prerogatives in order to strengthen their own control of the labor force. They became the *irreligiosos* who darkened the pages of so much church correspondence. This anticlericism remained the basic stance of many planters. But now, with the workforce scattered and on the move, others began to dream wistfully of the old days—of the colonial function of the *curas* and their mission to congregate the faithful into one place where they might be called upon when needed. "Expansion chapels" now appeared in relatively settled areas to encourage the peasants to stay put. The most prominent example of this was the cult of the hacienda San Antonio Xocneceh, outside Pustunich, but certainly there were others. Champotón was the oldest of European settlements on the peninsula, but by 1838 Antonio Dospesos, owner of a nearby rancho, was forced to erect a straw chapel and petition for a priest "in order that the inhabitants of that rancho might comply with the precept." The religious realm, once separate from and even opposed to the powers of the European settlers, now merged with its old rivals as the two sought to further their mutual interests.[31]

Antonio Mais was one of those who went out into the wilderness in search of souls. His confederate in this instance was a local sugar planter named Siriaco Megía. Seeing the Maya population disperse before them, Mais and Megía formed a plan to erect an open-air temple, a stone altar covered with a thatched roof, "situated almost in the middle of these parts." Megía donated the land from his rancho Xanbendzonot, while Mais agreed to send a minister there periodically, "so that there not be lost many of those souls who live and die like animals." The two men's mutual interest in the project derived from their express wish that the chapel attract both settled inhabitants and transients as well. The popularity of Xanbendzonot and the chapel we can only conjecture from subsequent events: rebels destroyed both during the Caste War.[32]

Tihosuco's economic transformations eventually led to political stability and rebellion. During the furor of the Imán revolt, Tihosuco had had its own separatist factions, in this case headed by an assistant priest named Simeón Guerrero, "the prime motor of revolution here." The centralist authorities arrested Guerrero and placed him under guard in the convent at Tekax. Eventually Guerrero returned to good standing when the separatist army prevailed; his later career is unknown, but the phenomenon of a petty clergyman "leading the disgraceful movements which have occurred in this village" would provide an example for even more audacious movements to follow.[33]

Still another revolt took place five years later, in 1843. Among those participating in the episode was Vito Pacheco, who apparently escaped punishment. Other guilty individuals are unknown, but authorities succeeded in confiscating their considerable stockpiles of material, including rifles, lead, powder, cauldrons, two mortars, and a cannon. This cache required seventy men to carry, and the authorities were uncertain whether to keep it or whether, given the weapons' potential for destabilizing the countryside, to pitch it into a *cenote*. This easy availability of arms along the frontier ultimately proved a key to peasant success in the Caste War, since peasant insurgents utilized well-stocked rifles and not simply rocks and machetes.[34]

TEPICH

Of the three southeastern towns identified with the rebellion, Tepich was by far the smallest. As a mere auxiliary, Tepich remained nothing but a tax pool for the church and state authorities at Tihosuco. Although most of the history of the community is now lost, we do know that Tepich was the scene of a long-standing dispute involving the *batab,* the minister, and the business of taxes which drew them together. In the late 1820s the *batab* of Tepich was a Maya named Juan Bautista Canul. At some point before July of 1833 an interim minister from Tihosuco, José Ignacio López, had removed Canul from office. In his words, Canul "managed by all the means that were in his reach as he was cacique of Tepich, to delay on a technicality, and with very bold notions, the collection of civil as well as ecclesiastical taxes." Canul challenged his removal, hence submitting the issue to the lethargic process of Spanish law. But he also seized on an unusual loophole: since his suspension was in dispute, López could not definitively assert that Canul was *not* the *batab* and therefore could not force him to pay church taxes like other Mayas. Canul procured an injunction to this effect from the *subdelegado* of Peto. So armed, he sat back on a two-year tax holiday while the suit moved glacially through channels.[35]

This stratagem infuriated López and the local judge. Changing their own tactics, they began to assert that Canul owed back taxes from the days before his appointment as *batab* (a claim which, if true, would have made his appointment unlikely). Finding himself outmaneuvered by López, Canul now moved to the offensive. He made incendiary speeches to the local Mayas, proclaiming that the priests were thieves who stole obvention money from all peasants. Such comments could hardly have failed to win approval from their intended audience, particularly coming from the man so recently charged with collecting taxes! Canul also devised a plot to throw López from the roof of the church the next time he ascended to make repairs. Finally, he burned the stocks in the town square, declaring that Indians should not be punished in such a manner. Ironically, while Canul engaged in rabble-rousing, the bishop was answering his protests with a letter upholding the tax exemption![36]

The Tepich incident was revealing in many ways. Perhaps most startling was the degree to which the Mayas of remote villages became adept at working the system. The mere fact that Canul challenged his dismissal suggested an assuredness with the legal process. More significantly, Canul was repeatedly able to go over the head of the local priest and judge. He did so to good effect, twice gaining written exemption from taxes. Both López and the judge seemed to acknowledge the Maya's combative tendencies by their language: "he has always been very cavilous and rebellious in this village," "as the querulous individual says," and so forth. This vocabulary, so common of rural creoles describing Indians, had the effect of acknowledging Indian resistance while simultaneously reducing it to something petty or merely spiteful. But Canul also knew how to turn a phrase to his advantage. When reporting that López had beaten him, he made clear that it was the bishop's orders that López abused. Nor was he above throwing in an occasional ironic dig. For example, when requesting an investigation, he asked "that a nearby *cura* be named in order that, venturing on commission into the village of Tihosuco, he ascertain all these scandalous deeds and others attributed to the good shepherd López."

Equally interesting was Canul's rabble-rousing once he ran afoul of the system. Perhaps Canul already had a social conscience about local taxpayers, or at least an idea of what was politically possible within his own community and people; after all, he had been fired for negligent collection. Another possible interpretation is that López, an interim *cura* and anxious for efficiency, had pressed Canul for a vigorous collection which the *batab* had found politically inexpedient. In either case, astute Maya of the Tihosuco parish received a lesson: the church tax system had within it the danger of compromising the *batabs*. Once that had taken place, public insurrection became a real possibility.

After this incident Tepich largely disappeared from the historical record. A report from the local magistrate in 1838 reports a widespread dispersal of the town's Indian population, mostly into small settlements safely removed from the demands for labor and taxes. However, the 1841 census makes it clear that Maya Indians continued to inhabit Tepich, and it is possible that the earlier report reflected a typical—and temporary—peasant response to the waves of cholera which struck between 1833 and 1835.[37]

We also know little of the man who would emerge here as a rebel caudillo. Although Cecilio Chi was the *batab* of Tepich when the war began, the 1832 census had listed him as a resident of Tihosuco. The census, a mere list of names, appears to have been performed by households, since last names appear in fragmented clusters. Chi's name appears directly below that of Juan José Chi, and it seems likely that he was then living with a relative, possibly a father or brother. Jacinto Pat's name appears beside no other Pat, and his living alone with his wife by this time probably indicates his increased status and prosperity. There may have even been kinship linkages between Pat and Chi. Cecilio Pat was himself married to a Teresa Chi.[38] Whatever the case, that the two principal caudillos of the rebellion knew each other some fifteen years before the war began is almost certain.

CHICHIMILÁ

The third radical community, Chichimilá, also had a history of peasant hostilities toward clerical control. Despite its proximity to Valladolid, Chichimilá had been in the forefront of peasant resistance during the years of the constitutional crisis, when peasants withheld taxes, *koché* service, and simple respect. A decade later, obventions there still proved difficult to collect.[39]

The best-documented episodes in Chichimilá's history involved its longtime *cura*, Juan de Dios Helguera. Helguera was an outspoken federalist whose views had left him open to political harassment after Mexico's centralist coup of 1830. Far more involved, however, were his disputes with local Mayas. In October 1837 peasants of Chichimilá and its auxiliaries Xoccén and Ebtún filed suit against the *cabecera*'s minister, Juan Pablo Escalante, for failure to carry out his appointed functions and for abuse of the local peasants. The suit dragged on for several years, eventually growing to include complaints against Helguera as well.[40] The peasants charged that Helguera was forcing them to contribute money to a defense fund so that he himself could carry on a suit against a local *vecino,* a suit over land titles which the peasants themselves had been willing to settle. The case was particularly interesting in that it included among peasant litigants several of the individuals who would later be apprehended as conspirators at the beginning of the Caste War. Chief among these was Manuel Antonio Ay, who participated in the suit on behalf of the peasants by reason of his literacy. The conclusion was also noteworthy: after lengthy investigations, the peasants agreed to drop their suit if Escalante would remove himself forever from the parish, a proposition which the minister accepted.[41] Helguera himself departed shortly afterward and died a natural death during the early years of the Caste War.[42]

By the beginning of the Imán revolt peasants such as those of Chichimilá and Xoccén had come to feel a new sense of personal empowerment in dealing with the clergy. On one hand, they had succeeded in removing their minister. On the other hand, the peasants' complaints also identified the ecclesiastical judges of Valladolid as their enemies. They considered them to have been responsible for obstructing their complaints against the local clergy. This mention is noteworthy since it helps explain the fact that peasants killed Valladolid's two highest-ranking clerics, Manuel López Constante and Alejandro Villamil, when the Caste War began. The events of the war were not necessarily indiscriminate jacqueries, but rather instances of peasant justice based on a history of local grievances.

Although Escalante was now out of the picture, Chichimilá continued to witness social disturbances involving clerics, *vecinos,* and Indian peasants. In late January 1844 the new minister, Pedro Pablo Alcocer, was playing cards in his house with three other local creoles, at four reales a hand. At about 7:30 that evening a local Maya named José Ay happened by and, "as he was addicted to the game," sat down to watch. By and by Alcocer and Julián Fernández got into an argument as to whether the priest was holding out four reales which Fernández had won. The quarrel soon degenerated into a brawl, and since Fernández was quite drunk, the minister had no trouble in defeating him.[43] The embittered Fernández launched a lawsuit against Alcocer, claiming that he had inexplicably attacked him with a knife. He was able to obtain a brief supporting document, in Maya, from the *batab* and *república* (who had not been present at the card game) supporting his claim. Feliciano Puc, the second *alcalde,* even claimed to have seen the whole event. The lingering anticlericism of Chichimilá provided ready participation in such legal harassments.[44]

Just prior to the outbreak of the war Chichimilá received a new *cura,* one Ramón Vivas. Vivas was himself a man of questionable reputation and was only now holding a curacy for the first time. Nine years earlier he had been expelled from the parish of Nabalam for flaunting the rules of celibacy, "since not content to live scandalously in his house with the woman whom he carried before the sights of all the people in a display, he was making the rounds of the evening dances with her." Transferred to Valladolid, Vivas corrected the excesses which had led to his dismissal and seemed to be on sound footing with his superiors. He managed to bring about only slight improvement in relations with local peasants but on occasion assisted future conspirator Manuel Antonio Ay in drafting letters. However, events in Chichimilá would soon prove beyond his control.[45]

TIXCACALCUPUL

Less understood are the conflicts of Tixcacalcupul, the village which lay between Chichimilá and Tepich. This particular town typified some of the more blatant contradictions between official intent and its application in reality. For example, rhetoric about education and its transformative power upon the Indians was often grandiose. But the realities of rural life lagged far behind liberal prognostications. A mere two years before the explosion of conflicts, the frustrated schoolteacher of Tixcacalcupul, heartland of the coming rebellion, reported that "regardless of my zeal, I perform double the work because of the total lack of Castilian; and I am forced to translate the Spanish to them in the Yucatec language, in order that they can understand."[46]

Land tenure was an underlying issue. During the 1820s Tixcacalcupul had joined Cancabdzonot in a lawsuit defending certain fields, which they believed to be theirs, against encroachment by peasants of Tepich.[47] Another suit pitted the *ayuntamientos* of Tixcacalcupul and Tekom against peasant communities to the south and west (Chikindzonot, Ekpetz, Tihosuco and Tepich) over alleged land invasions by the latter towns.[48] Finally, in 1844 the *república* successfully fought off the early (measurement) stages of a *denuncia* by a local estate owner.[49] Beyond these points, however, Tixcacalcupul, like most Yucatecan villages, lacks the comprehensive land titles and other records that would permit deeper analysis.

As elsewhere in the dramatic years of Yucatecan independence, factionalisms and hostilities had begun to plague the village. They erupted suddenly in 1845 over a relatively trivial incident. Unable or unwilling to contact a priest, a peasant from an outlying rancho paid a Maya *maestro cantor* to perform the burial service for his dead wife, whose cadaver, in the absence of legitimate burial, was quickly growing noisome. The minister, himself virtually unpaid, exploded with anger upon learning that a *maestro cantor* had received the burial fees, and declared that "in the coming elections for municipal *alcaldes* he was going to contribute with barrels of *aguardiente* in order that his [own] father would take the town's reigns of government, and crack down on *vecinos* as much as Indians." His rage doubtless reflected the unbearable tensions which now characterized rural life. It also provoked an equally violent counterreaction, as *cura, vecinos,* and three local *repúblicas de indígenas* rose up to testify against him, forcing his removal and imprisonment.[50] At least in this instance, the people of Tixcacalcupul were still able to find release by targeting a scapegoat from among their own. But the true source of the tensions—political factionalism, tax destabilization, and steadily dwindling land supply—still remained.

One additional conflict was the widespread resentment against the parish *cura,* Eusebio García Rejón, who used his power to interfere with local junta elections, as well as with the appointments in the Indian *repúblicas* of Tixcacalcupul, Tixcacal, Tekom, and Muchucax.[51] When the war finally erupted, peasant insurgents would kill Fr. García Rejón.

Why then the Caste War? These collective histories of Tihosuco, Tepich, and the other radical communities, cursory though they are, suggest several factors that help clarify the eruption of rural insurrection in the Oriente.

From certain perspectives these communities shared a great deal with towns and ranchos throughout the peninsula. All had histories of anticlericism, or at least of long-standing factional conflicts that had involved church, creole settlers, and the Mayas themselves. Far from being mere preserves of some pristine Maya culture, the villages had been actively integrated into the larger peninsular society since the late colonial period, and probably much earlier. All had *batabs* and *repúblicas* that participated heavily in the affairs of rural society. All enjoyed traditions of private Maya land ownership and peasant entrepreneurship. All witnessed varying degrees of land privatization. Here as elsewhere throughout Yucatán, municipal society was a place where various actors fought, made alliances, betrayed one another, and sought in the rulings of the state the means to advance their own interests. These features linked them more closely to communities of the north and east than is commonly recognized.

What distinguished the radical communities as likely source-points for revolt were special features of history and geography. Porfirian and modern academic writings have concurred in arguing that the war emerged among frontier communities which had not been subverted by the commercial transformations centered in the northwest. But in reality, these were *not* the remotest and most autonomous of Mayas. That distinction fell to the Mayas living in hamlets and ranchos nestled in the forests between Tihosuco and the Río Hondo; the people of those far-flung settlements would enter the war at a comparatively late date and would be quick to negotiate a separate peace when the opportunity arose.

The radical community's distinctiveness lay in their more intermediary position. They were neither the furthest nor the closest to the metropoles, but were situated at a strategic distance. Mayas of the insurgency's source-points had participated in a money economy since before the end of the colonial period, and their elites were intimately acquainted with local priests, *políticos,* and estate owners. But while sufficiently close for communication and trade, they were also removed from unwelcome scrutiny. In the absence of supervision, plots and cabals flourished like mushrooms in a dark cavern. Tihosuco in particular was a locus for discontent, with at least two political pronouncements between 1839 and 1843. Further to the southwest, Ichmul and Tiholop had already been disrupted by the separatist wars. The most isolated of Maya communities did not involve themselves in these earlier revolts.

Equally important were the economic influences which washed over the region. Political radicalization typically follows preexisting social and economic networks,[52] and this was no less true for the Caste War than for another insurrection. For decades they had been strategically located for the trade routes leading into Valladolid from Panabá to the north and Belize to the south. Some of this was a legitimate trade in commodities like corn and sugar, but much was not. Smuggled goods regularly passed through here. Mestizo *tratantes,* or peddlers, came to know and understand the sentiments of peasants living along their rural trade routes. Ambitious and not overly scrupulous locals grew wealthy from the traffic in contraband textiles and manufactured goods. Peasants of Tepich and Tihosuco and Chichimilá and Xoccén learned to know one another; they also learned of the guns and ammunition which the Belizeans were happy to sell. The cumulative influence of these trends was to allow the settlers of the Oriente to develop a regional identity considerably independent of Mérida and Campeche, though without necessarily eliminating the distinctions of race and class bequeathed from colonial days.

We can therefore stand the old reading on its head. It was the greater traditionality of the northwestern communities, their economic connection to Mérida, and their greater adhesion to old colonial practices which made them accept incrementally greater impositions by creoles. But it was the dynamic

eastern frontier where peasants were learning *new* and more daring forms of behavior—including tax resistance, mass mobilization, and political violence—
that made them threats to provincial stability. The Oriente represented inno-
vation of a distinctly explosive sort.

The availability of contraband weapons loomed all the more significant as
Yucatán plunged into its separatist wars. The central peasant recruiting grounds
for these wars were the north coast, particularly Tizimín and Espita, and the
towns from Valladolid to Tihosuco. The wars trained people of both the north
and south, in some cases failing to demobilize them. However, while the north
was separated from Belizean resources by Valladolid, the southern communities enjoyed easy access. Maya elites like Jacinto Pat and Cecilio Chi pondered
their opportunities as the fruits of the separatist wars—land, money, and
power—began to fall in disproportionate share to the creoles. Finally, elites
and masses alike were enjoying a splendid education in the arts of warfare. And
as the year 1846 approached, the final phase of that education now began.

THE BARRET REVOLT

The conditions attending Yucatán's reunion with Mexico in
1843 made further conflict inevitable. To begin with, there were many stresses
internal to the peninsula itself. The social and political balance which the
Spanish colonial regime had maintained had all but disappeared, giving rise to
ancient grievances and new competitions. There was renewed resistance and
initiative among the mass of poorer peasants. These dynamics directly jeopardized traditional Maya elites such as the *batabs* and the peasant church staff.
The struggle for local autonomy might have been held in check if not for the
manifest weakness and impoverishment of the Mérida government. Indeed,
the entire *denuncia* program merely advertised the fact that the government
had no means to reward its followers outside of an inherently limited homesteading program.

Another part of the destabilizing forces was external. Mexico's president,
General Antonio López de Santa Anna, had no love for the quarrelsome Yucatecans, perhaps the result of his unhappy exile there in the 1820s. But he
did need their money. Soon after reunification he reneged on open-port
agreements by subjecting Yucatecan products, including sugar and rum, to an
import tariff. This betrayal gave new life to secessionist sentiments throughout
the peninsula, and Yucatán split off again in late 1845.

Next came the United States invasion of Mexico. U.S. westward expansion into the peripheries of Mexico had brought repeated border disputes, ul-

timately resulting in formal war declarations on May 9, 1846. By the end of March 1847, General Winfield Scott had already seized Veracruz and was on his way to Mexico City.[53] Even though Yucatán had remained largely independent from the central Mexican government since 1840, the conflict encouraged instability, with the Yucatecans divided by mixed sentiments of fear, opportunism, and Hispanic resentment against U.S. aggression.

When the war with the United States began, Santa Anna once more offered reunification on terms highly favorable to Yucatecans. On January 1 of that year Miguel Barbachano, a wealthy merchant who had been educated in Europe and who had been active in politics throughout the 1840s, assumed the governorship and signed a new proclamation of union with a nation facing military rout, even disappearance. Thus Yucatán began the year 1846 with only faint prospects for political stability. These events would have been trying for even the most stable of societies. But by 1846 the pattern for insurrection was well established in Yucatán. As the state government grew weaker, elites struggled to assume power at local levels, usually recruiting Maya peasants with the promise of tax exemptions. Even though these teapot insurrections failed to spark larger revolt, they did rehearse the peasantry for its later and greater role.

First came the Solís rebellion of Valladolid. On the evening of January 5, 1846, a certain Juan Solís entered the plaza of San Juan at Valladolid, leading an army of fifty to seventy Mayas drawn from surrounding hamlets, armed with rifles, and recruited on the promise that their annual taxes would be reduced by one real. The army occupied the sacristy and "alarmed" the people living in the center of town, for whom the sack of 1840 was still a painful memory. Solís' real purpose, it seems, was to overturn the recent and controversial elections for Valladolid's *ayuntamiento*. However, he counted on victory through a mere show of arms and was unprepared to actually fight. The *alcalde* therefore succeeded in dispersing his mob. Solís withdrew to Chichimilá, where he and his two Maya confederates—Pedro Kuyoc and Luis Puc— were arrested.[54] A similar peasant revolt took place around Valladolid in July. Both episodes contained features which were gradually becoming the norm for Yucatecan rural society. These included sudden economic growth, war-related shortages and dislocations, territorial disputes between town and country, and the paradoxical dynamic of the state's increasing desperation for revenues against the peasantry's growing expectations of tax relief.[55]

Such adventures merely foreshadowed the larger urban-centered revolts. The factional disputes which had been brewing for a year at last boiled over on November 2, 1846, when disaffected *campechanos* pronounced against the Mérida-based government. For their leader they selected Domingo Barret, who was among other things a merchant and who in earlier times had con-tracted with the central Mexican government to supply and equip Yucatecan soldiers for the Texas wars.[56] Although the revolt found support in many parts of the peninsula, it had its political focus among merchants and other Cam-peche elites closely allied to ex-governor Santiago Méndez. With United States gunboats not far away, reunification placed them in extreme jeopardy. Moreover, the city's importers chafed at the high sugar tariffs constructed at their expense to benefit planters of the interior.[57]

Their revolt found ready sympathy among rural factions who sought to im-prove their own position by overturning the local power structure. The revolt successfully split the caudillos who had fought under Imán six years earlier: for-mer rebels of Tihosuco and Peto lined up behind Barret and Méndez, while of-ficers of the Tizimín area remained staunch *barbachanistas*. Instrumental in rais-ing this revolt were many of Imán's old friends, including Antonio Trujeque and Vito Pacheco, all of whom resorted to their proven tactic of levying peas-ant soldiers, once more with the promise of tax reductions. At the same time, *barbachanistas* everywhere seized the opportunity to brand Méndez as a traitor: "Those who pronounce in Campeche, at whose head has always been San-tiago Méndez, are forming an alliance with the Yankees against their legiti-mate government. Hear it well, Yucatecans."[58] Both Imán and his lieutenant Pastor Gamboa published broadsides denouncing the revolt as criminal.[59]

Mayas too entered the fray. It is impossible to determine how many peas-ants took up arms during the Barret revolt. Many carried guns; however, throughout the months of the insurrection the main experience for most peasants was probably not the exhilaration of combat, but rather the sudden and unpredictable terror of troops entering villages, men pressed into service, contributions gathered, and the community's already scarce corn requisitioned or simply stolen by passing soldiers. This last injustice was harshest, particu-larly when it enjoyed the support of local officialdom. Throughout April the magistrates and *subdelegados* tried to conduct inventories of the number of *cargos* of corn in their towns and *partidos* "in order to know whether the extrac-tion of this grain, whether for the interior or for foreign places, may by con-sequence produce shortages." As early as January, in the village of Tixpeual, the magistrate had the *batab* and *república* rounding up corn already made into tortillas "for the consumption of the valiant troops of the Most Honorable and Loyal City of Campeche." In Maxcanú the authorities found it necessary to "redouble" their "zeal and vigilance" in making the *república* stick with the task of collecting the personal contribution.[60] For good or bad, then, the war came to the peasants.

The Barret revolt scored rapid successes throughout the countryside. How-ever, the conflict reached its climax in the area of Valladolid, where peasants as well as impoverished creoles and mixed bloods resented the control of the city's aristocratic gentry and joined only too willingly in the hope of improv-ing their fortunes.

One who answered the call to revolt here was Bonifacio Novelo. Given his importance in the events of the next twenty years, it is worth a moment to consider the background of this remarkable individual. Yucatecan lore de-scribes Novelo as being either a mulatto or a mestizo, a point which can no longer be determined with any certainty. In 1841 Novelo, then twenty-six years old, was living in a poor barrio of Valladolid with his wife (María Ylaria Coronado, age twenty-three) and three small children (Claudio, Baluina, and Canuto). The Novelo clan was extensive in Valladolid and indeed throughout the entire southeast, but we know few details regarding their exact family structure. Bonifacio described himself as a *tratante,* that is, a peddler who sold goods in rural areas. The profession had brought him into intimate contact with the peasantry and its complex mentality. Unofficially he enjoyed a repu-tation as a smuggler and a troublemaker. Those who knew him regarded him as a highly intelligent individual; visitors to the rebel society of the 1860s de-scribed him as the most "*entendido*" of the Chan Santa Cruz leaders. Along with many other of his far-flung relatives, Novelo helped stage fraudulent municipal elections in Valladolid in the mid-1840s. During the Barret revolt, he seized the opportunity for social advancement, gaining the rank of lieu-tenant and organizing Maya regiments through the assistance of his close friend, Manuel Antonio Ay of Chichimilá. Under the command of Antonio Trujeque, Novelo became an officer over the peasant forces which were now poised to strike at Valladolid. He represented the classic petit bourgeois whose ability to communicate with both the high and low elements of soci-ety helped him to prosper in situations of revolution and upheaval.[61]

In the days prior to the attack on Valladolid the entire region around the city was charged with an air of panic and chaos. While many continued to flee to Mérida, others entrenched themselves in the plaza. "Bandits" roamed through the haciendas and ranchos of the surrounding countryside, "taking from their owners by force all that they desire, and leading off the estate workers, as has happened with Fr. D. José Nicolás Baeza and D. Pedro Pascual Gómez on their haciendas." Moreover, the commander of Valladolid's defenses now learned that an assault force of some seven hundred men had formed in Tihosuco. The most he could do to check their advance was to station sev-enty soldiers in Tixcacalcupul.[62]

These meager defenses proved useless. On January 15, pro-Barret forces overran Valladolid, once more sacking the town. Peasants raided not only private residences but also the shops and churches. Under the orders of Bonifacio Novelo, the invaders seized and executed Valladolid's patrician commander, Claudio Venegas. During the sack, peasants also took the opportunity to kill the elderly Fr. Manuel López Constante, whom they had identified as part of the Valladolid church hierarchy responsible for squelching their aforementioned lawsuits against Frs. Helguera and Escalante. The attack on López Constante was to raise considerable anguish among creoles. As the brother of Yucatán's first and most popular president, he symbolized the hitherto successful fusion of clergy and creole bourgeoisie. His death was gruesome testimony to how unraveled Yucatán's social fabric had become. Creole authorities tended to absolve peasants from responsibility, an almost instinctive return to the old dictum that Indians were "children with beards." Instead, blame focused on Novelo. Trujeque declared him an outlaw and shortly thereafter imprisoned him on charges of homicide.[63]

Improbably enough, one of those who had led the attack on Valladolid was Tihosuco's new minister, Marcos Áviles. Headstrong and imperious, Áviles had little use for self-effacing Christianity; in 1844 he went to court for physically abusing an elderly servant who had presumed to leave his employ without permission. While old-timers like Antonio Mais understood rural society enough to realize the inherent dangers of peasant mobilization, Áviles threw himself into these turbulent affairs with gusto. Trujeque had promised him the lucrative curacy of Peto in exchange for help in recruiting and directing peasant forces; what the government decreed, quipped Trujeque, the bishop could hardly refuse. Áviles apparently felt no contradiction in leading the volatile Maya peasants in what amounted to an anticlerical jacquerie, for he returned to Tihosuco and took part in the general victory celebration, much to Mais' disgust.[64] The tendency for lower-ranking clergy to associate with radical popular elements deepened—at least while those elements still seemed within the control of their creole leaders.

For the surrounding Maya communities the sack of Valladolid proved cathartic. Small insurrections and skirmishes continued for days, while those creoles not part of the army took to their houses or haciendas to wait for things to blow over. Everywhere settlers hoped that the regular army would soon restore control. But the change of mood was unmistakable. Back in Tihosuco, Mais found himself buying up small items from the sacked church—here an altarpiece, there a stole—rather like someone salvaging cargo after a shipwreck. In Tepich the peasants were openly boasting that they "could kill any priest they wanted," just as they had done with López Constante. The minister there had stopped saying mass and even refused to appear in public, since the peasants had flatly advised him that he was next. Nor would Mais order him to do otherwise, for fear that he himself would be blamed for the minister's death. Peasants also talked about raiding other towns, and a rumor surfaced that within fourteen days the entire Maya population would rise up in rebellion.[65]

On top of everything, Trujeque heaped public encomiums upon the Maya soldiers. Once the new government was in place, he declared, he would see to the formation of companies of armed and trained Maya soldiers throughout the *partido*. These companies would indeed come to pass, although not in the way that Trujeque had intended.[66]

It was at this same point that there occurred one of the darkest episodes in the long history of Yucatán's revolutions. In January of 1847, Pastor Gamboa was passing with his troops through the rolling country of Beneficios Bajos. Gamboa had been a lieutenant and understudy of Imán in the events of 1839–1841, and he enjoyed a history of working with peasant recruits in the back country. He also had a reputation as a violent and unpredictable man, particularly with those who attempted to restrain him. When in 1842 the *jefe político* of Tizimín refused to grant him requisitions until he received official instruction, Gamboa had him seized and robbed him of two hundred pesos. (Gamboa already possessed an annual two hundred pesos pension for life, a result of his military services, which he was fond of recounting in napoleonic terms.)[67] However, he did maintain a soldierly loyalty to the men who had served under him and at least to some degree stood by his recruiting promises: in late 1844 he filed complaints against the *batab* of Espita for trying to collect obventions from those who had been exempted for their service in Gamboa's company.[68]

On January 11 the *barbachanista* forces fought a pitched battle outside Tabi. The combined forces of Gamboa, Miguel Bolio, Felipe de la Cámara, and Patricio O'Horan successfully routed their enemies and occupied the parish.[69] Gamboa and his soldiers then entered the hamlet of Tabi. Most of the inhabitants had fled into the bush to avoid requisitions or impressment by the soldiers. The only ones who remained were certain members of the *república* and some women who had closed themselves up in their huts. Absent as well was the village's minister, José Dolores Cámara, himself a recent claimant of *baldío* lands.[70]

What followed was an atrocity. Around late morning or early afternoon the soldiers had begun making a sweep of the hamlet, rounding up all the women they could find and relocating them to the house of Fr. Cámara. As the women passed through the plaza, they saw Gamboa among "an infinity of soldiers and officials." He was then busy assigning orders to his men, and he instructed the few village men on hand that they were to go to meet him in Sotuta. In the plaza lay a number of dead bodies. Once the women reached Cámara's house, an unidentified peasant instructed them to come inside to avoid outrages by the soldiers. Shortly thereafter, the soldiers returned to the house, bringing with them a corpse. At first the women did not recognize the naked and savagely bloodied remains as the body of their *batab*, Ysidoro Tsib.

Exactly how many died in the killings at Tabi is unclear. The women stated that some of the bodies were of men from a different village. Papers of the investigation stated quite definitely that the *batab*, an *alcalde*, and the *escribano* had perished "by the most cruel and atrocious assassinations." But the question of who killed them appears less doubtful. It is fair to assume that the men of the *república* had died at the hands of Gamboa's soldiers, since their murders coincided with Gamboa's entry into the town. Of motives, Gamboa could have had only two: either he suspected the men of abetting his enemies, or else he believed they were withholding requisitions of grain or help in rounding up villagers as recruits.

The subsequent investigation was less than penetrating. The new government appointed Joaquín Cetina, judge of Tekax, to investigate the killings "which are attributed to Don Pastor Gamboa." Cetina assembled a panel of witnesses, one of whom was himself a Gamboa, and proceeded to take the testimony of the village women. This essentially threw the burden of solving the atrocity to the women themselves. All denied having any idea who perpetrated the killings or why, and only one claimed to have recognized Gamboa, the woman who had seen him in the plaza assigning details. Clearly, though, someone had accused Gamboa, given the above-cited remark of the government commission. Several days after the women's testimony, Cetina also took depositions of the late *batab*'s widow and son, but they were scarcely more illuminating. Thus, on February 10 Cetina reported back that Gamboa was, in fact, innocent.[71]

The Tabi atrocities have remained an unknown episode. They appear in none of the Yucatecan history books; we search in vain for them in Serapio Baqueiro's chronicle of the "great men" of independent Yucatán. And yet for the *batabs* and other peasant elites the event carried an unmistakable message. In earlier days, the *batab* had been a man of balance. He mediated between the demands of the two worlds: the creole need for labor and tribute and the peasant quest for subsistence and autonomy. The *batab*'s own material success depended on his ability to perform this balancing act. Moreover, for all their deprecations, for all their contempt toward the *batab*, the creoles in regular contact with the Maya communities understood the *batab*'s difficult position and even appreciated it. Without his help the intractability of the peasants, already notorious, would make extractions nearly impossible. This and only this explains why the *batabs* got away with so much, why they could take *curas* to court, and how they grew rich at the system's expense. But the *batab*'s position was deteriorating. The change had begun with the Bourbon reforms and accelerated after 1821. The significance of the Tabi massacre was that no *batab*, no village official, could hereafter count on the old tolerance as he went about his work. Given the need, ambitious creoles could make demands which the *batab* could no longer negotiate, and it could now be better said of Gamboa and his soldiers what Antonio Mais said about the Mayas: "Divine providence favors us with a brutal, fierce, and audacious people."[72] *Batabs* who failed to deliver could end up like Ysidoro Tsib: dead and mutilated, their murders forgotten after a public hand-washing. It was hardly surprising, then, to find a group of *batabs* immediately to the east of Tabi entertaining thoughts of radical change through the most radical of measures.

DENOUEMENT

By January 20 organized opposition to the Barret revolt had collapsed, and the Campeche clique now found itself in power. But the new government faced almost insurmountable problems in trying to balance its accounts while simultaneously restoring rural order. In the vicinity of Valladolid, armed peasants roamed the countryside inflicting mayhem and robbery. Homes in the region remained abandoned. To deal with this brigandage, Barret dispatched troops from the west coast. Although restoring a modicum of order, the commander still found the region in a desperate condition, with all archival material destroyed and the jails emptied of their prisoners. Their peacekeeping mission was in no way aided by the fact that reinforcements sent up from Peto took the opportunity to pillage several towns while en route.[73]

Meanwhile, the new regime wasted no time in antagonizing its rivals by open shows of favoritism. Barret arbitrarily struck some forty *barbachanista* officials from the public payroll; more to the point, he began preparations to relocate the seat of government to Campeche, thus depriving Mérida of its accustomed status as the Rome of the peninsula. Following Barbachano's self-imposed exile to Havana, Barret placed Mérida on conditions resembling martial law.[74]

Response to these heavy-handed manipulations came in the Ciudadela revolt of February 28. The uprising was led by *barbachanista* officers, principally

José Dolores Cetina and Felipe de la Cámara, and was seconded by no less a person than Imán himself. In addition to reinstatement of the Barbachano government, the rebels demanded reduction of civil taxes to a monthly real. They also promised to void all land *denuncias* not adjudicated by April 5, 1846. The promise was noteworthy, since caudillos such as Cetina and Imán had already secured their own *denuncias* and could now afford to pose as defenders of the people. They may have enticed many peasants as well, but their strategy was a serious blow to the aspirations of certain Mayas—including Jacinto Pat of Tihosuco, *who had not filed his own claim until August 1846.* Despite their populist program, the Ciudadela insurrectionists found that Barret not only firmly controlled the remainder of the army, but already enjoyed a network of rural support. By March 12, less than two weeks after its inception, the revolt collapsed. Cetina and other key officers fell prisoner, only to be exiled to Havana.[75] During the brief life of the Ciudadela revolt, Barret found it expedient to embrace their call for a halt to the *denuncia* process, promising in the same measure a restitution of wrongly alienated village lands.[76] After Barret's decree the land giveaways stopped completely and abruptly but gave signs of resuming in mid-July, only days before the outbreak of the Caste War proper.[77]

With the Ciudadela revolt barely behind him, the revolutionary governor got on with the business of cementing his regime. On April 28 Barret ordered an emergency assembly in the town of Ticul. Dispensing with electoral formalities, the assembly was to draw four or five political allies from each of the various departments, representatives who would meet to settle the most crucial problems of the new republic, namely: peasants, taxes, budgets, the army, and governmental reorganization.

Barret's opening address to the assembly on the 24th of May revealed that he lacked even the faintest clue as to how to resolve these issues. Regarding the question of church rents, Barret grew expansive over the benefits which religion provided for society ("it adorns the soul with the pure knowledge of its truths, dissipates ignorance, affirms security and protects learning"). Like millions before him, he appreciated the church's capacity for "inspiring the love of work." Yet the governor was less forthcoming in regard to feasible arrangements of finance. Recognizing the treasury's inability to salary the priests, he suggested an "absolute separation of church and state," coupled, paradoxically, with a plan to have the *curas* collect all taxes "with the help and protection of the authorities." At the same time, Barret argued that the civil taxes would resume once political upheavals were suppressed. Such vague and contradictory pronouncements merely advertised the ineffectual nature of the new regime.[78] Predictably, subsequent elections favored the Campeche clique, and Santiago Méndez assumed the presidency once more in mid-July.

More pressing was the issue of potential peasant uprisings. The peasant masses between Valladolid and Ichmul were armed and mobilized in February 1847 and were openly manifesting an assertive consciousness of their own power. Why then did the Caste War not begin until late July? Several factors help explain the delay. Perhaps the peasant masses, under the influence of Maya leaders, still felt themselves to be acting in concert with disaffected creole generals. Until the cessation of hostilities and the formal installation of the Barret government in May 1847, it would have seemed that the broad alliance was still fighting for goals which fundamentally appealed to the peasants. Only the subsequent repression of Maya leaders who had fought in the campaign would serve to destroy that alliance.

But there were other factors as well, chief among them being the cycles of agricultural labor on which rural life depended. In February the process of spring field preparations and planting were beginning, preparations which could not be avoided for any circumstance. Moreover, even for landless workers there was still the *zafra,* or sugar harvest, which extended from December to May; this meant money, or at least basic sustenance, for an unknown but presumably significant minority of the population.

It is possible that the influence of the annual birth-rate cycle played a role in delaying hostilities. As in many other agricultural societies, births here tended to decline in autumn and winter and peak in the summer months of June, July, and August. Yucatecan *curas* performed baptismal ceremonies and collected baptismal fees approximately one week after birth: fees for church services would not reach their annual high until the summer months. Revolutionary potential would thus peak when popular resentment over church fees was at its height. However, this must be balanced against other considerations. In many places, particularly in villages along the eastern frontier, peasants had quit paying taxes of any sort prior to the war's onset. Chichimilá was a good example. By June of 1847 Ramón Vivas, who had recently taken charge of the parish, had scarcely been able to collect thirty pesos from a population exceeding seven thousand people. Faced with the prospect of running church operations out of his own pocket, he asked to be relieved of the assignment, a request which was to find sudden and unexpected fulfillment.[79]

The same dilemma held true for civil taxes. By the time of the Caste War the *subdelegado* of Valladolid was petitioning for extra time to make good on a six thousand peso shortfall occasioned by the revolutions which had swept over the land.[80] Everyone understood that unpaid taxes meant unpaid troops.

Ironically, among those inconvenienced by the shortfalls were the Maya soldiers themselves, who in many instances had enlisted for cash payment as well as tax relief. Two days before the final eruption in Tepich, the Maya peasants of the rancho Yakulmis, outside Becanchén, were clamoring for the money still owed them from their service in 1843.[81] Doubtless the poverty of the new revolutionary government had much the same effect elsewhere. Land, itself of limited quantity and alienable only through the turgid legal process, could not meet the demands of everyone. Moreover, land programs placed the government in the untenable position of taking from some peasants to reward others. Thus the salary arrears owed to Yucatán's peasant defenders, together with the dubious plan for funding those salaries, threatened to turn the peninsula into a second Haiti, where armed bands had roamed since the 1791 revolution and where no president had ever gone unchallenged by pronouncing caudillos.

By mid-summer all these circumstances had changed. The annual work cycle was now at a low point, with the corn planted and the sugar harvested. Moreover, in summer the Méndez government moved to reassert the monthly one-real religious tax, having secured from the church a vague promise not to overcharge on minor obventions. During the Ticul assembly, Méndez himself had gone so far as to urge abolition of Maya taxes in order to quiet rural unrest: "Bring war to the palace to have peace in the countryside," he argued. Of course, the pressures of a sagging treasury soon dictated otherwise. But whatever pressures he may have felt, events would show that the decision to resume obventions was a colossal blunder. Méndez could scarcely have devised a policy more certain to provoke peasant outrage.[82]

Another straw which may have helped precipitate the Caste War was the death of *cura* Antonio Mais. The exact date of his death is unknown, but it appears to have taken place in late June or early July of 1847 and definitely preceded the war's beginning on July 30.[83] In many ways this elderly priest represented the frontier town's last link with the past. Mais was at least in his sixties at the time of his death. He had administrated most of the extensive 1803–1804 pastoral visit, had lived through the constitutional crisis, had succeeded brilliantly as an entrepreneurial priest, had survived any number of rivals and accusers, and had successfully established himself as an independent power in Ichmul and later Tihosuco. Whether the clientalist relationship he offered the peasants was the best they could desire is debatable. Mais demanded exorbitant taxes and maintained his own commercial estates within the bounds of the parish. However, he did constitute the only significant counterweight to men like Antonio Trujeque and Vito Pacheco, who had no interest whatsoever in rural tradition and stability. Moreover, he was one of the last of the old Spanish priests and the man who had approved Jacinto Pat and Cecilio Chi for their offices as *batabs*. Old obligations toward patronage died hard. Whatever restraint he may have exerted against the force of peasant rebellion disappeared with his death. And there was one last salient point regarding Mais' passing. Whereas some previous *curas* of the deep sugar territories had left generous legacies for their Indian parishioners, Mais died intestate, and a woman named Bonifacia Perera, who described herself as his long-time servant, spent the war years in legal battles to claim the estate.[84] The bitter irony of this could hardly have eluded his Maya parishioners.

In the meantime, Bonifacio Novelo was actively promoting the rebellion. Novelo had been arrested along with seven other members of the mob which sacked Valladolid, including kinsmen Eduardo and son Claudio Novelo, all on charges of murder. The jail also held an unusually large number of people, mostly Maya, charged with crimes in the wake of the Valladolid incident, serious offenses which included robbery, assault, and murder both real and attempted—testimony to the increasing anarchy of the southeast. But Novelo had escaped from prison shortly after his arrest in late January and was now traveling the back country, whipping up unrest among the peasants. Far from being repulsed by Novelo's role in the sack of Valladolid and his subsequent arrest, the peasants of the region found these to be impressive credentials. They listened attentively as Novelo talked of abolishing all taxes and by July had adopted the habit of calling him "Governor" in anticipation of changes that they would implement once a general insurrection had gone forward.[85]

Novelo's escape appears to have initiated a period of intensive planning. In an ominous inversion of the usual power structure, Maya peasants in Chichimilá had begun to shake down local creoles at five pesos apiece. Although the peasants made no comment as to their intentions, the "tax" would ultimately be used to buy war supplies from Belize. The *batab* and *república* began making these demands as early as May, summoning victims to face a junta of Mayas, while Novelo himself supervised from a hammock in the corner of the house. While all of this transpired, peasants lounged outside, drinking, intimidating the victims, and reverently invoking the name of Cecilio Chi, the militant *batab* of Tepich.[86]

Creoles first began to smell trouble when they observed bands of Chichimilá peasants, estimated to number around fifty each, setting out on the road to Tihosuco on the 12th and 13th of July. Rumor held that these peasants were bound for Culumpich, hacienda of Jacinto Pat. Within a few days the rumors grew to report that Pat, in league with the outlawed Novelo, was stockpiling contraband British rifles at the hacienda, while their confederates recruited peasant soldiers on the promise of reducing or abolishing all taxes.[87]

Suspicions quickly turned to Novelo's old allies, the Maya elites of the Chichimilá parish who had played so active a role in the litigations against the priests Helguera and Escalante. The chief suspect was "a notorious *caviloso,*" the new *batab* Manuel Antonio Ay, the same peasant who had been involved in plans to unseat the parish's *cura* and minister ten years before. As it happened, the authorities did not have to wait for long. On July 20, Ay and other peasants were at the hacienda Acambalam when the *alcalde* of Chichimilá observed a letter which had fallen out of Ay's hat. It was a note from Cecilio Chi announcing his plans to attack Tihosuco and requesting information on how many villages Ay had succeeded in recruiting for the conspiracy.[88] Ironically, the arrest followed hard upon the church's new calls for peasant piety. Only the day before these events the Mayas of the frontier towns had received notice, preached from the Sunday pulpit in Maya so that there could be no misunderstanding, that their religious observances would increase in 1848 with the institution of forty hours' devotion during Lent.[89]

Ay was quickly brought before the authorities in Valladolid. The surviving transcript of his trial presents confusing and often contradictory testimony, but some points clearly emerge.[90] Ay and several associates, including the town's *maestro de capilla* José Sebastián Tus as well as members of the extensive Puc clan, had taken active parts in the Imán revolt and the later battles of 1843 and 1846–1847. Ay was on close terms with Bonifacio Novelo and had organized local collections for a new rebellion, ostensibly for tax reduction. Ay ultimately acknowledged ownership of the letter from Chi, as well as other letters from Chi and Novelo found in his house, letters whose incriminating natures he tried unconvincingly to argue away. The plot apparently involved local non-Mayas such as Secundino Loria, a twenty-five-year-old laborer who had lived in the village throughout the tempestuous 1840s; but faced with charges of conspiracy, Loria saved himself by turning informant.[91]

On July 26, at five in the afternoon, the authorities passed Ay before a firing squad beside the outer wall of the church of Santa Ana in Valladolid. Accounts of his final moments differ. Some hold that the condemned man remained stoic to the end, while others say that he broke into tears, recanted his errors, and pleaded with his small son to remain loyal to the state. The authorities had heard rumors that local peasants would try to free Ay at the last moment; despite the sizable military guard posted to intimidate them, a large number of peasants did fill the streets to see the event but dispersed upon hearing the volley of the rifles.[92]

After the execution, the soldiers carried Ay's body to Chichimilá. Ay's widow and son (the same who had witnessed his execution) came out to meet the procession but were denied possession of the corpse. The captain of the cavalry escort, Felipe Cámara de Zavala, discovered that the white families of Chichimilá were in the final stages of evacuation. Maya peasants of the town had been in open revolt since about 3:00 that afternoon, and only the presence of the escort succeeded in restraining them. On the following morning, after the traditional ceremony in which villagers were brought to view the body of an executed criminal, Cámara ordered Ay's corpse to be buried under the shade of a ceiba tree in the plaza.[93]

The day after these dramatic events, the strident *barbachanista* colonel José Dolores Cetina returned from exile in Havana. Cetina once more proclaimed against the Campeche government and in favor of the plan of the earlier Ciudadela revolt. Then, assembling some three hundred men in Tizimín, he began a march to Valladolid, the city where peasant forces had shattered Barbachano's government in January. But Cetina found Valladolid garrisoned by three government columns under the command of Eulogio Rosado.[94] Checkmated, Cetina was wisely preparing to negotiate surrender when he suddenly found himself invited to join forces with Rosado in what creoles feared to be a looming peasant war. Indeed, rather than quelling popular fears, Ay's execution precipitated a dragnet for co-conspirators. Ay had in many ways been a temporary substitute for Novelo, whom officials feared and hated more than any Maya. To all it seemed that some cataclysm was imminent:

> *In these towns the Indians menace the white race with impudence,*
> *and if these Indians go forward with a general uprising, we will*
> *be unable to count on the forces necessary to suppress them, and in*
> *the towns, haciendas, ranchos and roads nothing will be found but*
> *the blood and stiffening cadavers of the whites.*[95]

This, at least, was the view of the *jefe político,* Felipe Rosado. Trujeque and Vito Pacheco therefore set out with a posse to seize Jacinto Pat and Cecilio Chi. They found Pat on his hacienda Culumpich but curiously enough failed to arrest him. The traditional interpretation holds that Pat was in a state of such perfect composure that Trujeque and Pacheco decided the reports to be false. But it is at least equally plausible that old political loyalties stayed their hand or that Pat was surrounded by adherents and was in no position to be intimidated. Indeed, there was a curious timidity in all of Trujeque's policings, a hesitancy perhaps motivated by fear of provoking a mass uprising.

The next target was Cecilio Chi. Again, Trujeque avoided a head-on confrontation. He instead sent a messenger summoning Chi to Tihosuco to carry out the disarming of his troops, left fully equipped since the sack of Valladolid. Exactly why the weapons had remained in peasant hands is unclear.

Perhaps the times were too unsettled for local elites to make such demands; or perhaps they remembered the firestorm of protest the peasants of Tepich had raised when authorities confiscated their weapons after the 1843 mobilization.[96] But armed they were. Chi responded to this transparent ruse by withdrawing, along with his soldiers, to his hacienda outside of town and posting sentries throughout the countryside. Trujeque did at last force himself to enter Tepich with a small mounted force but found a scene like that of Tabi months before. The men had deserted, leaving only the women and children. As with Gamboa's troops in Tabi, the fear, frustration, and lack of resistance tempted men into atrocities, this time the rape of a young girl who was found running along the road which reportedly led to Chi's hacienda. In addition, the soldiers burned the peasants' houses and scattered their furniture and scanty possessions.[97]

On the 28th of July Trujeque's posse rounded up five more suspects: Calletano Xicum, Juan de Mata Chan, and José María Pan of Tepich; Lorenzo Yc of Ekpetz; and Luisano Galas of Valladolid. Between their arrest and their formal interrogation the peasant sack of Tepich (July 30) intervened, and the line of questioning pursued by the *alcalde* of Tihosuco very much reflected widespread creole fears of conspiracy and impending revolt.[98] The information which resulted from these interrogations was a combination of hard fact and creole fantasy; the latter aspect was either concocted by the Tihosuco creoles in their reports, reported under duress, or else drawn out through leading questions in a situation in which the detainees, eager to save themselves by satisfying their captors, simply told them what they knew they wanted to hear. For example, it is unlikely (though not necessarily impossible) that Pat and Chi had spoken of planning to kill only male creoles, to marry themselves to the white widows, and to relegate Maya women to the role of servants.[99]

However, the bulk of the testimony cannot be so easily dismissed, particularly since it proved an accurate blueprint for later events. The detainees reported that a series of meetings had taken place—not at Jacinto Pat's hacienda in Tihosuco, as the porfirian historians always reported, but in a home (presumably Chi's) on the outskirts of Tepich. Cecilio Chi had presided at these events, although one informant reported that Chi had begun the meetings but that Pat himself had "dictated" them. Apparently the initial conspiracy focused on two broad initiatives. Chi was to coordinate the rebellion in Tepich, Chichimilá, Tixcacalcupul, Uayma, Muchucux, Tiholop, and Tinum—all villages to the north and west of Tihosuco. Chi's alleged confederate in Tixcacalcupul was Francisco Dzul. All the detainees denied knowing the names of other leaders, although one implicated the "*sargento*" of Ekpetz. Second,

Pat, together with his sons Silvestre and Esteban, was to lead the villages of Tihosuco, Tituc, Polyuc, and Chunhuhub, as well as the ranchos Catz, Santa María, and X-Canul. Again, there would seem to be some support for these allegations in later historical events, since Chi did in fact dominate military affairs toward the north and center, while Pat's influence prevailed south of Tihosuco, in the area that is now west-central Quintana Roo. In addition to assuming military command in the south, Pat was also said to have extended the offer to supply Chi with material in the form of powder and lead. This too has a grounding in the known facts, since Pat was a man of means and was conveniently located for a clandestine trade with Belize. It is possible that Chi, a man geographically closer to the center of creole society, further removed from the hinterlands, and apparently the junior member of the Pat-Chi partnership, needed more convincing and support. After all, it was he who was to command peasant forces in the very heartland of the peninsula and against large creole towns. Pat's sphere of influence consisted of the inaccessible communities to the south. Chi's legendary ferocity may therefore have been a consequence of his more vulnerable situation, semi-dependent on Pat's aid, and generally unable to take calculated gambles on prisoners and parleys. These facts, rather than some innate bloodthirst, may better account for Chi's draconian reputation.

Another factor in these machinations was the collection of disaffected non-Mayas from Valladolid. The leader of this group was Bonifacio Novelo; the other two mentioned were Pedro Pablo Mendoza and José María Mendoza, cronies of Novelo since the days of the Imán revolt.[100] According to the Tepich detainees, Novelo had for some time been recruiting peasants for a general uprising. Although allied with Cecilio Chi, Novelo called for himself to be made governor, presumably for life, with the Mendozas acting as his seconds.[101]

However, by mid-August these revelations had come too late for creoles hoping to prevent a peasant uprising. As soon as news of Trujeque's militia reached Tepich, Cecilio Chi gathered together his adherents and withdrew from town. Then, quite unexpectedly, in the early morning hours of July 30, 1847, Chi's forces descended upon Tepich. This time the massacre was general. Insurgents slaughtered all members of the twenty-five to thirty creole families, killing everyone who was not recognizably a Maya peasant: whites, mulattos, men, women, children, all perished. "Only one individual, a certain Alejo Arana, managed to escape the slaughter and run to Tihosuco, where he served as bearer of the fatal news."[102]

As the August heat bore down upon the Yucatecan frontier in the days that followed, it became clear that this summer would not end as had so many hundreds of summers before. A fear now settled over the towns and hamlets like dust. Men prepared their weapons; whole families loaded their belongings on mule trains and made for the west or else disappeared into the woods and forests, making for secret locations where they believed they could remain safe. But for Yucatán itself there was no secret location. The only place was at the edge of an immense turbulence, a time of troubles which would rage for decades and which would separate the Yucatecans, at once frantic and hopeful, from the placidity of their colonial past.

Conclusions

In virtually all lands the countryside wears a mask of tranquillity. And yet when the rural world is held to historical scrutiny, it writhes with the themes of usurpation and tyranny, manipulation and resistance. Nowhere is this more true than in Yucatán.

The Caste War which followed Chi's strike on Tepich defies easy characterization—that is, aside from its extreme violence. The conflict involved foreign interventions, alliances of Mayas and non-Mayas, double-dealing rebel leaders, and opportunistic power struggles on both sides. It is also difficult to place the war into neat periods. Although creoles had retaken most of their lost territory by 1853, the Maya rebels successfully established independent territories in the eastern forests, where they maintained highly militant tribal villages under the unifying symbol of the Speaking Cross. Fighting continued at different levels of intensity for several decades, with raids, massacres, and reprisals becoming the normal features of frontier life. Unable to oust the People of the Cross, Yucatecans settled down to their lucrative henequen industry and contented themselves with the recriminations and public hand-wringings which Juan Mateos' poetry so brilliantly exemplified.[1] This state of affairs continued up to and beyond the coming of the Mexican Revolution in 1910. Only in the 1930s did rebel communities reach a peaceful understanding with the Mexican government.[2]

Unfortunately, the events of the war, every bit as dramatic as epic history should be, exceed the scope of this study. My purpose here has been to explore the social fabric which underlay rural society in the first half of the nineteenth century and to explain how the weaknesses in that fabric enabled the rebellion of 1847. In a subsequent work I will explore both the military events of war and the restructuring of rural society. For the moment, there remains only to review the major features of rural Yucatán from the early nineteenth century to the assault on Tepich.

Late colonial Yucatán assumed a social formation somewhat different from that of central Mexico. By 1821 the peninsula had purged the old Franciscan church structure and had replaced it with a less autonomous secular hierarchy. The seculars had strong links with Yucatán's emerging *hacendado* class. Priests and entrepreneurs enjoyed close familial relations. Moreover, the priests, through their control of *capellanía* money and peasant church fees, functioned as a key element of the peninsula's banking system. By 1821 the clergy itself enjoyed a tradition of landowning, and rural pastors often held peasant-worked properties within the confines of their own parishes. The Yucatecan church was neither weakened nor insignificant; instead, it had fused itself with the agrarian bourgeoisie during the economic growth period of the Bourbon reforms.

Control over the peasantry began to fracture during the brief period of Spanish constitutionalism, when a group of intellectuals and urban elites— the so-called *sanjuanista* party—maneuvered the peninsula's governor into a broad interpretation of constitutional decrees, thereby abolishing all peasant religious fees. They apparently intended to encourage rural elites such as the clergy to break from the Spanish metropole. Although the *sanjuanistas* fell to later repression, their tactics produced the desired effect, for by 1821 formerly reactionary clergymen were now leading a modified liberal party. Yucatecan independence came without so much as a rifle shot. The old liberals and their new converts now united in reimposing the church-tax system on the peasants, thus proving that the *indigenismo* of the earlier *sanjuanistas* was mere rhetoric.

Of greater interest was the peasant reaction to these events. Disgruntled peasants seized upon the opportunity to end their participation in the Spanish Catholic system altogether. The rural clergy, disconcerted by the abolition of obventions in 1813–1814, blamed any lack of peasant cooperation on creole "jacobins." But while peasants were indeed willing to establish favorable alliances with creole liberals, most evidence suggests that resistance after 1812 consisted of autonomous action by the Maya communities, or factions within communities. After 1814 rural authorities succeeded in reasserting partial control. Peasant resistance to taxes of church and state became the leitmotif of the next three decades, with chronic debt-dodging, lawsuits, and millenarian rumors that "the authorities" had abolished all taxes.

In sum, the process of independence did not pass over the indigenous peasantry like wind passing over some insensate stone. Just as Hidalgo's revolt permanently altered the world of the Bajío's squatters and tenant farmers, so too did the activities of the *sanjuanistas* involve peasant participation that quickly escaped elite control. The expectations of this period were never to die. In fact, the episode became a precedent to which later peasants (and later demagogues) could appeal.

Rural Yucatán was never a simple binary division between Maya and Spaniard, "ladino" and "macehual," or rich and poor. Between the extremes of class and of ethnicity stretched a network of intermediaries whose role was to communicate the wealth, the orders, and the information of this country world. The network included minor officials, ministers, peddlers, and above all Maya elites such as the *república de indígenas* and the peasant church staff. They were all Janus-faced individuals, addressing both the highs and lows of their world, and their activities helped preserve the peace. Municipal politics served as the sphere in which they (and all other elements) converged and interacted. In sum, the saga of the "castes," so entrenched in the minds of historians and in the popular memory, is a distortion of the way this rural society actually functioned.

A central figure in virtually all disputes and uprisings was the Maya *batab,* or cacique. The *batab* constituted one of the last remaining vestiges of pre-Columbian Maya authority. He was typically a man of property and enjoyed some command of Spanish and perhaps literacy, but his strongest asset was his ability to serve as a broker between the Maya and creole worlds. Taxes, labor drafts, and forced requisitions of commodities all hinged on his performance. *Batabs* took much of their income from commissions on collection of civil and religious taxes. Between 1821 and 1841 creoles managed to avoid major peasant conflicts in no small part because they remained successful in coopting this class of potential Maya leadership. Similarly, within the official cults and church religious staffs, peasants expected material rewards and sought to establish the best possible situation for themselves. When church patronage failed, peasant loyalties evaporated.

The process of commercialization begun under the Bourbon monarchs and continued by their less-regal heirs did not undermine rural stability because it assailed communal identities, or at least not exclusively because of that. Its disruptive effect struck at that network of brokers and power balancers that had helped regulate the old colonial world. To a large degree it obviated the old cultural power center of the rural world, the church. Creoles themselves fell into bitter struggles to purge the last remnants of this weakening body and to step into the opening power vacuum. In so doing, they helped rehearse the peasantry for its role as an insurgent force. But at the same time the fluctuations of power undermined peasant elites whose status had largely come to depend on patronage from both church and state.

In virtually all parts of the countryside, the Mayas (and everyone else) experienced the growth as a conflict between centralized power and local autonomy. Colonial tradition had invested authority into the old elites located in Mérida and Campeche, or in smaller networks found in provincial *cabeceras*. In a social sense, authority meant deference: the right to sit on *cabildos*, occupy elected office, and assume leadership generally in local affairs. In more material regards, it meant the ability to control taxes and labor and the right to regulate access to land. Yucatán's various constitutions provided mechanisms for staking out local autonomy through village incorporation, but these failed to keep pace with the rapid economic growth in the south and the east. The quest for local autonomy had the potential for uniting marginal elites with the rural Maya peasantry. Political instabilities which emerged in hamlet after hamlet suddenly exploded when Yucatán staged its larger revolt from Mexico. Here as elsewhere, processes of political fragmentation showed an alarming momentum, as leaders who began separatist revolts soon found themselves overtaken by newer and more radical movements.

The equilibrium of rural society began to destabilize in 1839, when a group of provincial elites near Valladolid staged a revolt against Mexico and its client-government in Mérida. Finding his revolt nearly extinguished, Colonel Santiago Imán resorted to a last desperate gamble: he mobilized Maya peasants as soldiers, promising land reforms and the complete abolition of church taxes. *Batab*-directed peasant mobilizations turned the tide, and by 1840 Yucatán had won its independence.

Like many formulas for short-term glory, Santiago Imán's revolt had disastrous consequences in the longer view. It sowed discord among rural elites, some of whom profited from the rebellion and some of whom lost. The net result was a succession of attempted coups and revolts which proved difficult to arrest. Imán's revolt also acquainted the peasants with the arts of mobilization and warfare. It reawakened expectations of liberation, as one peasant community after another refused to pay taxes. It compromised the financial position of the rural clergymen, who now found themselves forced to raise church "user fees" to compensate for lost tax revenues. The tax destabilizations and land grabs also seriously jeopardized the position of the *batab*. These individuals had always made their living partly on tax concessions. As taxes grew progressively more uncollectable, the prestige and percentages available to the *batab* dwindled to critical levels. The balancing act of the *batab* became more difficult, and the 1830s and 1840s witnessed a rapid turnover in the position, often through forced removal.

Finally, Imán's revolt also hastened the long-postponed centerpiece of the liberal agenda: land alienation. The new government loosened terms of acquisition and credit, and grants of public land (*denuncias*) became the favored means of paying soldiers after 1843. The largest of the *denuncias* were filed by priests, generals, and *latifundistas*. Numerous Mayas who had served in the war also filed for land. However, land alienation was a complex process. In some cases *denuncias* failed to translate instantly into changes in modes of production, while in other cases the new titles simply legitimized land usage patterns that had existed for some time. Peasants themselves reacted to the land rush in a variety of non-revolutionary ways, such as obtaining safe titles for village properties and founding new communities whose surrounding lands qualified for legal protection. Finally, although land was certainly a core issue, unrest typically erupted over related social and economic matters, particularly the tax controversy.

The backbone of revolutionary instigation was a conspiracy among the *batabs* of a string of eastern communities, notably Chichimilá, Tepich, and Tihosuco. The peasants of these communities manifested a capacity for concerted action that to some degree reflected a larger regional consciousness of the Oriente, a consciousness born of a set of social and economic ties independent of Mérida's hegemony. But this regional identity could not entirely counteract the deep conflicts therein. Tihosuco was not only a smugglers' crossroads but also the scene of a three-way struggle involving ambitious creoles, uncooperative peasants, and a powerful but aging *cura*. In Tepich, virtual war over taxes had broken out between the *batab* and the minister in the 1830s. Peasants of Chichimilá had also carried on a long-standing campaign against clerical authorities in Valladolid, and it is hardly coincidence that these authorities should be among the first victims of peasant jacqueries. It was amid these circumstances that the Caste War's original leaders emerged.

The importance of the *batabs'* crumbling status cannot be overestimated in tracing the origins of the Caste War. The *batabs* found themselves left behind in the Yucatecan land grab and forced into the sad position of collecting uncollectable taxes. And for the first time since the Montejos cut a bloody swath through the countryside, the *batabs* now found themselves hunted down and killed for failing to cooperate. Doubtless the land alienations would have roused some sort of rural conflict, whatever the position of indigenous leaders. The Maya could indeed be audacious, even brutal and fierce—just as Antonio Mais had said. But they were not a magical people, and there is no reason to believe that their revolt would have assumed the force or purpose that it did had not Yucatecan development allowed these Maya brokers to remain in power for as long as they did. Instead, the Caste War might have manifested itself in broken tools and stolen cows or as a series of sporadic uprisings soon suffocated by some rural constabulary. Still another possibility would have been a scenario similar to the one Brazilians are currently enacting in the Amazon jungle: peasants and small farmers would have gradually pressed into the eastern rainforests, stripping the land of its ancient treegrowth and burning out the soil, only to have their milpas absorbed by the ranches and sugar plantations which were coming up behind them. As it happened, however, these alternative courses were not to be. The themes of usurpation and power so often rehearsed in rural society received sudden vent, shattering the visions of prosperity which had charmed the elite of Yucatán and sending those elites in search of new strategies for dominating a yet uncontrolled countryside.

Notes

INTRODUCTION

1. Centro de Apoyo a la Investigación Histórica de Yucatán (CAIHY), "Composición leída por D. Juan A. Mateos la noche del 18 de octubre de 1866, en función a beneficio de las viudas y huérfanos de los valientes, que sucumbieron en el asedio de Tihosuco" (Mérida: L. Ancona, 1866), 7. All translations from Spanish and Maya are mine.

2. John Lynch, *The Spanish American Revolutions, 1808–1826* (New York: W. W. Norton and Co., 1986), 341–356.

3. The sixteenth-century bishop of the spiritual conquest, Diego de Landa, referred to Yucatán as "one living rock." "*Mayab t'an*" signifies "the land of the Maya speech." The epithet "land of pheasant and deer," another phrase from Landa, served as the name of a popular novel by Yucatecan writer Miguel Bolio.

4. Eligio Ancona, *Historia de Yucatán desde la época más remota hasta nuestros días* (Mérida: Gobierno del Estado de Yucatán, 1917), vol. 1, 246.

5. Sidney Mintz, *Sweetness and Power: The Place of Sugar in Modern History* (New York: Viking, 1985), passim; Stuart B. Schwartz, *Sugar Plantations in the Formation of Brazilian Society: Bahia, 1550–1835* (Cambridge: Cambridge University Press, 1985), 160–201; Richard S. Dunn, *Sugar and Slaves: The Rise of the Planter Class in the English West Indies, 1624–1713* (New York: W. W. Norton and Company, 1972), 59–83; Manuel Moreno Fraginals, *The Sugarmill: The Socioeconomic Complex of Sugar in Cuba, 1760–1860,* trans. Cedric Belfrage (New York: Monthly Review Press, 1967), passim; C. L. R. James, *The Black Jacobins: Toussaint L'Ouverture and the San Domingo Revolution* (New York: Random House, 1963), 45–57.

6. Howard F. Cline, "Regionalism and Society in Yucatán, 1825–1847: A Study of 'Progressivism' and the Origins of the Caste War" (Ph.D. diss., Harvard, 1947).

7. Lawrence James Remmers, "Henequen, the Caste War, and Economy of Yucatan, 1846–1883: The Roots of Dependence in a Mexican Region" (Ph.D. diss., University of California, Los Angeles, 1981), 309–327.

8. Robert W. Patch, "A Colonial Regime: Maya and Spaniard in Yucatan" (Ph.D. diss., Princeton University, 1979); Nancy M. Farriss, *Maya Society under Colonial Rule: The Collective Enterprise of Survival* (Princeton: Princeton University Press, 1984); Robert W. Patch, "Agrarian Change in Eighteenth-Century Yucatan," *Hispanic American Historical Review* 65, 1 (1985), 21–49; Matthew Bennett Restall, "The World of the *Cah:* Postconquest Yucatec Maya Society" (Ph.D. diss., University of California, Los Angeles, 1992); and Robert R. Patch, *Maya and Spaniard in Yucatán, 1648–1812* (Stanford: Stanford University Press, 1993).

9. Nelson Reed, *The Caste War of Yucatan* (Stanford: Stanford University Press, 1964); Ramón Berzunza Pinto, *Guerra social en Yucatán* (Mexico City: Costa-Amic, 1965); Moisés González Navarro, *Raza y tierra: La guerra de castas y el henequén* (Mexico City: El Colegio de México, 1970).

10. Victoria Bricker, *The Indian Christ, the Indian King: The Historic Substrate of Maya Myth and Ritual* (Austin: University of Texas Press, 1981), 87–118; Philip C. Thompson, "Tekanto in the Eighteenth Century" (Ph.D. diss., Tulane University, 1978).

11. To a large extent González Navarro can also be identified with this view. See also Renán Irigoyen, "El henequén y la guerra de castas," *Orbe* 4, 15 (1948), 38–45; Irigoyen, "Fue el auge del henequén producto de la guerra de castas?" *Orbe* 4, 9 (1947), 62–65; Remmers, 1981.

12. The vision of these years as a distinct and essential period is the legacy of Howard F. Cline's "Regionalism and Society." More recently, studies by Yucatecan scholars have begun to refocus attention to life between the end of the Spanish empire and the beginnings of the Caste War. See Pedro Bracamonte y Sosa, "Amos y sirvientes: Las haciendas de Yucatán, 1800–1860" (Thesis, Universidad Autónoma de Yucatán, 1989); Bracamonte y Sosa, "Sirvientes y ganado en las haciendas yucatecas (1821–1847)," *Boletín E.C.A.U.D.Y.* 12, 70 (1985), 3–15; Ermilio Cantón Sosa and José Armando Chi Estrella, "Los orígenes de la institución militar en el Yucatán independiente: La milicia activa en el Partido de Tizimín (1823–1840)" (Thesis, Universidad Autónoma de Yucatán, 1993); Beatriz Eugenia Carrillo y Herrera, "Iglesia y sociedad yucateca en el siglo XIX (1800–1840)" (Thesis, Universidad Autónoma de Yucatán, 1993); José Arturo Güémez Pineda, "Resistencia indígena en Yucatán: El caso del abigeato en el distrito de Mérida, 1821–1847" (Thesis, Universidad Autónoma de Yucatán, 1978); Silvia Mercedes Marrufo Noh, "La hacienda productora de caña de azúcar en Yucatán, 1821–1860" (Thesis, Universidad Autónoma de Yucatán, 1989).

13. Robert W. Patch, "Decolonization, the Agrarian Problem, and the Origins of the Caste War, 1812–1847," in Jeffery T. Brannon and Gilbert M. Joseph, eds., *Land, Labor, and Capital in Modern Yucatán: Essays in Regional History and Political Economy* (Tuscaloosa: University of Alabama Press, 1991), 51–82. Patch estimates 459,923 hectares (70–71).

14. Herman W. Konrad, "Capitalism on the Tropical-Forest Frontier: Quintana Roo, 1880s to 1930," in Jeffery T. Brannon and Gilbert M. Joseph, eds., *Land, Labor,*

and Capital in Modern Yucatán: Essays in Regional History and Political Economy (Tusca-loosa: University of Alabama Press, 1991), 145.

15. Cline, "Regionalism and Society," 599–601; Reed, *Caste War,* 23–24.

16. I have followed Farriss' example by using the anglicized plural *batabs* instead of the Spanish *batabes* or the Maya *batabo'ob.*

17. I offer this observation with some embarrassment, for my notion of peasant elites as leaders is hardly original or surprising. The definitive statement of this concept is Eric R. Wolf's theory that peasant revolts spring from a potentially revolutionary class of "middle peasants." See Wolf, *Peasant Wars of the Twentieth Century* (New York: Harper and Row, 1969), 291–292. But I find little documentary evidence to allow the three-tiered schema suggested by Wolf and have preferred to rely on a two-strata concept.

18. Farriss, *Maya Society,* 39–47.

19. *You will intermarry with them;*
    You will wear their clothes;
    And you will put on their hats,
    And you will speak their language.
    Nevertheless there will be trade:
    War trading
    At the time of the sprouting flowers,
    Of the flowers of the cross;
    But no one of us will rest,
    And on the day of the painted flowers,
    Then will be their lamentation.

Munro S. Edmonson, trans., *The Ancient Future of the Itza: The Book of Chilam Balam of Tizimin* (Austin: University of Texas Press, 1982), 174–175.

20. Much of the blame here lies with Yucatán's patrician historians of the past century. Authors like Justo Sierra O'Reilly, Serapio Baqueiro, Eligio Ancona, and Juan Francisco Molina Solís saw the Maya peasants as intractable vestiges of barbarism. True positivists, they could not imagine that peasants would meaningfully interact with the history of civilization and progress.

The first and most accomplished of these authors, Justo Sierra O'Reilly, was born in the remote village of Bolonchén. Sierra O'Reilly became a lawyer, married the daughter of Governor Santiago Méndez, and went on to serve as president of the Yu-catecan congress. He presided over much of the liberal legislation of the 1840s, edited some of Yucatán's first literary magazines, and published the first Yucatecan novel. More infamous is his role in the diplomatic history of the Caste War, during which he was assigned to negotiate the annexation of Yucatán to the United States. His princi-pal historical work is *Los indios de Yucatán: Consideraciones históricas sobre la influencia del elemento indígena en la organización social del país* (Mérida: Compañía Tipográfica Yu-cateca, 1954). Begun as an extended treatise on the origins of the Caste War, *Los indios* never goes beyond a detailed description of the *sanjuanista* episode of 1812–1821. He was also the father of the intellectual apologist for porfirian Mexico, Justo Sierra Méndez. Sierra O'Reilly's statue, erected shortly before the revolution, presides over the intersection of the Paseo de Montejo and Avenida Colón in Mérida.

The second great patrician historian, Serapio Baqueiro, made his principal contribution in *Ensayo histórico sobre las revoluciones de Yucatán desde el año de 1840 hasta 1864* vols. 1 and 2 (Mérida: Manuel Heredia Argüelles, 1878 and 1879) and vol. 3 (Mérida, Tipografía de G. Canto, 1887). Baqueiro was himself the son of one of the leading generals of Yucatecan troops during the war (Cirilo Baqueiro) and enjoyed access to numerous documents which, presumably, are not extant.

Finally, two patrician historians attempted to present the grand sweep of Yucatecan history. The first of these was Eligio Ancona. His *Historia de Yucatán desde la época más remota hasta nuestros días* (Mérida: Gobierno del Estado de Yucatán, 1917, 5 vols.) remains an impressive work and a rich source of information on events following 1821. Ancona went on to serve as governor of Yucatán following the state's restoration to Mexico. During the late porfirian times, Juan Francisco Molina Solís published a three-volume study entitled *Historia de Yucatán durante la dominación española* (Mérida: Imprenta de la Lotería del Estado, 1904–1913).

21. Pedro Manuel Regil, *Memoria instructiva sobre el comercio general de la provincia de Yucatán y particular del puerto de Campeche* (1811); Policarpo Antonio de Echánove, *Cuadro estadístico de Yucatán en 1814* (1814); José María Regil y Alonso Manuel Peón, *Estadística de Yucatán* (1853).

22. The two most important were *El museo yucateco* (1841) and *El registro yucateco* (1845), both edited by Justo Sierra O'Reilly.

23. Notions of peasant passivity find reinforcement in the writings of the American traveler John Lloyd Stephens, whose various travelogues have wielded an enormous influence over Yucatecan histories. His *Incidents of Travel in Central America, Chiapas and Yucatan* (New York: Dover Publications, 1963, orig. 1840) and subsequent *Incidents of Travel in Yucatan* (New York: Dover Publications, 1963, orig. 1843) not only became popular fare in the United States, but also among Mérida's intelligencia. In 1847 the British House of Parliament's report on foreign relations lifted Stephens' comments verbatim for its section dealing with Yucatan.

Incidents of Travel merits its reputation as a classic. Stephens was a keen observer of surface events, and the modern historian must reckon with his views on innumerable points. But Stephens' ability to peer beneath the surface into the more subtle (and often more definitive) dynamics of peasant-elite interactions often led him to grievous misunderstandings which have remained with us to the present day. One example will suffice. In 1842 Stephens visited the southern village of Nohcacab and portrayed it as the perfect bastion of peasant torpitude and indifference. Typical was his view on peasant participation in local politics, where "Indian alcaldes are frequently elected without being aware that they have been held up for the suffrages of their fellow-citizens" (*Incidents of Travel*, vol. 1, 205). What Stephens could not have known—and what the historical record indisputably shows—was that the peasants of Nohcacab were compulsive litigants. Indeed, the village had a tradition of quarrels and rebellions extend-ing back to the 1810s and probably much earlier.

Similarly, few who have read Stephens' account of the hacienda Uxmal can forget the scene of Maya servants slavishly tending to the feet of their master Simón Peón. They were, in a phrase Stephens took from Peón himself, "*muy dócil*" (ibid., 139). But within a year of Stephens' visit many of these same peasants were on trial for running amok and killing the estate's *mayordomo,* then doing the same on the adjacent property. Docility often concealed a world of resentment and hostility which the foreign trav-eler failed to perceive in his overnight visits. Undoubtedly we can forgive Stephens for not exploring court transcripts and notarial archives. But the larger point is that our own critical readings must now go beyond those of the nineteenth-century traveler. We must apply the newer concepts of peasants as active historical agents to the study of the Caste War's formative decades.

24. Farriss, *Maya Society,* 4–6; Inga Clendinnen, *Ambivalent Conquests: Maya and Spaniard in Yucatan, 1517–1570* (Cambridge: Cambridge University Press, 1987), 139–153; most recently, Restall, "World of the *Cah,*" 1992.

25. Eric Wolf, *Europe and the People without History* (Berkeley: University of Cali-fornia Press, 1982), 17.

26. My study employs a largely materialist reading. As models of peasant commu-nity fragmentation I have profited in particular from several studies: Sheldon Annis, *God and Production in a Guatemalan Town* (Austin: University of Texas Press, 1987); Thomas Benjamin, *A Rich Land, A Poor People: Politics and Society in Modern Chiapas* (Albuquerque: University of New Mexico Press, 1989); Herbert S. Klein, *Haciendas and Ayllus: Rural Society in the Bolivian Andes in the Eighteenth and Nineteenth Centuries* (Stanford: Stanford University Press, 1993); Florencia A. Mallon, *The Defense of the Community in Peru's Central Highlands: Peasant Struggle and Capitalist Transition, 1860–1940* (Princeton: Princeton University Press, 1983); William P. Mitchell, *Peasants on the Edge: Crop, Cult, and Crisis in the Andes* (Austin: University of Texas Press, 1991); Frans Schyrer, *The Rancheros of Pisaflores: The History of a Peasant Bourgeoisie in Twentieth-Century Mexico* (Toronto: University of Toronto Press, 1980); Irene Silverblatt, *Moon, Sun, and Witches: Gender Ideologies and Class in Inca and Colonial Peru* (Princeton: Princeton University Press, 1987); Carol A. Smith, ed., *Guatemalan Indians and the State: 1540 to 1988* (Austin: University of Texas Press, 1990); and Waldemar Smith, *The Fiesta System and Economic Change* (New York: Columbia University Press, 1977).

27. See bibliography for a listing of archival sources.

1. A RURAL SOCIETY IN THE NEW CENTURY

1. Diego de Landa, *Relación de las cosas de Yucatán,* ed. Miguel Rivera Dorado (Madrid: Hermanos García Noblejas, 1985), 181.

2. Regil, *Memoria instructiva,* 9.

3. Regil, *Memoria instructiva*, 2.

4. Patch, "Agrarian Change," 31; Stephens, *Incidents of Travel*, vol. 1, 48; Federico de Waldeck, *Viaje pintoresco y arqueológico a la provincia de Yucatán (América central) durante los años 1834 y 1836*, trans. Manuel Mestre Ghigliazze (Mérida: Compañía Tipográfica Yucateca, 1930, orig. 1837), 89–90. Records of the Mérida dog-killer can be found in CAIHY, "Manuscritos."

5. Waldeck, *Viaje pintoresco*, 33.

6. Marta Espejo-Ponce Hunt, "Colonial Yucatan: Town and Region in the Seventeenth Century" (Ph.D. diss., University of California, Los Angeles, 1974) 547–549; Cline, "Regionalism and Society," 284–285, 304, 305–306, 307–311; B. A. Norman, *Rambles in Yucatan; or, Notes of Travel through the Peninsula, Including a Visit to the Remarkable Ruins of Chi-Chen, Kabah, Zayi, and Uxmal* (New York: J. & H. G. Langley, 1843), 209; Waldeck, *Viaje pintoresco*, 25–27.

7. "Viaje a Bolonchen-ticul," *Museo yucateco* I, 1841, 218; CAIHY, XLV, 034, 1864.

8. Hunt, "Colonial Yucatan," 424–429; Patch, "Agrarian Change," 41; Norman, *Rambles in Yucatan*, 75–82; Ancona, *Historia de Yucatán*, vol. 2, 178–180.

9. Cline, "Regionalism and Society," 311–335; Ralph L. Roys, *The Titles of Ebtun* (Washington, D.C.: Carnegie Institute of Washington, 1939).

10. Rosemary L. Batt, "The Rise and Fall of the Planter Class in Espita, 1900–1924," in Jeffery T. Brannon and Gilbert M. Joseph, *Land, Labor, and Capital in Modern Yucatán: Essays in Regional History and Political Economy* (Tuscaloosa: University of Alabama Press, 1991), 198.

11. Remmers, "Henequen, the Caste War, and Economy," 106–107. The liberal leader Francisco Bates was himself from Sierra Alta and maintained political connections with the region after independence (Ancona, *Historia de Yucatán*, vol. 3, 192).

12. Peter Gerhard, *The Southeast Frontier of New Spain* (Norman: University of Oklahoma Press, 1993, orig. 1979) 78–79, 84–85; Norman, *Rambles in Yucatan*, 135–136; CAIHY, XLVIII, 011, "Informes del inspector de escuelas públicas," Sept. 20, 1865.

13. Ralph L. Roys, *The Political Geography of the Yucatán Maya* (Washington, D.C.: Carnegie Institute of Washington, 1957), 135–142.

14. *Registro yucateco*, I (1845), 215.

15. *Registro yucateco*, IV (1845), 314.

16. Sergio Quezada, "Encomienda, cabildo, y gubernatura indígena en Yucatán, 1541–1583," *Historia mexicana* 34, 4 (1985), 662–684.

17. In part this misconception traces back to the comments of Stephens. En route from Valladolid to Chemax, Stephens saw ragged hunters emerging from the woods:

> *Naked, armed with long guns, and with deer and wild boars slung on their backs, their aspect was the most truculent of any people we had seen. They were some of the Indians who had risen at the call of General Iman, and they seemed ready at any moment for battle (Stephens,* Incidents of Travel, *137).*

Of course, the famous traveler had no way of knowing who these particular individuals were and certainly could not have known whether they had taken part in any rebellions. But borrowing on Stephens, subsequent accounts have portrayed these as constituents of some remote tribe known as the Huits. These same Huits would later come to be identified as the source of peasant insurgency.

The term "*huit*" apparently derives from a nickname for peasant recruits during the Yucatecan wars of the 1840s. Baqueiro writes of revolutionary creoles who "with the object of putting into practice their network of guerrillas, accompanied by their *huithes*, as the Indians who lent their services to the war were then called" (Baqueiro, *Ensayo histórico*, vol. 1, I, 86–87). According to the Cordemex dictionary of the Maya language, the term "wits" generically refers to mountains or backwoods, or the people thereof. The Cordemex also reports that in the sixteenth century the term was synonymous with the people of the region of Ah K'in Ch'el, the region of the northern coast and *not* the south or east. Many of the rebellious creoles of the 1840s came from this region and presumably identified their peasant recruits not by an actual tribal patronymic, but by what had come to be a nickname for rustics. See *Diccionario Maya Cordemex*, ed. Alfredo Barrera Vásquez (Mérida: Ediciones Cordemex, 1980), 924–925; Roys, *Political Geography*, 79–91.

18. Carol Steichen Dumond and Don E. Dumond, in their editorial passages in *Demography and Parish Affairs in Yucatan, 1797–1879: Documents from the Archivo de la Mitra Emeritense, Selected by Joaquín de Arrigunaga Peón* (University of Oregon Anthropological Papers no. 27, 1982), provide a useful glossary of the late colonial church's tax terminologies; see 333–338. Other mentions of tax methods derive from my observations on the material contained in this same volume.

19. Clendinnen, *Ambivalent Conquests*, 58–71.

20. Farriss, *Maya Society*, 199–223.

21. Dumond and Dumond, *Demography*, 263.

22. According to Stephens, Becanchén had grown to six thousand by the time of his visit in 1841. See Stephens, *Incidents of Travel*, vol. 2, 5, 152; Dumond and Dumond, *Demography*, 440.

23. Indeed, this problem holds true for virtually all aspects of rural vocabulary, Maya or Spanish.

24. William Parish Robertson, *A Visit to Mexico, by the West India Islands, Yucatan, and United States, with Observations and Adventures on the Way* (London: Simpkin, Marshall & Co., 1853), vol. 1, 146–147.

25. Norman, *Rambles in Yucatan*, 136–137.

26. Matters of racial distribution are murky, though some observations are possible. Part of the problem confronting demographers is that racial taxonomies were seldom consistent or precise in the first decades of the nineteenth century. The most thorough division adopted four categories: *español* (occasionally written as *español/americano/ europeo*, reflecting the persistent creole fantasy of stocking the peninsula with immigrant yeomen); *mestizo; mulato, pardo, negro,* or some combination of the three; and finally, *indio*, or *maya*. The term *pardo* signified an Indian-black mix; *mulato* indicated

black-Spaniard. At times the tabulation lumps *español* and *mestizo* together, a fact which indicated not so much an equivalent social status, but rather a common language and cultural orientation, separate from those of the indigenous Maya. One final point of interest here is the occasional *indios hidalgos,* Mayas who had earned some sort of honorific position through their (or more likely, their ancestors') cooperation with the Spanish. These Indians enjoyed exemption from obventions. After 1821 the government forbade classification by race, and the *curas* appear to have conformed to this dictum, save for the common separation of *indio* from *español.*

27. Typical in this regard was Tihosuco; in 1806 the parish *cabecera* contained ninety-six *pardos,* while the estates contained none. Even in the more accessible parish of Tekantó, only eight *pardos* and no *mestizos* lived on the parish's six haciendas. Of nine towns whose racial demographics for 1813 are fairly complete, we find the highest percentage of Indians in Tihosuco, the town furthest from Mérida. The lowest percentages of Indians occur in Kopomá and Ticul, both on well-developed trade routes. See Dumond and Dumond, *Demography,* 223, 431.

28. Morris Steggerda, *The Maya Indians of Yucatan* (Washington, D.C.: Carnegie Institute of Washington, 1941), 93-94.

29. In the parish rolls of Espita, 1806, we find 385 unmarried Indians under age sixteen, but only 36 between ages sixteen and twenty-five, and only 15 bachelors twenty-five years or older. In Tekantó, 1813, bachelors disappear altogether after age twenty-five. Widowhood was a common but nevertheless temporary state between marriages. Turning to Espita once more, we find 30 girls already widowed by age sixteen! See Dumond and Dumond, *Demography,* 72.

30. For example, the haciendas of the parish of Tixcacalcupul, 1808, had 284 men and 269 women; thirteen years later, hacienda women outnumbered men 149 to 130. However, there were exceptions. In Uayma, 1807, we find 240 male Indians on haciendas, but only 30 women. See Dumond and Dumond, *Demography,* 273, 275, 293.

31. Ralph L. Roys, *The Indian Background of Colonial Yucatan* (Norman: University of Oklahoma Press, 1972, orig. 1943), 61-63, 148-160.

32. In 1803, of the sixteen extant parish reports on tax collection, ten *curas* reported that their work was done by the *batab,* with or without the assistance of other village officials. In two cases the *cura* collected them personally. One hired the *maestro de capilla,* an unusual arrangement, since the *maestro* was an Indian church assistant in the business of memorizing, teaching, and reciting prayers (Archivo Histórico de la Arquidiócesis de Yucatán [AHAY], Visitas pastorales [VP], 5, exp. 53, 1804). See also Farriss, *Maya Society,* 359.

33. Archivo Notarial del Estado de Yucatán (ANEY), Feb. 19, 1816, 54-57.

34. When particular items seemed justified by larger state budget priorities, the *república* could and did apply for supplemental funds from Mérida. For example, the *batab* and *república* of remote Polyuc petitioned for fifty pesos to complete the town's *audiencia* house (Archivo General del Estado de Yucatán [AGEY], Fondo Colonial [FC], Correspondencia de los gobernadores [CG], II, 1, Mar. 6, 1818).

35. Records of the civil hierarchy of Tekantó have led to speculation that the succession of office followed an elaborate pattern synchronizing the Spanish year with the pre-Columbian Maya calendar. See Thompson, "Tekanto." While intriguing, the argument is not entirely convincing. See chapter 4 below for additional information on methods of election. For an account of the history of the Pat family, see below, chapter 6.

36. AGEY, FC, Ayuntamiento (A), I, 5, Feb. 18, 1811.

37. Farriss, *Maya Society,* 355–386.

38. Clendinnen, *Ambivalent Conquests,* 40–42.

39. Grant D. Jones, *Maya Resistance to Spanish Rule: Time and History on a Colonial Frontier* (Albuquerque: University of New Mexico Press, 1989).

40. For information on the minor episodes between 1548 and 1761, see Ancona, *Historia de Yucatán,* vol. 2, 86–87, 89, 91, 146.

41. ANEY, Oct. 23, 1761, 302–305; June 9, 1764, 568.

42. The best examination of the Jacinto Canek rebellion of 1761 is in Bricker, *Indian Christ,* 70–76. Significant new information also appears in Patch *Maya and Spaniard,* 156–157, 210, 227–229. In addition, see Nancy M. Farriss, "Remembering the Future, Anticipating the Past: History, Time, and Cosmology among the Maya of Yucatan," *Comparative Studies in Society and History* 29, 3 (1987), 566–593. Further analysis can be found in Patch, "Colonial Regime," 391–394.

43. See chapter 4 for further information on this episode.

44. Archivo General de la Nación de México (AGNM), Bienes Nacionales (BN), XX, 10, 1830.

45. Cline, "Regionalism and Society," 391–394; Patch, "Agrarian Change," 30–36; Eric Van Young, *Hacienda and Market in Eighteenth-Century Mexico: The Rural Economy of the Guadalajara Region, 1675–1820* (Berkeley: University of California Press, 1981), passim.

46. Patch, "Agrarian Change," 34–35.

47. AGEY, FC, Impuestos propios y arbitrios (IPA), I, 7, June 14, 1813.

48. AGEY, FC, Tierras (T), I, 12, Dec. 6, 1823.

49. Patch, "Agrarian Change," 42–44; Bracamonte y Sosa, "Sirvientes y ganado," 8–12.

50. Bracamonte y Sosa, "Amos y sirvientes," 274.

51. Dumond and Dumond, *Demography,* 309–310.

52. ANEY, Mar. 6, 1811, 80–81.

53. The only systematic accounting of these properties for the early nineteenth century is found in the 1811 censuses, which offer detailed breakdowns of size, location, and ownership for six *partidos* (Camino Real, Champotón, Costa, Bolonchencauich, Sierra Baja, and Valladolid). While it would be preferable to examine all *partidos* over a greater span of years (particularly into the crucial 1840s), these censuses offer some clear patterns regarding individually owned peasant land.

54. It is risky to draw conclusions from these two *partidos,* since the omission of one or two estates radically alters the percentages (and given the haphazardness of all Yucatecan census operations, omissions were inevitable).

55. If this were the case, it would be unlikely to find them listed individually on the harvest-tax roster, as indeed they appear.

56. AGEY, FC, IPA, II, 45.

57. The ratio of private to communal was 79:46.

58. *Registro yucateco,* I, 174.

59. Restall ("World of the *Cah,*" 249–250) argues for collective family ownership by the heirs, with land "sometimes being placed nominally in the hands of a familial group representative." I would suspect, however, that the long-term effect was not significantly different from that obtained by dividing it among the several heirs.

60. ANEY, Dec. 1, 1832, no page numbers (1814–1815 documents).

61. ANEY, Jan. 14, 1832, 7–13; Sept. 18, 1833, 131.

62. ANEY, Apr. 7, 1825, 300–330.

63. Cline, "Regionalism and Society," 127.

64. At the time of the 1803–1804 *visita* the average tenure was a little over seven years, while the most common term of office was a mere four years. Three-quarters of the rural priests had served in a particular location for eight years or less. The number of *curas* sampled at any given time would doubtless be on their first assignment and would still have had the potential for years in the same location.

65. Santiago Ciriaco Esquivel of Valladolid suffered from gonorrhea (AHAY, Decretos y oficios [DO], microfilm roll [r.] 109, Feb. 4, 1845). I add this note for the benefit of a skeptical reader.

66. AHAY, Visitas pastorales (VP), 5, exp. 32, 1804.

67. AGNM, BN, IX, 23, Dec. 1, 1837.

68. For example, see the accounts of Tekax, a prosperous and heavily Indian parish, 1841 (Dumond and Dumond, *Demography,* 434–435). Fr. Silvestre Antonio Dondé supported a *coadjutor,* two ministers, a *maestro de capilla,* an organist, a gravedigger, and a carpenter.

69. Billie R. DeWalt, "Changes in the Cargo System of Mesoamerica," *Anthropological Quarterly* 48, 2 (1975), 90–94; Robert M. Hill II and John Monaghan, *Continuities in Highland Maya Social Organization: Ethnohistory in Sacapulas, Guatemala* (Philadelphia: University of Pennsylvania Press, 1987), 20–22.

The only set of parish records specifically identifying the church staff by name is the 1826 *matrícula* of Tzucacab. However, this reveals nothing more than the facts that they were married, reserved from taxes, and linked by patronymic to others in the village, none of which is terribly surprising (AGNM, BN, XXXI, 13, 1826). The Tzucacab *matrícula* is noteworthy for the Maya marginalia indicating which of the villagers were dead, sick, or fugitive.

70. Norman, *Rambles in Yucatan,* 21.

71. AHAY, "Cuentas de fábrica del curato de Tihosuco comprensivas desde 23 de marzo de 1817 hasta 30 de abril de 1827" (CF), passim; DO, box 19, May 9, 1836; DO, r. 94, July 13, 1815. On the *maestros cantores,* see Anne C. Collins, "The *Maestros Cantores* in Yucatan," in *Anthropology and History in Yucatan,* ed. Grant D. Jones (Austin: University of Texas Press, 1977), 233–247.

72. Farriss, *Maya Society,* 41. The loss of *doctrina* contributions would become one of the most bitter complaints of rural *curas,* perhaps because the shortage of castor oil cut into their source of illumination. See chapter 2 for related information.

73. CAIHY, Decretos, no. 23, Jan. 21, 1822, 109; Mar. 7, 1822, 208; Jan. 9, 1822, 106.

74. By the beginning of the nineteenth century, Yucatecan tax collectors still honored the distinction of *indios hidalgos,* the tax-exempt status awarded to selected peasant elites. However, records of *indios hidalgos* are fragmentary at best, making analysis of matters such as number and distribution impossible. See Ch. 4 below.

75. James C. Scott, *The Moral Economy of the Peasant: Rebellion and Subsistence in Southeast Asia* (New Haven: Yale University Press, 1976), 46–47.

76. *When misery came,*
    When Christianity came
    From these many Christians
    Who arrived
    With the true divinity,
    The True God.
    For this indeed was the beginning of misery
    For us,
    The beginning of tribute,
    The beginning of limosna.

Munro S. Edmonson, translator and annotator, *Heaven Born Merida and Its Destiny: The Book of Chilam Balam of Chumayel* (Austin: University of Texas Press, 1986), 199. Edmonson translates *limosna* as "tithe," which I have corrected here.

77. AHAY, VP, box 5.

78. One example of this is found in AHAY, CF.

79. For further information on *capellanías* in the nineteenth century, see Carrillo y Herrera, 117–192.

80. Genny Mercedes Negroe Sierra, "La cofradía de Yucatán en el siglo XVIII" (Thesis, Universidad Autónoma de Yucatán, 1984), 38; Adriaan C. Van Oss, *Catholic Colonialism: A Parish History of Guatemala, 1524–1821* (Cambridge: Cambridge University Press, 1986), 79–108.

81. Farriss, *Maya Society,* 96, 438; ANEY, Jan. 5, 1817, 322–325; ANEY, Oct. 31, 1814, 192–195; ANEY, Feb. 19, 1816, 54–57; AHAY, DO, r. 94, Apr. 22, 1815. The reader will immediately perceive that the structure of Yucatán's clerical wealth differed from that of the central Mexico church. The principal works on this much larger church organization are Michael P. Costeloe, *Church Wealth in Mexico: A Study of the 'Juzgado de Capellanías' in the Archbishopric of Mexico, 1800–1856* (Cambridge: At the University Press, 1967), and Jan. Bazant, *Alienation of Church Wealth in Mexico: Social and Economic Aspects of the Liberal Revolution, 1856–1875,* trans. and ed. Michael P. Costeloe (Cambridge: At the University Press, 1971). Both describe a situation in

which church wealth was primarily corporate, not individual; neither deal at any length with conditions in Yucatán.

82. For example, two brothers of Oligario Molina were priests. See Alan Wells, *Yucatán's Gilded Age: Haciendas, Henequen, and International Harvester, 1860–1915* (Albuquerque: University of New Mexico Press, 1985), 68.

83. AHAY, DO, r. 94, Apr. 22, 1815; July 4, 1815.

84. Ibid., July 4, 1815.

85. Fallon reports a 3 percent deduction in the eighteenth century. This apparently increased after the turn of the century. See Michael J. Fallon, "The Secular Clergy in the Diocese of Yucatan: 1750–1800" (Ph.D. diss., Catholic University of America, 1979), 55.

86. Dumond and Dumond, *Demography,* 434.

87. Cline, "Regionalism and Society," 195–197; AGNM, BN, XXXVIII, 13, 1844. One of the *visita* queries had dealt with how obventions were collected. Unfortunately, this remark could refer either to the type of payment or to number, size, or timing of payments. Thirteen *curas* responded that Indians paid "as they were able." We may be reading normative values here and not real practice, since the *curas* were probably stressing that they did not coerce the Indians. Only one village, Telchac, specifically stated that Indians paid in both corn and money. Money payment was the accepted practice in eight *cabeceras:* Kopoma, Oxkutzcab, Tekax, Ticul, Mani, Motul, Sotuta, and Tsonot Pip. There does appear to be some association between high rents and more advanced monetization. The first four were moderately rich to rich parishes; the next three yielded three thousand annual pesos each, while the revenues of Tsonot Pip are unknown.

88. Van Oss, *Catholic Colonialism,* 85–87; Dumond and Dumond, *Demography,* 309–451; AHAY, CF. Regarding the *musil* tax (which also appears in the documents as *mulsil,* see Woodrow W. Borah, *Justice by Insurance: The General Indian Court of Colonial Mexico and the Legal Aides of the Half-Real* (Berkeley: University of California Press, 1983), 364–365.

89. *Koché* travel invariably caught the attention of foreign travelers to Yucatán; surprisingly, however, it appears only incidentally in the extant primary documents.

90. AHAY, DO, r. 105, Feb. 6, 1838.

2. RETURN TO PAGAN ANTIQUITY

1. AGEY, FC, Varios (V), 1, 18, May 1813.

2. Letter from José Ortiz, José María Domínguez, and Ignacio Manzanilla, Mar. 3, 1814. Reprinted in J. Ignacio Rubio Mañé, *Los sanjuanistas de Yucatán* (no bibliographical information, 1971).

3. AHAY, DO, r. 94, Apr. 2, 1812.

4. AGNM, BN, XXI, 17, Jan. 1812. According to a November 9, 1809, inventory, the disputed rancho San Juan Sinhil contained forty-five boxes of *panela*, a still with copper tubing, three dozen clay molds for making sugar, a *trapiche* house with two serviceable mills, four mules, one hundred *mecates* readied for sugar planting, and one hundred more readied for corn. The combination of sugar and foodstuffs was typical of Yucatecan sugar estates, which seldom achieved the level of pure commercialization envisioned in Eric R. Wolf and Sidney W. Mintz, "Haciendas and Plantations in Middle America and the Antilles," *Social and Economic Studies* 6, (1957), 380−412. The internalization of peasant subsistence production within the ostensibly commercial enterprises reflected the Maya peasants' stronger bargaining power vis-à-vis slaves or purely proletarianized labor.

5. AHAY, DO, r. 96, Mar. 25, 1815. See chapter 3 below for a discussion of Solís' will and the aftermath of his death on the local peasants.

6. Roys, *Titles of Ebtun,* 177−255.

7. ANEY, Nov. 18, 1811, 358−359.

8. Crescencio Carrillo y Ancoca, *El obispado de Yucatán: Historia de su fundación y de sus obispos desde el siglo XVI hasta el XIX* (Mérida, R. Caballero, 1895), 118. Rubio Mañé, *Sanjuanistas de Yucatán,* 65−66, also provides information on the life and character of Estévez y Ugarte's assistant Antonio Mais, important in the later history of Yucatán.

9. Regil, *Memoria instructiva,* 5−18; Bracamonte y Sosa, "Amos y sirvientes," 41−42.

10. Yucatán followed in less pronounced fashion the colonial model found elsewhere. See, for example, the discussion of Peruvian officials in Steve J. Stern, *Peru's Indian Peoples and the Challenge of Spanish Conquest: Huamanga to 1640* (Madison: University of Wisconsin Press, 1982), 92−98. In the Villa Alta region of Oaxaca, Mexico, the system operated through the Spanish *alcaldes mayores;* see John K. Chance, *Conquest of the Sierra: Spaniards and Indians in Colonial Oaxaca* (Norman: University of Oklahoma Press, 1989), 103−111.

11. Bracamonte y Sosa, "Amos y sirvientes," 53.

12. ANEY, Apr. 4, 1815, Aug. 25, 1815, other dates. On colonial protections, see Borah, *Justice by Insurance,* 351−368; Farriss, *Maya Society,* 272−285; Charles Gibson, *The Aztecs under Spanish Rule: A History of the Indians of the Valley of Mexico, 1519−1810* (Stanford: Stanford University Press, 1964), 220−299; and Colin M. MacLachlan, *Criminal Justice in Eighteenth-Century Mexico: A Study of the Tribunal of the Acordada* (Berkeley: University of California Press, 1974). While Spanish policy permitted colonials to squeeze certain amounts of land from the Indians, it nonetheless kept large amounts of Indian property from alienation.

13. There is as yet not available means for offering a quantitative breakdown of anticlericism among estate owners. Estate owners' hostility to clerical control is known largely through anecdotal sources.

14. AGEY, FC, T, exp. 17, 1817.

15. Lorenzo de Zavala acted as attorney for the interests of various rural elites at this time (ANEY, May 17, 1813, 110–113). Pablo Moreno came from a family of estate owners in Valladolid; see Moreno's will in ANEY, Apr. 18, 1833, 314–315.

16. On the formation of the *sanjuanista* party, see Sierra O'Reilly, *Indios de Yucatán,* 39–44. For a more recent analysis of Yucatecan political factions involved in the constitutional crisis, see Paul Joseph Reid, "The Constitution of Cádiz and the Independence of Yucatán," *The Americas* 36, 1 (1979), 22–38.

17. Latin American Library, Tulane University (TUL), Yucatán Collection, 1, 21, Apr. 20, 1912; May 20, 1812.

18. Antonio Gramsci, *Selections from the Prison Notebooks,* trans. and ed. Quinten Hoare and Geoffrey Nowell Smith (London: Lawrence & Wishart, 1971). See also, George Rudé, *Ideology and Popular Protest* (New York: Pantheon Books, 1980); and T. J. Jackson Lears, "The Concept of Cultural Hegemony: Problems and Possibilities," *American Historical Review* 90, 3 (1985), 567–593.

19. James C. Scott, *Weapons of the Weak: Everyday Forms of Peasant Resistance* (New Haven: Yale University Press, 1985), especially 304–350.

20. On the proclamation, see Sierra O'Reilly, *Indios de Yucatán,* 59–65.

21. Dumond and Dumond, *Demography,* 363–364.

22. Ibid., 379–380.

23. Ibid., 443–444.

24. Ibid., 386.

25. It is difficult to wholly accept Ranajit Guha's "mirror-image" view of the language between masters and subalterns. However, certain reversals of values are clear at times, this being just such a case. See Guha, *Elementary Aspects of Peasant Insurgency in Colonial India* (Delhi: Oxford University Press, 1983), 15–16.

26. Dumond and Dumond, *Demography,* 366, 380, 400.

27. CAIHY, exp. box I, 7, misc. dates, 1813.

28. Ibid.

29. Dumond and Dumond, *Demography,* 363, 437, 450.

30. AHAY, DO, r. 107, July 7, 1816; r. 94, Oct. 6, 1816.

31. Ibid., r. 94, Jan. 21, 1815.

32. AGEY, FC, Correspondencia de diversas autoridades (CDA), Subdelegaciones, II, 1A, Jan. 1, 1814, 6 (Telá, parish of Tihosuco).

33. Ibid., FC, V, I, 16, Sept. 18, 1813; May 4, 1813; 17, May 22, 1813.

34. Ibid.

35. The information regarding these short-lived *ayuntamientos* comes from AGEY, FC, IPA, misc. dates and *expedientes.* The Maya-dominated *ayuntamientos* were Nunkiní (I, 40, Oct. 28, 1813), Tixhualahtún (II, 13, Nov. 5, 1813), Celul (II, 14, Dec. 13, 1813), Chumayel (II, 24, Jan. 17, 1814), Kancabdzonot (II, 38, Mar. 21, 1814), Dzitás (II, 41, May 26, 1814), Hocabá (II, 44, June 7, 1814), and Dzitbalché (I, 15, Aug. 4, 1813).

36. AGEY, FC, IPA, I, 40, Oct. 28, 1813; II, 30, Jan. 31, 1814.

37. Ibid., I, 8, Sept. 15, 1813.

38. ANEY, Mar. 14, 1814, 80–84; Mar. 16, 1814, 87–88; Mar. 21, 1814, 89–90. From Tihosuco came twenty-nine; from Yaxcabá, thirty-three; from Sacalum, six (naming an additional twenty-nine others as interested parties); from Dzitbalché, four (stating that they were acting on behalf of the entire village); and from Tixcacaltuyú, forty-five. In at least one case, the emissaries were *república* members within their villages. Lorenzo Naa and Policarpo Tsib, the first and second *alcaldes,* served as delegates of Yaxcabá. *Regidor* Valentín Ek led Tixcacaltuyú's representatives.

39. Ferdinand reconfirmed this ruling in a letter to Bishop Estévez y Ugarte in October 1815 (TEX, MAC-44, Oct. 12, 1815).

40. AGEY, FC, A, I, 20, Aug. 17, 1814.

41. Sierra O'Reilly, *Indios de Yucatán,* 161–162.

42. Ibid.

43. As argued by Ted Robert Gurr, *Why Men Rebel* (Princeton: Princeton University Press, 1970), 92–122.

44. AHAY, DO, r. 107, July 7, 1816; r. 94, Oct. 6, 1816.

45. AGNM, BN, XXVI, 14, Feb. 8, 1819.

46. AGEY, FC, V, I, 25, Feb. 13, 1816.

47. Ibid., FC, V, I, 31, Jan. 15, 1819.

48. The behavior of Yucatán's rural elites calls to mind the case of the Haji of Sedaka who, in their quest for new affluence, began to violate long-standing moral economies, provoking subtle forms of "daily resistance" among the poorer peasants. See James C. Scott, *Weapons of the Weak: Everyday Forms of Peasant Resistance* (New Haven: Yale University Press, 1985), 13–27.

49. CAIHY, Decretos, no. 41, Mar. 17, 1821, 80. Throughout the document, the name of the town varies between Sacalum and Sacalaca.

50. AHAY, DO, r. 94, July 15, 1816.

51. Ibid., r. 94, Sept. 26, 1815; r. 94, Nov. 1, 1815; r. 107, undated letter c. 1816.

52. Caste War caudillos such as Manuel Antonio Ay and Jacinto Pat had witnessed the constitutional crisis in their early to mid-teens (at least according to one account, Ay was fourteen in 1813, presumably a few years older than Ay). See below, chapter 6, for biographical information on the principal Caste War leaders.

53. Dumond and Dumond, *Demography,* 375.

54. Fallon, "Secular Clergy," 73.

55. AHAY, Concursos a Curatos (CC), 34, Mar. 30, 1818.

56. Ibid., Mar. 30, 1818.

57. Ibid., Apr. 3, 1818; Apr. 5, 1818; Apr. 27, 1818.

58. Ibid., undated.

59. CAIHY, Decretos, no. 41, Mar. 29, 1821, 94.

60. AHAY, DO, box 11, c. July 9, 1822; box 11, July 10, 1822. I have translated the word *calaboza* as "dungeon" and the word *cárcel* as "jail." While neither term has an exclusive or steadfast meaning, the peasants were clearly suggesting a terrible place of confinement, while Bravo tried to portray it as a place for momentary detentions.

61. Ibid., July 12, 1822.

62. Dumond and Dumond, *Demography,* 367.

63. AHAY, DO, box 13, July 15, 1827; July 24, 1827; Dec. 11, 1827. CAIHY, Decretos, no. 23, July 31, 1821, 24–25; Aug. 9, 1821, 36–37. Dumond and Dumond, *Demography,* 376.

64. AHAY, VP, 5, exp. 49, 1804; Dumond and Dumond, *Demography,* 427; AHAY, DO, box 12, c. Apr. 12, 1825 (date of forwarding letter); Apr. 19, 1825; c. May 17, 1825; May 23, 1825.

65. Dumond and Dumond, *Demography,* 427.

66. The tendency of peasants in times of social upheaval to read their own expectations into less than millenarian events finds many parallels in history. See, among others, Georges Lefebvre, *The Coming of the French Revolution,* trans. R. R. Palmer (Princeton: Princeton University Press, 1967, orig. 1939), 143. On a more theoretical level, see James C. Scott, *Weapons of the Weak,* 332–335.

67. Regarding the attempts of various conservatives to infiltrate the liberal, or *sanjuanista,* party, see Sierra O'Reilly, *Indios de Yucatán,* 169–172.

68. See, for example, the anxious correspondence from Pich (AGEY, FC, A, I, 44, 1820).

69. Ancona, *Historia de Yucatán,* vol. 3, 129–185.

70. The *curas* responded energetically and in concert when the government toyed with the idea of organizing a single tax with a subvention paid out to support the clergy. See TEX, no. 56, "Representación que los curas de la provincia de Yucatán hicieron al Illmo. sr. obispo doctor D. Pedro Agustín Estévez y Ugarte," July 4, 1822.

71. Tithes in particular remained a reliable source of church revenue throughout the crisis: partial receipts for the years 1812–1813 total some 36,000 pesos. See ANEY, misc. dates, Jan.–Apr. 1813.

3. THE OTHER SIDE
OF THE GOLDEN AGE

1. Ancona, *Historia de Yucatán,* vol. 3, 228–229.

2. AGNM, BN, IX, 23, 11–17, 1837.

3. Ancona, *Historia de Yucatán,* vol. 3, 225–236.

4. See ibid. 220–224, for a summary of the essential provisions of the 1825 Yucatecan constitution.

5. Waldeck, *Viaje pintoresco,* 39–40.

6. Ibid., 32.

7. Carrillo y Ancona, *El obispado,* 994–1007; Michael P. Costeloe, *The Central Republic in Mexico, 1835–1846: Hombres de Bien in the Age of Santa Anna* (Cambridge: Cambridge University Press, 1993), 36.

8. Ancona, *Historia de Yucatán,* vol. 3, 245–248. In many ways, the centralists expedited the liberal agenda by renewing the attack on rural *cofradía* properties.

9. AGEY, Documentos del Congreso (DC), Acuerdos, r. 20, Oct. 8, 1823, 30.

10. Ibid., FC, IPA, I, 10, Aug. 2, 1813.

11. Ibid., PE, T, I, 8, May 26, 1823.

12. Franklin P. Knight, *Slave Society in Cuba during the Nineteenth Century* (Madison: University of Wisconsin Press, 1970), 14–15.

13. AGEY, PE, Gobernación (G), XIII, 22, July 22, 1836.

14. CAIHY, exp. box III, 99, Dec. 28, 1833.

15. Güémez Pineda, "Resistencia indígena." As an example of land invasion, see documents on peasants occupying land claimed by the hacienda Yamuch, near Chapab (AGEY, FC, T, I, 25, Sept. 25, 1821).

16. See, for example, the dispute taking place outside Hunucmá, AGEY, PE, T, I, 20, July 27, 1831. We also find an extended case of land expropriation outside of Cantamayec, where José Antonio Ac was turned out of land bequeathed to him by his grandparents, though apparently with no title. The *subdelegado* justified attacking Ac's house and seizing his few possessions on the grounds that Ac had been poaching on local haciendas. The Maya was able to prevent complete destruction by arriving at the last moment with one of the village's Indian *alcaldes,* apparently a kinsman (AGEY, PE, G, IX, 16, Apr. 11, 1837).

17. AGEY, PE, T, I, 30, July 11, 1837.

18. Ibid., I, 25, Mar. 18, 1834. These scattered folios represent what was once an enormous corpus of paperwork regarding estate growth (Ibid., I, 12, 1823; I, 24, 1831; I, 31, 1837; I, 32, 1837).

19. ANEY, Nov. 2, 1830, 169–171.

20. On the physical description of the hacienda, see Bracamonte y Sosa, "Amos y sirvientes," 190–239.

21. CAIHY, "Documentos 1819–1865," Nov. 1837, "Lista de los individuos (todos ciudadanos mejicanos) que en cumplimiento de la ley de 4 de abril han pedido al Gobierno terrenos pertenecientes a la república en clase de hipoteca . . ."

22. Ibid., Correspondencia, July 14, 1825, 168; July 26, 1825, 170; Aug. 10, 1825, 171; Aug. 22, 1825, 173–174; Sept. 10, 1825, 175; Aug. 12, 1825, 179; Sept. 16, 1825, 177–178; Oct. 17, 1825, 182. Additional background information on Yucatán's early efforts to combat smallpox can be found in Sherburne F. Cook, "Francisco Xavier Balmis and the Introduction of Vaccination to Latin America," *Bulletin of the History of Medicine* 11, 5 (1942), 543–560, and part 2, 12, 1 (1942), 70–101.

23. AGEY, PE, A, I, 35, Aug. 2, 1825.

24. Archivo Municipal de Campeche (AMC), exp. III, Dec. 31, 1844.

25. Maya proclivities for these types of marriages—particularly for widowed men to marry the sister of their late wife—are amply documented in an unclassified AHAY manuscript entitled "Libro en que se toma razón de las dispensas de parentezco comenzado el 24 de abril de 1834 hasta 23 de mayo de 1841."

26. AHAY, DO, r. 105, June 25, 1838.

27. Michael Taussig, *Shamanism, Colonialism, and the Wild Man: A Study in Terror and Healing* (Chicago: University of Chicago Press, 1987), 60–66.

28. Scott, *Moral Economy,* 180–192.

29. ANEY, June 21, 1815, 91–101.

30. Ibid., Jan. 11, 1816, 331–334; Jan. 5, 1817, 322–325.

31. Ibid., June 21, 1815, 91–101; AHAY, VP, 5, exp. 48, 1804.

32. ANEY, July 14, 1818, 276–287; I am indebted to Matthew Restall of Boston College for calling this document to my attention.

33. Ibid., June 5, 1831, 409, 429–430; Dec. 30, 1834, 151–155.

34. Ibid., Aug. 10, 1835, 97–100.

35. Silvia Mercedes Marrufa Noh, "La hacienda productora de caña de azúcar en Yucatán, 1821–1860" (Thesis, Universidad Autónoma de Yucatán, 1989), 77–78.

36. AGEY, DC, Acuerdos, Oct. 14, 1823, 30.

37. Stephens, *Incidents of Travel*, vol. 1, 150.

38. Anticipation turned to disappointment, for at the end of the job the Mayas discovered that they could not roll out the barrel. Dondé's *mayordomo* complained that the work was not to his satisfaction, and his master consequently withheld pay. The Mayas took their claims to court, where the magistrate appointed a commission to resolve the matter within eight days. Of that commission's ultimate conclusions we know nothing (CAIHY, "Juicios," Jan. 3, 1822, 65).

39. AGEY, PE, "Nunkiní," misc. dates, Mar. 1845.

40. Ibid., PE, Gobernación (G), XIII, 2, Sept. 9, 1840. An affidavit of eight hacienda employees, together with Chuc's surviving account of a sizable forty-pesos debt, testify that things had indeed occurred as Chuc had described.

41. Ibid., DC, Acuerdos, r. 20, Aug. 1, 1823, 17.

42. Wells, *Yucatan's Gilded Age*, 151–182; Gilbert M. Joseph, *Revolution from Without: Yucatán, Mexico, and the United States, 1880–1924* (Cambridge: Cambridge University Press, 1982), 71–82.

43. AGEY, Justicia (J), III, 12, July 20, 1831.

44. Ibid., III, 13, Aug. 4, 1831.

45. Ibid., III, 14, Aug. 16, 1831; Aug. 21, 1831; Aug. 24, 1831.

46. On the belief in evil winds, see Robert Redfield *The Folk Culture of Yucatan* (Chicago: University of Chicago Press, 1941), 305–306. Belief in evil winds is alive and well in contemporary Yucatán, in both rural and urban sectors.

47. AGEY, PE, G, III, 20, July 27, 1831.

48. AHAY, DO, r. 105, May 19, 1838.

49. Deep, permanent burial has seldom been a practice here, particularly in country churchyards. Bodies are buried in shallow graves; the bones are later disinterred to make room for new burials, a process which occasions no particular distress or mourning.

50. CAIHY, Decretos, no. 41, June 5, 1821, 164; no. 23, Sept. 4, 1821, 52–53; no. 41, Jan. 42, 1821, 8.

51. Cantón Sosa and Chi Estrella, "Los orígenes de la institución militar," 12–21, 42–46, 59–62.

52. Salvador Rodríguez Losa, "Cuadro IX: Población de Yucatán, Censos," appendix, no page numbers; "Cuadro estadístico de la provincia de Yucatán, según los in-

formes que me fueron dados por Sres. Espinosa, Rejón, Hernández, y según mis propias observaciones," in Waldeck, *Viaje pintoresco,* no page numbers.

53. David J. Robinson and Carolyn G. McGovern, "La migración regional yucateca en la época colonial: El caso de San Francisco de Umán," *Historia Mexicana* 30, 1 (1980), 99–125.

54. The most thorough study of Maya migrations is Farriss, *Maya Society,* 199–223; see also James W. Yrder, "Internal Migration in Yucatán: Interpretation of Historical Demography and Current Patterns," in *Anthropology and History in Yucatan,* ed. Grant D. Jones (Austin: University of Texas Press, 1977), 191–231.

55. AGEY, PE, box 17, G, Aug. 4, 1844.

56. Ibid., PE, box 2, A, IV, 29, Apr. 26, 1840.

57. Ibid., PE, box 19, A, Jefatura Política, Nov. 6, 1845.

58. Ibid., PE, box 20, G, May 8, 1845; May 25, 1845.

59. AHAY, Asuntos Terminados (AT), 12, exp. 16, Nov. 21, 1835.

60. Ibid., AT, 12, exp. 16, Jan. 14, 1832; Jan. 16, 1838; Feb. 8, 1836.

61. CAIHY, CCA, no. 95, 1842, 1–9.

62. AHAY, AP, 3, May 5, 1838.

63. AHAY, AP, 3, May 5, 1838.

64. AHAY, AP, 3, misc. dates.

65. Reed, *Caste War,* 11.

66. AGEY, PE, G, IX, 19, Apr. 17, 1837.

67. CAIHY, Decretos, no. 41, Feb. 20, 1821, 44; Mar. 12, 1821, 73–74. The incident took place in Sacalaca, a fairly remote community.

68. See, for example, the case of Timucuy in CAIHY, Decretos, no. 41, Feb. 1, 1821, 18.

69. CAIHY, Decretos, no. 41, May 12, 1821, 142.

70. Landa reported that slave girls in particular were fair game for the nobility's desires. See Landa, *Relación de las cosas,* 87.

71. See, for example, the case of the runaway son and stepmother, AGEY, PE, J, II, 16, Aug. 16, 1842. They fled from Mamá to an estate in remote Peto, where they were legally defended against extradition by Felipe Rosado, who would play an important role in the early months of the Caste War.

72. Thomas P. Anderson, *Matanza: El Salvador's Communist Revolt of 1932* (Lincoln: University of Nebraska Press, 1971), 13–14; Carol Andreas, "Women at War," *NACLA Report on the Americas* 24, 4 (1990/1991), 20–27.

73. AGEY, DC, Acuerdos, Aug. 17, 1827, 65–66.

74. CAIHY, Decretos, no. 41, Apr. 13, 1821, 142.

75. Ibid., May 7, 1821, 132–133.

76. Ibid., June 15, 1821, 171.

77. Güémez Pineda, "Resistencia indígena."

78. ANEY, Apr. 11, 1825, 110–112.

79. Regil y Peón, *Estadística de Yucatán,* 108.

80. Typical in this regard was Miguel Chan of Kulul, in the *partido* of Campeche (CAIHY, Decretos, no. 41, May 11, 1821, 140).

81. Norman, *Rambles in Yucatan,* 135–136.

82. As suggested by Theda Skocpol; see *States and Social Revolutions: A Comparative Analysis of France, Russia, and China* (Cambridge: Cambridge University Press, 1979), 47–51, 112–117.

83. Stephens, *Incidents of Travel,* vol. 1, 204.

84. Their names were Juan Anastasio Keb, Juan Kuyoc, Lorenzo Ceh, Vicente Canché, and Juan Poot of the barrio San Mateo; and Manuel Antonio Kuyoc, Valentín Canché, Pablo Tsib, and Mariano Canché of the barrio Santa Barbara.

85. AGEY, J, III, 17, Mar. 21, 1832.

4. DILEMMAS OF THE MAYA ELITE

1. TUL, Yucatecan Collection, 1, 25, Feb. 15, 1812.

2. AGEY, PE, G, II, 47, Jan. 24, 1831.

3. Roys, *Indian Background,* 130, 149–150.

4. AGEY, PE, J, I, 5, Dec. 29, 1842.

5. AHAY, DO, r. 108, Oct. 8, 1844.

6. Roys, *Indian Background,* cites a reference to a large hidalgo class in 1766 (148). On the rich peasant, see Wolf, *Peasant Wars.* Documentary evidence for a privileged class of hidalgos is slender. Virtually the only reference is a stray comment from the village of Temosón, just prior to independence, complaining that hidalgos were shirking their responsibility for community patrol (CAIHY, Decretos, no. 41, Apr. 13, 1821, 142). We also find listings of "hidalgos by birth" in Libre Unión, Kantunil, Xanabá, and Santa Elena (previously Nohcacab); see AGEY, PE, box 34, Poblaciones, misc. dates 1849.

7. ANEY, Nov. 7, 1820, 19.

8. AGEY, Fondo Justicia (FJ), XII, 57, Mar. 21, 1821.

9. AGNM, BN, X, 53, "Matrícula de Peto, año de 1826." The woman's name was María Castro; she and her husband Salvador Cocom had both fled the parish and were unavailable for taxes under any conditions.

10. AGEY, FC, CG, II, 4, June 24, 1820, 89–90. In addition, see the identical complaint from Homún, same documents and date, 93.

11. See the complaint from Yaxkukul, in AGEY, FC, CG, III, 4A, July 20, 1820, 190–191.

12. AGEY, DC, Acuerdos, Nov. 5, 1827, 71–73.

13. AHAY, DO, box 12, July 7, 1825; Feb. 16, 1826.

14. AGEY, PE, Empleos (E), II, 57, Nov. 12, 1830.

15. Ibid., box 15, A, Jan. 11, 1844; Nov. 23, 1844.

16. Thompson, "Tekanto," 258–259.

17. ANEY, Dec. 30, 1817, 20.

18. AHAY, CC, 34, Aug. 2, 1818.

19. ANEY, Feb. 25, 1826.

20. ANEY, July 7, 1826.

21. AGEY, PE, box 106, G, "Irregularidades," Jan. 10, 1865. The document appears to refer to traditional practices and probably represents pre–Caste War electoral policies.

22. Thompson, "Tekanto," 367–400; see also Thompson, "The Structure of the Civil Hierarchy in Tekanto, Yucatan, 1785–1820," *Estudios de la cultura maya* 16 (1985), 183–197.

23. AGEY, PE, E, II, 40, Mar. 24, 1829 (Tihosuco); 44, Apr. 24, 1829 (Tiholop); 45, Apr. 29, 1829 (Tepich); and 46, May 15, 1829 (Telá).

24. AGEY, PE, box 2, A, III, 30, Jan. 26, 1835. On the highland Maya cargo systems, see Frank Cancian, *Economics and Prestige in a Maya Community: The Religious Cargo Systems in Zinacantan* (Stanford: Stanford University Press, 1965), 97–106; Waldemar R. Smith, *The Fiesta System and Economic Change* (New York: Columbia University Press, 1977), 24–28; Jan. Rus and Robert Wasserstrom, "Civil-Religious Hierarchies in Central Chiapas: A Critical Perspective," *American Ethnologist* 7, 3 (1980), 467–472.

25. CAIHY, exp. III, 93, Nov. 23, 1833. While *subdelegados* enjoyed 8 percent of the tax revenues from *vecinos,* the *repúblicas* continued per an earlier decree of July 26, 1824 (not extant).

26. Restall, "World of the *Cah,*" 196–203.

27. AGEY, PE, G, Oct. 20, 1840.

28. ANEY, Aug. 25, 1846, 432–434.

29. AGNM, BN, XIII, 30, 1827.

30. ANEY, Aug. 18, 1846, 224–225.

31. Dzul borrowed money from creoles, but he loaned it to them as well and sued when they failed to pay. While battling the *subdelegado* of Peto, Dzul was simultaneously carrying on a suit to collect an outstanding loan from Manuel María Montalvo of Chunhuhub. In this latter case Dzul used Fr. Mariano Brito as his legal representative. See ANEY, Nov. 7, 1836, no page numbers; Dec. 16, 1836, 277.

32. AGEY, FJ, XI, 1, Nov. 21, 1836; Dec. 20, 1836.

33. AGEY, FC, CG, III, 1, Apr. 4, 1818; Apr. 7, 1818.

34. Roys, *Political Geography,* 138. For more information on the Pat family in Tihosuco, see chapter 6.

35. AGEY, FJ, I, 3, Mar. 8, 1842.

36. AGEY, PE, E, II, 51, Sept. 18, 1829. When Tomás May resigned his office as the *batab* of Huhí, near Sotuta, he composed a resignation letter which reviewed his history as an official as evidence that he had "done enough." Hence the information presented here.

37. Ibid., box 25, G, Jefe Superior Político (JSP), Feb. 23, 1847.

38. Ibid., box 27, G, "Caciques," Feb. 23, 1847.

39. Ibid., E, II, 65, Oct. 18, 1838.

40. AHAY, DO, r. 116, Feb. 1, 1840.

41. For a thorough exploration of literacy and the Maya world, see Restall, "World of the *Cah*."

42. AGNM, BN, XXXI, 13, "Matrícula del pueblo de Tzucacab, año de 1826"; X, 53, "Matrícula de Peto, año de 1826."

43. AGEY, PE, G, I, 25, May 22, 1841. In the Tekax court dockets for 1844, we find at least one Maya on trial for counterfeiting (AGEY, 1845).

44. AGEY, FC, Diputaciones Provinciales (DP), II, 5, Aug. 5, 1820.

45. AGEY, PE, T, I, 19, Apr. 24, 1831.

46. Again, for an examination of the extant colonial documents, see Restall, "World of the *Cah*," passim.

47. AGEY, FC, Propios y arbitrios, I, 40, Sept. 28, 1813.

48. AGEY, box 72, G, "Caciques," Feb. 6, 1847; Feb. 11, 1847. There is an extensive body of literature relating literacy with political and cultural domination. See Farriss, "Remembering the Future," 566–593; Jack Goody and Ian Watt, "The Consequences of Literacy," in *Literacy in Traditional Societies,* ed. Jack Goody (Cambridge: Cambridge University Press, 1968), 27–68; Claude Levi-Strauss, *Tristes Tropiques,* trans. John and Doreen Weightman (New York: Atheneum, 1973), 294–304; and Patricia Seed, "'Failing to Marvel': Atahualpa's Encounter with the Word," *Latin American Research Review* 26, 1 (1991), 7–32.

49. AGNM, BN, XXXV, 5, misc. dates, Nov.–Dec. 1824. During this period Apan rose from *teniente* in earliest documents to *batab* in the later.

50. In the succeeding volume I intend to explore post-1847 rural leadership roles in both the pacified and rebel areas. Until then a number of studies are available. See Grant D. Jones, "Revolution and Continuity in Santa Cruz Maya Society," *American Ethnologist* 1 (1974), 659–683; Don E. Dumond, "Independent Maya of the Late Nineteenth Century: Chiefdoms and Power Politics," in Grant D. Jones, ed., *Anthropology and History in Yucatan* (Austin: University of Texas Press, 1977), 103–138; Grant D. Jones, "Levels of Settlement Alliance among the San Pedro Maya of Western Belize and Eastern Petén, 1857–1936," in Jones, ed., (1977), 139–189; and Barbara Angel, "The Reconstruction of Rural Society in the Aftermath of the Mayan Rebellion of 1847," *Journal of the Canadian Historical Association* 4 (1993), 33–53.

51. AHAY, CC, 35, July 8, 1841.

52. Years later, responding to an inquiry, Glory himself rather coyly remarked that Trujillo, now long departed, had undergone a complete reformation of character, "and I do not doubt that he maintains himself thus even now" (ibid.).

53. Variations on this theme were endless. Anastasio Tsib of Chemax, on behalf of the Mayas of both the ranchos Cocom and Catzim, came before the authorities protesting having to pay for both the local school and the patriotic contribution. To this the authorities speedily replied that the two were separate, not mutually exclusive, and that the *rancheros* had better pay up. See CAIHY, Decretos, no. 41, Apr. 3, 1821, 103.

54. Juan Tomás Chan had received the commission to collect the patriotic contribution for Timun. One payer became so furious that he physically assaulted the mem-

bers of the town's *ayuntamiento*. Chan, perhaps hoping to set an example for other tax resisters, filed suit against the unnamed assailant, but because he had not been one of those attacked, the court threw out the case. See CAIHY, Decretos, no. 23, Jan. 14, 1822, 107.

55. AGEY, DC, Correspondencia, 1831–1835, Jan. 27, 1834, 78. Today Yaxcopoil is a popular tourist attraction and is well worth the visit.

56. AHAY, DO, box 12, Nov. 25, 1825; Dec. 14, 1825. Faced with this prodigious body of testimony, the cathedral merely sent Acevedo a reprimand.

57. AGEY, FC, DP, I, 5, Aug. 5, 1820.

58. Ibid., Correspondencia de diversas autoridades, I, 3, Sept. 14, 1801.

59. Ibid., Correspondencia, III, 1, Jan. 23, 1818. The nature of the conflict is unknown.

60. We find a case of reiterated commands for collection, for example, in AGEY, FC, CG, Maní, June 24, 1820.

61. AGEY, PE, G, 13, 13, Oct. 12, 1840.

62. TUL, Yucatecan Collection, 2, 7, July 17, 1844; Sept. 5, 1844.

63. CAIHY, Decretos, no. 61, Apr. 19, 1845, 188.

64. AGEY, PE, box 28, G, "Correspondencia con los jefes y oficiales militares," Jan. 7, 1848; FC, "Correspondencia," 1847–1848, Jan. 1, 1848, 31.

65. AGEY, II, G, 47, Jan. 24, 1831.

66. The project which angered the Hopelchén peasants was the construction of a town cistern, of little interest to rancho peasants who enjoyed their own private *cenote*. See AGEY, PE, J, II, 14, June 17, 1842.

67. AGEY, PE, G, XII, 27, misc. dates.

68. The recourse to threats of "secret attacks" from without had deep appeal to the peasant psychology, rooted as it was in an intense localism and a continual fear that the good things of the world lay under constant threat of plots and malevolent schemes. See George M. Foster, "Peasant Society and the Image of the Limited Good," *American Anthropologist* 67 (1965), 293–315.

69. AHAY, DO, r. 116, Aug. 16, 1841; AHAY, CC, 35, Oct. 27, 1845.

70. AHAY, CC, 35, June 26, 1846; July 6, 1846; July 7, 1846.

71. Letitia Reina, *Las rebeliones campesinas en México (1819–1906)* (Mexico City: Siglo Veintiuno, 1980), 403.

72. Sierra O'Reilly, *Indios de Yucatán*, 98–99; AHAY, CC, 34, 1814, misc. dates. We do not find Granado Baeza interfering with sales of local Indian land, such as the purchase of Yaxuelá described in chapter 2.

73. AGEY, PE, G, I, 29, July 1, 1827.

74. As described in Phillip Baer and William R. Marrifield, *Two Studies on the Lacandones of Mexico* (Norman: Summer Institute of Linguistics, 1971); R. Jon McGee, *Life, Ritual, and Religion among the Lacandon Maya* (Belmont, Calif.: Wadsworth Publishing Co., 1990); Victor Perera and Robert D. Bruce, *The Last Lords of Palenque: The Lacandon Mayas of the Mexican Rain Forest* (Boston: Little, Brown and Company, 1982), 10–34.

75. AHAY, CC, no number, exp. 124, Jan. 18, 1805. See also Stephens, *Incidents of Travel*, vol. 1, 269.

76. AGEY, PE, G, IV, 12, May 3, 1832; CAIHY, Decretos, no. 61, Apr. 19, 1844, 10; AHAY, AT, 13, exp. 32, Apr. 5, 1845; AHAY, AT, 13, exp. 33, Apr. 26, 1845.

77. The best documented was an 1824 complaint to the governor. The plaintiffs were Pedro Chable's two sons, now acting as spokesmen for their small settlement of *milperos* in a spot called Taná, outside of Nevelá and, at least in their argument, within the parochial confines of Tixcacaltuyú. Their problem was the *alcalde* of nearby Tixmeuac, a certain Ancelmo Hernández. This man harassed them continually, they charged, "obligating them to the most scandalous burdens, to satisfy all sorts of contributions, [even] after we verified the receipts in the aforementioned Tixcacaltuyú, of which we are ancient residents indeed." Their father, Pedro, had come with a legalized copy of a paper proving that Taná fell within Tixcacaltuyú; he gave it to the local Indian *alcalde* Francisco Moo, whose efforts on behalf of the Maya of Taná landed him in jail, and there the matter stood. Significantly, the Taná Indians had already tried one interesting maneuver. An earlier complaint had gone before congress in April of the previous year, and they had waited all this time for the response which never came (AHAY, CC, 34, Mar. 24, 1824).

78. In this case what we must judge from is undoubtedly a Spanish translation of an original Maya document.

79. From Governor José Crespo's account of the Jacinto Canek uprising, Mar. 12, 1762, reprinted in *Diario de Yucatán*, Nov. 22, 1936, 12–13.

80. The document speaks of it being abandoned "more than seventy years," which would place its abandonment prior to the rebellion itself. This was almost certainly a mistake on the part of the petitioners.

81. The data for *batab* resignations appears primarily in the sections "Caciques" and "Empleos," misc. dates.

5. THE IMÁN REVOLT

1. Norman, *Rambles of Yucatan*, 233–234.

2. AGEY, PE, box 5, G, IV, 101, Mar. 30, 1841.

3. Remmers, "Henequen, the Caste War, and Economy," 208. The details of the Imán revolt appear in Baqueiro, *Ensayo histórico*, vol. 1, 49–120.

4. Costeloe, *Central Republic in Mexico*, 46–54. The reconquest of Texas would remain the leitmotiv of Mexican politics until the collapse of the conservative central republic.

5. CAIHY, "Correspondencia de Valladolid," Apr. 14, 1838, 38–39; May 25, 1838, 41–42; May 26, 1838, 42–43.

6. Baqueiro, *Ensayo histórico*, vol. 1, 23–25; Ancona, *Historia de Yucatán*, vol. 3, 261–265; Carrillo y Ancona, *El obispado*, 1016–1017.

7. In March 1820, for example, Faustino Imán purchased the hacienda Santa Guadalupe Ochil, located between Mérida and the coastal village of Chuburná, for four hundred pesos. See AGNM, BN, 163, 14, Mar. 15, 1820.

8. AGEY, PE, box 2, CP, III, 23, May 15, 1841.

9. A tip of the historical hat to my colleague Dan Snell for illuminating this point.

10. Cantón Sosa and Chi Estrella, "Orígenes de la institución militar," 144–146.

11. TUL, "Yucatecan Letters," 3, 15, 9, Sept. 11, 1825.

12. AGEY, PE, J, EV, 14, 1837.

13. AHAY, DO, r. 104, Feb. 15, 1840.

14. Details of the Imán revolt appear in AGEY, PE, G, 11, 23, Jan. 7, 1840, "Información sumaria hecha en averiguación . . ."

15. Baqueiro, *Ensayo histórico,* vol. 1, 26–27, 29, 30–31.

16. AGNM, BN, II, 5, Nov. 27, 1845.

17. AGEY, FC, Criminal, III, 3, misc. dates, 1821. This well-documented episode throws an ironic touch on one of the legends of Yucatecan history. During the Caste War negotiations of 1848, the insurgent leader Jacinto Pat made his now-famous accusation that a priest named Herrera saddled and rode peasants like horses. Evidence for a priest named Herrera operating in the vicinity of Tihosuco is now lacking; Herrera and his saddle may well have been an invention, or possibly the accusation represents some folk memory of a real event. At any rate, it is clear that the priests were not the only ones capable of such abuses.

18. AGEY, PE, Correspondencia, I, 4, Nov. 12, 1822.

19. On the Campeche militia and desertions from the Mexican army, see Waldeck, *Viaje pintoresco,* 31, 97.

20. William L. Clements Library, University of Michigan, MI, "Collection," Aug. 11, 1846.

21. AGEY, box 13, G, Apr. 20, 1843; Fidelio Quintal Martín, ed., "Proceso y ejecución de Manuel Ay Tec, caudillo campesino de Chichimilá, Yucatán," *Boletín E.C.A.U.D.Y.* 13, 76 (1986), 27.

22. Baqueiro, *Ensayo histórico,* vol. 1, 30–31.

23. AHAY, DO, r. 105, Sept. 2, 1839; Oct. 2, 1839.

24. AHAY, DO, r. 99, Sept. 8, 1835.

25. Regarding these lawsuits, see chapter 6, below.

26. Baqueiro, *Ensayo histórico,* vol. 1, 37.

27. AHAY, DO, r. 104, July 24, 1840.

28. Ibid., r. 104, Jan. 14, 1840.

29. Ibid., r. 104, Mar. 3, 1840.

30. Ibid., r. 107, May 1, 1843; May 3, 1843.

31. I have not seen the original Maya letter to this, which is apparently to be found in CAIHY (dated June 20, 1843). A translation appears in Fidelio Quintal Martín, *Correspondencia de la guerra de castas* (Mérida: Ediciones de la Universidad Autónoma de Yucatán, 1992), 15.

32. Baqueiro, *Ensayo histórico,* vol. 1, 84–90.

33. AGEY, PE, 1843 Plebiscite, misc. pages.

34. AHAY, DO, r. 109, Apr. 14, 1846.

35. Ibid., r. 104, Dec. 9, 1840.

36. CAIHY, exp. box VI, 33, Apr. 5, 1841.

37. Ibid., exp. box VII, 30, Nov. 16, 1843.

38. Patch, "Decolonization," 71.

39. ANEY, Sept. 30, 1844, 242–243; Oct. 8, 1844, 250; Mar. 17, 1845, 68–69; Oct. 7, 1845, 73–75; Oct. 11, 1845, 92–93; Mar. 9, 1846, 94–96; Jan. 13, 1847, 2–4.

40. Ibid., Jan. 10, 1845, 2–3; Mar. 9, 1846, 94–96; Dec. 20, 1844, 344–347.

41. Ibid., Feb. 19, 1816, 74–76.

42. See below, chapter 6, for biographical details of the life of Mais.

43. I have listed the *curas* in the order in which they received their claims. See ANEY, May 24, 1844, 108; July 9, 1844, 154–157; Dec. 6, 1844, 323–326; Dec. 13, 1844, 331; Dec. 14, 1844, 334; Dec. 18, 1844, 336–338; Jan. 28, 1845, 22; Apr. 3, 1845, 94; May 9, 1845, 125–126, May 26, 1845, 136; Sept. 30, 1845, 56–57; Oct. 1, 1845, 57–60; Oct. 4, 1845, 102–104; Oct. 13, 1845, 418; Jan. 3, 1845, 23; Feb. 19, 1846, 74–76; Mar. 13, 1846, 98–100; Mar. 31, 1846, 113; Apr. 20, 1846, 66; May 26, 1846, 100–102; June 12, 1846, 72; July 13, 1846, 343; July 17, 1847, 73–75. The claim of Manuel Antonio Sierra O'Reilly appears in ibid., Sept. 22, 1845, 37–39.

44. Ibid., July 17, 1847, 73–75.

45. AGEY, PE, box 19, G, JP, "Correspondencia," Oct. 17, 1845 (Peto); CAIHY, Decretos, no. 61, Aug. 22, 1844, 74 (Xanabá).

46. ANEY, Jan. 13, 1845, 2–4.

47. Ibid., Oct. 17, 1846, 180.

48. Ibid., July 31, 1844, 170; Mar. 15, 1845, 68; Sept. 15, 1846, 255–256.

49. Ibid., Mar. 2, 1847, 49–50.

50. Fifteen lay in the vicinity of Chancenote alone, eight in Cenotillo. On the Badillo *denuncia,* see ANEY, May 1, 1845, 240–241.

51. AGEY, PE, T, I, 33, Mar. 10, 1840.

52. ANEY, Jan. 28, 1845, 22.

53. Ibid., Aug. 25, 1846, 432–434; Feb. 15, 1847, 338.

54. This point can be inferred from the cases of Tihosuco and Yaxcabá, where *batabs* filed their claims at the same time as local officials with whom they had standing political alliances. See CAIHY, "Registro de las denuncias de terrenos baldíos," 49, 54.

55. CAIHY, Decretos, no. 61, June 19, 1847; Dec. 5, 1845, 257.

56. ANEY, Oct. 9, 1846, 259–260.

57. Ibid., Feb. 9, 1846, 56–57.

58. Examples of this are numerous, and I shall only cite a few instances of what could be extended to a rather tedious list. Outside of Peto, José Antonio Pérez filed for and received a quarter-league of land in which he had already set up his ranchos Santa Rosa and San Pedro (ANEY, Aug. 16, 1842, 214–215). Similarly, *cura* Antonio

Mais of Tihosuco sought legitimate title to land where he had already set up *"un establecimiento de agricultura"* (ANEY, Jan. 28, 1845, 22).

59. A multitude of peasant complaints survive, largely as brief notations of pending or concluded legal actions, in a CAIHY manuscript entitled "Decretos 1844–1845." These notations trace the legal battles of fifty-two different communities.

60. CAIHY, Decretos, no. 61, Oct. 23, 1845, 245; Oct. 11, 1844, 105.

61. AGEY, FC, A, I, 5, Apr. 24, 1813. As early as 1831 the *república* of Pisté was petitioning for measurement. If this early petition was representative, it may have been tempting for authorities in Mérida to pigeon-hole such demands by referring them back to the *subdelegado,* who could halt further inquiry through a variety of pretexts. In this case, *subdelegado* Agustín Acereto reported back that the *república* had withdrawn its support for the request. Either they had been bought off or intimidated. Thus the *república* itself would have to assume the initiative and costs of reinitiating the complaint (AGEY, PE, T, I, 19, May 10, 1831).

62. AGEY, PE, J, IV, 26, July 16, 1840; CAIHY, Decretos, Oct. 31, 1844, 121.

63. Patch, "Decolonization," 74–75.

64. See "Ley de 30 de octubre de 1843, declarando libre y reglamentando el trabajo de los sirvientes," and "Ley de 12 de mayo de 1847, sobre sirvientes y jornaleros," University of Alabama, Yucatecan microfilm collection, roll 49.

65. AGEY, PE, Decretos y leyes, I, 2, July 7, 1842; J, II, 13, Aug. 16, 1842.

66. Patch, "Decolonization," 65–66.

67. CAIHY, Decretos, no. 61, June 19, 1845, 210.

68. AGEY, Box 20, G, Apr. 23, 1845; May 3, 1845; CAIHY, Decretos, no. 61, May 6, 1845; June 27, 1845, 211.

69. AGEY, PE, T, I, 3, Mar. 8, 1842. Village acquisition of surrounding properties had been underway since at least 1837.

70. The point was not as strange as it seems. The glottal occlusions, so essential to rendering meaning in Maya, are missing in Spanish. Thus the transition to Spanish is as disconcerting for the Maya as is learning an unstressed language for the Spaniard.

71. AHAY, DO, r. 107, Dec. 20, 1840. See also Nov. 16, 1840; Nov. 24, 1840; Nov. 30, 1840.

72. AHAY, DO, r. 104, Jan. 14, 1840.

73. Ibid., r. 116, Jan. 27, 1840.

74. Only in March of 1841 did he resume the initiative. At that time Dondé wrote to Governor Méndez, explaining that he planned to resume the work and sought an official blessing. After all, it was he himself who had voluntarily exempted widows and unmarried women as early as 1836, a noteworthy example of preemptive reform. While reminding the governor that *batabs* enjoyed the privilege of confiscating and selling off personal property to pay off bad debts, he claimed that he had specifically forbade such practices among his collectors, instructing them instead to accept whatever the peasants had to offer as piecemeal installments. And was it not revealing that while the jails were full of people who owed on the contribution, there was not a

single case of arrest for back debt on obventions? See AGEY, PE, box 5, G, IV, 101, Mar. 30, 1841.

75. Ibid., G, XI, 32, Apr. 13, 1840; box 12, G, Apr. 17, 1843.

76. In Ticul the local officials attributed the resurgence of typhus to two factors: the susceptibility of the Indians, particularly in the rainy season, and the presence of so many Mexican deserters, who, it was commonly held, could not tolerate the tropics (Ibid., box 12, G, July 29, 1843). Outbreaks also occurred in Calotmul, 1844 (Ibid., box 17, G, Jan. 2, 1844).

77. Remmers, "Henequen, the Caste War and Economy," 210. Evidence of rural hardship in 1843 also appears in the correspondence of those who lived indirectly on church revenues. María Mónica Tovar, an elderly mother living in Tizimín, found that scarcity in her son's parish of Hopelchén had resulted in her monthly allotment ending along with his salary. As she pleaded with the bishop's office, "Señor, be persuaded that only my broken health, which is what keeps me from doubling myself over in work in search of subsistence, and the shortage of grain, obliges me to bother you" (AHAY, DO, r. 107, May 2, 1843).

78. Ancona, *Historia de Yucatán,* vol. 3, 280.

79. Norman, *Rambles in Yucatan,* 27.

80. Stephens, *Incidents of Travel,* vol. 1, 43–44.

81. CAIHY, Expedientes, box VI, 25, Sept. 9, 1840.

82. AHAY, DO, r. 104, Oct. 3, 1840. As with laws and reforms since the Laws of Burgos, it is doubtful that this decree was completely and thoroughly applied. It seems more likely that *subdelegados* came to dominate the process when local circumstances permitted.

83. Ibid., r. 106, June 3, 1842; r. 107, Nov. 5, 1842. If records of these various taxes exist, they would provide an extraordinary index of distribution of wealth. But I have found no evidence that they or any other detailed tax records exist for the early national period.

84. Cline, "Regionalism and Society," 634–637.

85. AHAY, DO, r. 107, May 2, 1843.

86. Ibid., r. 107, May 12, 1843; May 24, 1843; July 7, 1843.

87. Ibid., r. 107, July 13, 1843.

88. For the last complaints on this score, see ibid., r. 107, Aug. 22, 1843; Aug. 17, 1843; Aug. 21, 1843; also, see above regarding the episode of the Ichmul revolt. Restoration of some level of church taxes may have had a hand in quieting the strike by the *fiscales* and *maestros cantores.*

89. Ibid., r. 10, Aug. 28, 1842. See also the case of Conkal, in AHAY, AT, box 13, exp. 47, May 26, 1847.

90. Ibid., r. 107, Sept. 18, 1843.

91. See, for example, CAIHY, CCA, no. 74, "Exposición que el Sr. P. José Sotero Brito hace como cura interino de la parroquia de Peto, al Excmo. Sr. Gobernador sobre la necesidad, de una contribución religiosa" (Mérida: Carlos M. Flores, 1840).

92. AHAY, AT, 13, July 14, 1843.

93. AGNM, BN, XXXVIII, 15, Oct. 2, 1844.

94. CAIHY, no. 300, José María Barrera to José Canuto Vela, Apr. 7, 1850.

95. AHAY, DO, r. 108, Feb. 26, 1846.

96. Ibid., r. 108, Oct. 4, 1846.

97. Ibid., r. 107, Aug. 21, 1843. The *cura* in question was José Antonio García.

98. Ibid., r. 107, Aug. 8, 1843.

99. AGEY, PE, G, I, 25, May 22, 1841.

100. Ibid.

101. AGEY, PE, box 16, G, Oct. 29, 1844.

102. CAIHY, Decretos, no. 61, Dec. 19, 1844, 144.

103. Ibid., Dec. 19, 1844, 144; Apr. 30, 1845, 92; May 12, 1845, 197; Aug. 26, 1845, 228. Yet another example of *batabs* ignoring the new tax allowances comes from Cusumá. See AGEY, PE, G, "Caciques," XII, 12, July 13, 1840.

As with the 1813–1814 crisis, peasant protest quickly became generalized. The Xul peasants also protested that the *alcalde* was forcing them to build a cistern "which is neither beneficial nor necessary to us, because we have among our people a cave where we can easily find spring water for the benefit of our families." (AGEY, PE, box 8, J, II, 14, June 17, 1842). I am inclined to doubt that this referred to the vast Xtacumbilxunán cave visited by Stephens. This was too far to be of daily use for Xul and could hardly be termed accessible even for those living close by, owing to its prodigious depth.

Peasants also tried other ways of maximizing their gains from the Imán revolt. At least some Maya widows were able to obtain pensions on the grounds that their husbands had died in the fighting of 1842. This was the case with Josefa Tun and María and Cecilia May of Hobayam (AGEY, PE, box 20, G, C, Jan. 21, 1845).

104. CAIHY, Decretos, no. 61, Aug. 29, 1844.

105. AGEY, PE, G, "Caciques," XIII, 6, Sept. 26, 1840.

106. Ibid., PE, E, II, 65, Oct. 18, 1838; G, XI, 6, Nov. 6, 1838; G, "Caciques," XIII, 15, Oct. 20, 1840.

107. AHAY, DO, r. 116, Feb. 1, 1840.

108. Consider, for example, the escape from Tiholop, in which three prisoners not only broke free but also made off with their keeper's guns (AGEY, PE, J, II, 12, Oct. 13, 1842).

109. AGEY, PE, A, IV, 30, May 4, 1840.

110. See, for example, Victoriano Rodríguez' successful attempt to move his rancho Hobonox from Tituc to Kancabchén, citing innumerable but unspecified injuries from the former (AGEY, PE, G, III, 65, Oct. 27, 1842).

111. The pattern was similar to that described for rural Colombia in the years between the Thousand Days' War and the *violencia*. See Charles W. Bergquist, *Coffee and Conflict in Colombia, 1886–1910* (Durham: Duke University Press, 1986), 96.

112. CAIHY, "Correspondencia de Valladolid," July 29, 1837, 10.

113. AGEY, PE, A, I, 31, Jan. 10, 1841; 25, Feb. 3, 1841.

114. Ibid., G, V, 130, May 15, 1841.

115. Ibid., A, I, 32, Feb. 14, 1841; 26, Mar. 3, 1841.

116. Bonifacio Novelo's signature appears on a petition defending the legitimacy of Valladolid's 1841 *ayuntamiento* elections. See ibid., May 7, 1841. See also ibid., A, I, 2, May 25, 1841; 21, June 1, 1841.

117. Ibid., J, I, 3, misc. dates, Mar. 1842; "Correspondencia de la jefetura política del partido de Yaxcabá . . . ," I, 7, misc. dates, Mar. 1842.

118. CAIHY, Decretos, no. 61, Dec. 18, 1844, 143; June 14, 1845, 207.

119. AGEY, PE, G, XII, Aug. 6, 1840.

120. Stephens, *Incidents of Travel,* vol. 1, 139–142; AGEY, PE, box 17, G, Oct. 20, 1844.

121. AGEY, PE, T, XIV, 49, Dec. 5, 1843.

122. Ibid., 1844 court dockets for Tekax, Sept. 16, 1845. The listing is presumably only partial.

123. CAIHY, Decretos, no. 61, Mar. 27, 1844, 14–15. Meanwhile, the demand for *fagina*—or its equivalent—continued, often without regard for the limits of municipal jurisdiction. The *alcalde* of San Antonio Xul, for example, demanded contributions of wood from the peasants of the remote rancho San Hermenegildo Put, but in this case the peasants were able to secure an administrative injunction against the *alcalde* (CAIHY, Decretos, no. 61, July 11, 1845, 215–216). Bernardino Poot of Chikindzonot was not so fortunate in trying to escape the forced labor of jail construction, though, and was summarily ordered back to work. Other town Indians repeated Poot's demand the following month but were also denied (CAIHY, Decretos, no. 61, Aug. 4, 1845, 221; Sept. 10, 1845, 233).

124. AGEY, PE, "Nunkiní," misc. dates, Mar. 1845.

125. Norman, *Rambles in Yucatan,* 233–234.

126. Ibid.

6. "THE DEVIL WILL OVERTAKE US"

1. AHAY, DO, r. 109, Feb. 6, 1847.

2. AGEY, PE, July 22, 1847.

3. The statues were erected in 1984 in honor of the tenth anniversary of the state of Quintana Roo (personal interview with Nelson Reed, who was one of the ceremony's honored guests, Mar. 24, 1993). For an instructive article on the church architecture of Tihosuco, see Jorge Victoria Ojeda, "Arquitectura religiosa en Tihosuco, Quintana Roo. Notas y comentarios sobre este importante conjunto colonial," *Boletín E.C.A.U.D.Y.* 16, 93 (1988), 9–27.

4. *Registro yucateco* 1 (1845), 214–215.

5. AGEY, FC, "Correspondencia de los gobernadores, varios partidos," III, Mar. 3, 1818.

6. Norman, *Rambles in Yucatan,* 53–54, 66.

7. AGEY, FC, Fondo Militar, I, 16, Mar. 21, 1801.

8. Ibid., FC, "Correspondencia de various autoridades," I, 3, Mar. 30, 1801; May 18, 1801; May 31, 1801; Aug. 5, 1801.

9. Ibid., box 18, Nov. 19, 1844; Aug. 20, 1844.

10. On the activities of Andrés Rubio, see AGEY, PE, J, IV, Jan. 18, 1836. Cline discusses the deleterious effect of smuggling and foreign competition in his article "The 'Aurora Yucateca' and the Spirit of Enterprise in Yucatan, 1821–1847, *Hispanic American Historical Review* 47 (1948), 30–60. According to calculations published in the newspaper *Los pueblos,* a measure of cloth costing sixteen pesos in Jamaica or Belize sold for thirty-one pesos in Mérida, hardly a disincentive to smuggling (*Los pueblos,* I, 31, June 6, 1840, 2–3).

11. Angel E. Cal, "Capital-Labor Relations on a Colonial Frontier: Nineteenth-Century Northern Belize," in Jeffery T. Bannon and Gilbert M. Joseph, *Land, Labor, and Capital in Modern Yucatán: Essays in Regional History and Political Economy* (Tuscaloosa: University of Alabama Press, 1991), 92; see also Baqueiro, *Ensayo histórico* vol. 2, 145–146.

12. AGEY, DC, Sesiones, Jan. 3, 1834, 90.

13. Remmers, "Henequen, the Caste War, and Economy," 211–213.

14. CAIHY, "Estados de los extranjeros residentes en este departamento," Dec. 5, 1838, no page numbers; Rubio Mañé, *Sanjuanistas de Yucatán,* 65–67. Some confirmation of these events comes from Mais himself, for in his subsequent application to the curacy of Ichmul he complained that the liberals had turned his students against him.

15. ANEY, Jan. 22, 1829, 8–9.

16. AHAY, VP, exps. 44, 57, 69; ANEY, Jan. 28, 1845, 22; AHAY, DO, r. 109, Nov. 23, 1847.

17. AHAY, DO, box 17A, Sept. 26, 1835. Documents of Tihosuco illustrate the point that peasants often had their own version of history quite at variance from the official accounts produced in cities. The case in point concerns the career of Mais. In July of 1835 the Mérida newspaper *El cometa, o terror de los tiranos* ran an article beatifying Mais for his efforts in redistributing food to his parishioners at Tihosuco during the cholera epidemic. "Divine Providence will recompense the said ecclesiastic for his acts of charity and virtue," it asserted, and perhaps the prediction had a germ of truth: the Tihosuco rebels did wait until Mais' death to begin their offensive. But once begun, Mais' property became a prime target (AHAY, DO, box 17, July 23, 1835; *Cometa,* II, no. 92, 368). Tihosuco suffered another minor smallpox outbreak in June 1842, striking down some twenty-five adults and children. Vaccine soon arrived, and Mais applied it with good results (AGEY, PE, G, IV, 110, June 12, 1842).

18. AGEY, PE, G, "Varios," 128, Jan. 25, 1841. Villages undergoing construction included Sabán, Tituc, Polyuc, Chunhuhub, Sacalaca, Tahdziú, Tiholop, and Tzucacab.

19. AHAY, CC, 35, May 23, 1846. Local creole rivalries sometimes took strange twists. One feature which made this possible was the Spanish system of arrest warrants.

Authorities could either arrest individuals *de oficio,* that is, acting under suspicion of probable guilt, or else through a *fianza* of accusation, in which the accusing party posted bond as security against frivolous complaint. In April of 1845 Vito Pacheco and Eusebio Megía arrested Miguel López for "conspiracy." While still imprisoned, López put up a writ of *fianza* against Pacheco and Megía for abuse of authority, and thus all three waited in jail together. See AGEY, box 19, G, Juzgados, Apr. 16, 1845.

20. AGEY, FC, IPA, I, 37, Sept. 23, 1813.

21. AGEY, PE, E, II, 40, Mar. 24, 1829. I am skeptical of identifying Francisco and Jacinto Pat as the same person and favor a later date for Jacinto Pat's appointment as *batab.* Record of Pat's marriage can be found in the 1828 *matrícula* of Tihosuco, a document which I discovered in the church archive, currently stored in a box of assorted and unclassified materials. During my research in Mérida in 1990–1991, I was able to copy this matrícula in its entirety.

22. From Joaquín Castillo Peraza, "Artículos sueltos" (Mérida: Tipografía G. Canto, 1899), 27–29, quoted in Fidelio Quintal Martín, "Biografías campesinas del siglo XIX," *Boletín E.C.A.U.D.Y.* 9 (1982), 46–48.

23. The name Panabá suggests some acquaintance with the village of the same name on Yucatán's northeast coast.

24. The hacienda Culumpich is mentioned repeatedly in transcripts of the interrogation of Manuel Antonio Ay in July 1847. See Quintal Martín, ed., "Proceso y ejecución." Regarding Pat's ranch and his *denuncia,* see CAIHY, no. 129, "1845 a 1846: Registro de las denuncias de terrenos baldíos," Aug. 18, 1846, 49; Nov. 21, 1846, 64.

25. AGEY, PE, A, VII, 24, Feb. 9, 1841.

26. Ibid., G, XII, 15, July 18, 1840; box 14, A, Dec. 31, 1843; box 15, G, Jan. 21, 1844. To the contrary, Cecilio Chi did not appear on the Tepich plebiscite, nor did Manuel Antonio Ay on that of Chichimilá.

27. AGEY, PE, box 29, G, 5, June 7, 1848.

28. CAIHY, "Documentos de Yucatán," July 17, 1843.

29. The history of Hunukú parallels the formation of ad hoc communities like Tonolá in Somoza-era Nicaragua. See Jeffrey L. Gould, *To Lead as Equals: Rural Protest and Political Consciousness in Chinandega, Nicaragua, 1912–1979* (Chapel Hill: University of North Carolina Press, 1990), 158–160.

30. Dumond and Dumond, *Demography,* 262; CAIHY, "Estado que manifiesta las leguas de distancia,"; ANEY, misc. dates, 1844–1846; CAIHY, "Registro de las denuncias," misc. dates. Of the land surveyed in the Tihosuco region, only one document remains, a cursory map of the *paraje* Pichquén, whose survey was ordered by a certain Alfonso Vázquez. This, a square league of property between Tepich and Tihosuco, was awarded on Feb. 23, 1844 (see ANEY, above date, 15–18).

31. AHAY, DO, r. 105, June 8, 1838.

32. Ibid., r. 117, Nov. 20, 1841. The rancho's name fails to appear among the decidedly brief 1854 list of surviving Tihosuco properties. See CAIHY, "Noticia circunstanciada de todas las poblaciones que componen este distrito [Tekax]," June 14, 1854.

33. AHAY, DO, r. 105, June 27, 1839; June 22, 1839.

34. MI, "Collection," Aug. 11, 1846; AGEY, PE, box 16, G, Jan. 9, 1844.

35. AGNM, BN, XX, 42, July 22, 1830; 30–33, 1832.

36. The local judge eventually caught up with Canul and had him escorted to the minister for punishment. Canul was planning to level the *cura* with his trump card, the bishop's letter upholding his tax exemption; but the minister ignored the letter and launched into a torrent of abuse, including harsh language and blows (AGNM, BN, XX, 42, Mar. 23, 1832; May 2, 1832; July 24, 1832).

37. This report is cited and discussed in Patch, "Decolonization," 59.

38. AGEY, PE, Censos y padrones (CP), I, 12, Oct. 15, 1832, 11, 12; 1828 Tihosuco *matrícula,* no page numbers.

39. AGEY, DC, Acuerdos, Mar. 10, 1824, 76.

40. Helguera was in fact in the habit of exporting his Indian church staff abroad to assist less-developed parishes. His sacristans undertook the arduous journey to Mérida to purchase holy oils for the *cura* of Labcah, who had no help of their own (AHAY, DO, r. 107, c. Dec. 1842). But the anecdote reveals more than merely the power of Helguera. Indian elites from the eastern communities were not the isolated *"huits"* often featured in the literature, but individuals conversant with the metropole and well traveled in the context of their society.

41. AGNM, BN, XXXVII, 15, misc. dates, 1837; IV, 22, misc. dates, 1839. The problem in linking the Manuel Antonio Ay of the 1839 documents with the Manuel Antonio Ay who was tried and executed for conspiracy in 1847 is age. The former listed his age as forty. The latter claimed to be twenty-seven at the time of his death. Peasant communities tended not to duplicate names. The likely explanation is that one of the two ages listed was an error or that the earlier Manuel Antonio Ay was father to the later Ay and that some tradition of radicalism and political leadership existed within the family.

42. Helguera, whose last clerical post was *cura* of Xcan, died a war refugee in Carmen in December 1849 (AHAY, DO, r. 114, Dec. 26, 1849).

43. AGNM, BN, XXXVIII, 13, Feb. 17, 1844.

44. Ibid., Feb. 1, 1844; Feb. 2, 1844.

45. AHAY, DO, r. 105, Feb. 7, 1838; r. 107, June 6, 1843; Quintal Martín, ed., "Proceso y ejecución."

46. AGEY, PE, box 19, G, Aug. 26, 1845.

47. Ibid., DC, Acuerdos, r. 20, Mar. 30, 1824, 88.

48. Ibid., DC, Acuerdos, r. 20, Nov. 20, 1823, 40.

49. CAIHY, Decretos, no. 61, Sept. 26, 1844, 95.

50. AGNM, BN, II, 3, Apr. 29, 1845.

51. AHAY, DO, r. 104, Sept. 17, 1841.

52. Timothy Wickham-Crowley, *Guerrillas and Revolution in Latin America: A Comparative Study of Insurgents and Regimes since 1956* (Princeton: Princeton University Press, 1992), 138–153.

53. The most comprehensive account of this subject is still Justin H. Smith, *The War with Mexico,* (New York: Macmillan, 1919).

54. The appeal of his brother Vicente Solís Novelo failed to free him (AGEY, FJ, May 6, 1846). These rebels were apparently related to the later and more famous revolutionary Bonifacio Novelo. The Novelo clan in Valladolid was extensive.

55. AGEY, PE, report from Agustín Acereto, *subdelegado* of Valladolid, June 15, 1847.

56. AGEY, DC, Sesiones, Jan. 9, 1834, 91.

57. On the Barret revolt, see Ancona, *Historia de Yucatán,* vol. 2, 335–353.

58. MI, "Collection," Dec. 13, 1846.

59. Ibid., Dec. 3, 1846; Dec. 15, 1846; Dec. 28, 1846.

60. AGEY, PE, box 26, J, Justicia Militar (JM), Jan. 24, 1847; box 23, G, Apr. 6, 1847; Nov. 28, 1846.

61. AGEY, PE, CP, VI, 74, May 18, 1841, 29; TEX, García Collection, G559, June 1878.

62. AGEY, PE, box 25, G, JP, Jan. 12, 1847.

63. Ancona, *Historia de Yucatán,* vol. 3, 341–343.

64. AGNM, BN, XXXVIII, 10, 1844, misc. dates; AHAY, DO, r. 120, Feb. 6, 1847. The ironies of Fr. Aviles and the sack of Valladolid were not necessarily unique. Strains of discontent appeared elsewhere among the poorer elements of the clergy, the rural ministers who enjoyed little stake in parish wealth and who labored only for a fixed and relatively small salary. Younger than their more-established superiors, they came to maturity in a time of increasing anarchy and political violence. Aviles had a counterpart in the Tixmeuac minister José Bruno Romero, who had formed an alliance with local anticlerical discontents. Although Romero did not join them in publicly ridiculing the *cura* during processions through the village, his political links were sufficiently close to force the *cura* to have him recalled (AHAY, DO, r. 106, Apr. 12, 1842). Subsequent litigation revealed that the dispute was rooted in control of parish accounts. Even after Romero's departure, *cura* Antonio de los Ríos, prominent sugar entrepreneur, initiated a lawsuit of malfeasance against his former assistant, only desisting when his attorney persuaded him to drop the case, "it being the more prudent strategy to end this business than to continue it, owing to the baleful and incalculable consequences which originate from litigation" (AHAY, DO, r. 107, Aug. 28, 1843).

65. Ibid., r. 109, Feb. 13, 1847; Feb. 6, 1847.

66. Ibid.

67. AGEY, PE, box 17, 6, Sept. 30, 1844; box 8, I, 17, Sept. 2, 1842.

68. CAIHY, Decretos, no. 61, Sept. 29, 1844, 136–137.

69. MI, "Collection," Jan. 11, 1847.

70. AGEY, PE, box 26, J, JM, Jan. 22, 1847. All material regarding the Tabi killings derives from this same group of documents. It is worth noting here that Cámara had been a non-presence in the years leading up to the war. As early as 1843 *vecinos* had complained that the *cura*'s ill-health was resulting in almost total church neglect, including infrequent church hours, and neglect of the town's celebrated virgin cult. Cámara was in fact suspended in May of that year and only permitted to celebrate masses or perform marriages when other priests from Sotuta were absolutely unavailable. He

regained his clerical authority over Tabi at some time before 1846 (AHAY, DO, r. 107, Jan. 23, 1843; May 19, 1843).

71. AGEY, PE, box 26, J, Feb. 10, 1847.

72. AHAY, DO, r. 109, June 7, 1847.

73. Baqueiro, *Ensayo histórico*, vol. 1, 190–193, 196–199.

74. Ibid., 196, 199–200.

75. Ibid., 201–211.

76. CAIHY, Expedientes, box VII, 89, Mar. 5, 1847.

77. The last *denuncia* awarded before the eruption of the Caste War was handled by Fr. Domingo Silvos Escalante, *cura* of Espita, on behalf of his brother Vicente. It awarded an undetermined amount of property outside Sucilá, which was already bounded on all four sides by haciendas and ranchos (ANEY, July 17, 1847, 73–75).

78. CAIHY, "Mensaje de gobernador provisional, a la asamblea extraordinaria, en su instalación en el pueblo de Ticul, el 24 de mayo de 1847" (Mérida: Castillo y Compañía, 1847), 10–11, 15–17.

79. AHAY, CC, 35, June 1, 1847.

80. AGEY, PE, box 28, report from Agustín Acereto, *subdelegado* of Valladolid, June 15, 1847.

81. AGEY, PE, report from Valladolid, 1847.

82. Baqueiro, *Ensayo histórico*, vol. 1, 222; Cline, "Regionalism and Society," 637. Méndez' actual words were, "Guerra a los palacios para que haya paz en las cabañas."

83. The last known letter from Mais came on June 19; it concerned the licenses for his new minister, Fr. Aguilar (AHAY, DO, r. 109, June 19, 1847).

84. ANEY, Aug. 9, 1849, 98–99.

85. AGEY, PE, Valladolid court docket, Apr. 24, 1847; box 26, J, Apr. 24, 1847.

86. Baqueiro, *Ensayo histórico*, vol. 1, 230.

87. Quintal Martín, ed., "Proceso y ejecución," 28–29.

88. Bricker (*Indian Christ*, 95–97) has argued that the letter was not the conspiratorial communiqué that creoles believed and that the Caste War itself grew out of defensive actions. However, I am inclined to doubt this reading. I base my opinion on Ay's trial transcripts; the high military preparedness of the insurgents; the shrewd, almost opportunistic nature of Jacinto Pat and other *batabs;* and the assertiveness of the eastern peasantry, particularly those who had been involved in the recent military mobilizations.

89. Quintal Martín, ed., "Proceso y ejecución," passim; AHAY, DO, r. 109, July 20, 1847.

90. Lack of additional evidence makes the transcript's many contradictions and ambiguities nearly impossible to resolve. I am of the opinion that all witnesses were lying to some extent and that all had more knowledge than they cared to admit regarding local illegalities and pending rebellion. This also holds true for Manuel Antonio Ay's accusers as well.

91. Quintal Martín, ed., "Proceso y ejecución," misc. pages; AGEY, PE, box 39, Poblaciones-Chichimilá, Aug. 25, 1841.

92. Baqueiro, *Ensayo histórico*, vol. 1, 231–232.

93. Ibid., 232.

94. Ibid., 226–227. It is impossible to determine with any exactness the date of Cetina's return. However, the events in Chichimilá and Tepich do not appear to have been under his direction or urging. Indeed, he seems to have been utterly unaware of them before approaching Valladolid.

95. AGEY, PE, letter of José Eulogio Rosado.

96. CAIHY, Decretos, no. 61, Mar. 26, 1844, 14–15. Kauá had raised a similar protest (Ibid., Sept. 28, 1844, 97).

97. Baqueiro, *Ensayo histórico*, vol. 1, 238.

98. The following account derives from the testimony in AGEY, PE, box 26, J, Aug. 1847.

99. This may have been a case of the "negative consciousness" which Guha has identified as a common feature of early peasant rebellions: rather than striving to obliterate the culture of the dominant class, the peasants merely seek to seize that culture for themselves. See Guha, *Elementary Aspects*, 18–20, 28–36.

100. AGEY, PE, A, I, 2, May 25, 1841; 21, June 1, 1841.

101. AGEY, PE, box 26, J, Aug. 14, 1847; G, July 22, 1847.

102. Ancona, *Historia de Yucatán*, vol. 4, 19.

CONCLUSIONS

1. On the later Yucatecan henequen industry, see González Navarro, *Raza y tierra,* 169–225; Remmers, "Henequen, the Caste War, and Economy," 562–704; and Wells, *Yucatán's Gilded Age.*

2. On revolutionary events in Yucatán, see Joseph, *Revolution from Without,* and James C. Carey, *The Mexican Revolution in Yucatán, 1915–1924* (Boulder: Westview Press, 1984). On the last years of the Caste War rebels, see Paul Sullivan, *Unfinished Conversations: Mayas and Foreigners between Two Wars* (Berkeley: University of California Press, 1991), 131–159.

Bibliography

ARCHIVES

AGEY   Archivo General del Estado de Yucatán
- DC   Documentos del Congreso
- FC   Fondo Colonial
  - A   Ayuntamientos
  - CDA   Correspondencia de Diversas Autoridades
  - CG   Correspondencia de los Gobernadores
  - CR   Criminal
  - DP   Diputaciones Provinciales
  - FM   Fondo Militar
  - IPA   Impuestos Propios y Arbitrios
  - T   Tierras
  - V   Varios
- FJ   Fondo Justicia
- PE   Poder Ejecutivo
  - A   Ayuntamientos
  - CP   Censos y Padrones
  - DL   Decretos y Leyes
  - E   Empleos
  - G   Gobernación
  - I   Iglesia
  - J   Justicia
  - M   Militia
  - T   Tierras
  - V   Varios

Poder Ejecutivo material for the years 1821–1840 is classified by volume and *expediente* numbers, here designated by roman and arabic numerals, respectively. Material for the years 1840–1865 is classified in sequentially numbered boxes.

AGNM   Archivo General de la Nación de México
      BN   Bienes Nacionales
AHAY   Archivo Histórico de la Arquidiócesis de Yucatán
      AP   Asuntos Parroquiales
      AT   Asuntos Terminados
      CAP   Capellanías
      CC   Concursos a Curatos
      CF   Cuentas de Fábrica
      DO   Decretos y Oficios
      DV   Documentos Varios
      DP   Dispensas de Parentezco
      OC   Oficinas de Cofradía
      VP   Visitas Pastorales
AMC   Archivo Municipal de Campeche
ANEY   Archivo Notarial del Estado de Yucatán
CAIHY   Centro de Apoyo a la Investigación Histórica de Yucatán
      CCA   Colección Carrillo y Ancona
MI   William L. Clements Library, University of Michigan
TEX   Nettie Lee Benson Library, University of Texas
TUL   Latin American Library, Tulane University

THESES AND DISSERTATIONS

Bracamonte y Sosa, Pedro. "Amos y sirvientes: Las haciendas de Yucatán, 1800–1860." Thesis, Universidad Autónoma de Yucatán, 1989.

Cantón Sosa, Ermilio, and José Armando Chi Estrella. "Los orígenes de la institución militar en el Yucatán independiente: La milicia activa en el Partido de Tizimín (1823–1840)." Thesis, Universidad Autónoma de Yucatán, 1993.

Carrillo y Herrera, Beatriz Eugenia. "Iglesia y sociedad yucateca en el siglo XIX (1800–1840)." Thesis, Universidad Autónoma de Yucatán, 1993.

Cline, Howard F. "Regionalism and Society in Yucatan, 1825–1847: A Study of 'Progressivism' and the Origins of the Caste War." Ph.D. diss., Harvard, 1947.

Fallon, Michael J. "The Secular Clergy in the Diocese of Yucatan: 1750–1800." Ph.D. diss., Catholic University of America, 1979.

Güémez Pineda, José Arturo. "Resistencia indígena en Yucatán: El caso del abigeato en el distrito de Mérida, 1821–1847." Thesis, Universidad Autónoma de Yucatán, 1978.

Hunt, Marta Espejo-Ponce. "Colonial Yucatan: Town and Region in the Seventeenth Century." Ph.D. diss., UCLA, 1974.

Marrufo Noh, Silvia Mercedes. "La hacienda productora de caña de azúcar en Yucatán, 1821–1860." Thesis, Universidad Autónoma de Yucatán, 1989.

Negroe Sierra, Genny Mercedes. "La cofradía de Yucatán en el siglo XVIII." Thesis, Universidad Autónoma de Yucatán, 1984.

Patch, Robert W. "A Colonial Regime: Maya and Spaniard in Yucatan." Ph.D. diss., Princeton University, 1979.

Remmers, Lawrence James. "Henequen, the Caste War, and Economy of Yucatan, 1846–1883: The Roots of Dependence in a Mexican Region." Ph.D. diss., UCLA, 1981.

Restall, Matthew Bennett. "The World of the *Cah:* Postconquest Yucatec Maya Society." Ph.D. diss., UCLA, 1992.

Santiago Pacheco, Edgar Augusto. "La política eclesiástica borbónica y la secularización de parroquias franciscanas en Yucatán: 1750–1825." Thesis, Universidad Autónoma de Yucatán, 1992.

Thompson, Philip C. "Tekanto in the Eighteenth Century." Ph.D. diss., Tulane University, 1978.

STATISTICAL ABSTRACTS

Echánove, Policarpo Antonio de. *Cuadro estadístico de Yucatán en 1814.* 1814.

Regil, José María, y Alonso Manuel Peón. *Estadística de Yucatán.* 1853.

Regil, Pedro Manuel. *Memoria instructiva sobre el comercio general de la provincia de Yucatán y particular del puerto de Campeche.* 1811.

INTERVIEWS

Interview with Mr. Nelson Reed, St. Louis, Missouri, March 24, 1993.

SECONDARY LITERATURE

Ancona, Eligio. *Historia de Yucatán desde la época más remota hasta nuestros días.* 4 vols. Mérida: Gobierno del Estado de Yucatán, 1917.

Anderson, Thomas P. *Matanza: El Salvador's Communist Revolt of 1932.* Lincoln: University of Nebraska Press, 1971.

Andreas, Carol. "Women at War." *NACLA Report on the Americas* 24, 4 (1990/1991), 20–27.

Angel, Barbara. "The Reconstruction of Rural Society in the Aftermath of the Mayan Rebellion of 1847." *Journal of the Canadian Historical Association* 4 (1993), 33–53.

Annis, Sheldon. *God and Production in a Guatemalan Town.* Austin: University of Texas Press, 1987.

Arrigunaga Coello, Maritza. *Catálogo de las fotocopias de los documentos y periódicos yucatecos en la Biblioteca de la Universidad de Texas en Arlington.* Arlington: University of Texas at Arlington Press, 1983.

Baer, Phillip, and William R. Marrifield. *Two Studies on the Lacandones of Mexico.* Norman, Okla.: Summer Institute of Linguistics, 1971.

Baqueiro, Serapio. *Ensayo histórico sobre las revoluciones de Yucatán desde el año de 1840 hasta 1864.* Mérida: Manuel Heredia Argüelles, 1878, 1879 (vols. 1 and 2); Tipografía de G. Canto, 1887 (vol. 3).

Batt, Rosemary L. "The Rise and Fall of the Planter Class in Espita, 1900–1924." In *Land, Labor, and Capital in Modern Yucatán: Essays in Regional History and Political Economy.* Ed. Jeffery T. Brannon and Gilbert M. Joseph. Tuscaloosa: University of Alabama Press, 1991, 197–219.

Bazant, Jan. *Alienation of Church Wealth in Mexico: Social and Economic Aspects of the Liberal Revolution, 1856–1875.* Trans. and ed. Michael P. Costeloe. Cambridge: At the University Press, 1971.

Benjamin, Thomas. *A Rich Land, A Poor People: Politics and Society in Modern Chiapas.* Albuquerque: University of New Mexico Press, 1989.

Bergquist, Charles W. *Coffee and Conflict in Colombia, 1886–1910.* Durham: Duke University Press, 1986.

Berzunza Pinto, Ramón. *Guerra social en Yucatán.* Mexico City: Costa-Amic, 1965.

Bolland, O. Nigel. *The Formation of a Colonial Society: Belize, from Conquest to Crown Colony.* Baltimore: Johns Hopkins University Press, 1977.

Borah, Woodrow W. *Justice by Insurance: The General Indian Court of Colonial Mexico and the Legal Aides of the Half-Real.* Berkeley: University of California Press, 1983.

Boserup, Ester. *The Conditions of Agricultural Growth: The Economics of Agrarian Change under Population Pressure.* Chicago: Aldine Publishing Company, 1965.

Bracamonte y Sosa, Pedro. "Sirvientes y ganado en las haciendas yucatecas (1821–1847)." *Boletín E.C.A.U.D.Y.* 12, 70 (1985), 3–15.

Bricker, Victoria. "The History of a Myth and the Myth of History." In *Anthropology and History in Yucatan.* Ed. Grant D. Jones. Austin: University of Texas Press, 1977, 251–258.

———. *The Indian Christ, the Indian King: The Historic Substrate of Maya Myth and Ritual.* Austin: University of Texas Press, 1981.

Brundage, Burr Cartwright. *Empire of the Inca.* Norman: University of Oklahoma Press, 1963.

Burns, Allan F. "The Caste War in the 1970's: Present-Day Accounts from Village Quintana Roo." In *Anthropology and History in Yucatan.* Ed. Grant D. Jones. Austin: University of Texas Press, 1977, 259–273.

———. *An Epoch of Miracles: Oral Literature of the Yucatec Maya.* Austin: University of Texas Press, 1983.

Cal, Angel E. "Capital-Labor Relations on a Colonial Frontier: Nineteenth-Century Northern Belize." In *Land, Labor, and Capital in Modern Yucatán: Essays in Regional*

History and Political Economy. Ed. Jeffery T. Brannon and Gilbert M. Joseph. Tuscaloosa: University of Alabama Press, 1991, 83–106.

Cancian, Frank. *Economics and Prestige in a Maya Community: The Religious Cargo Systems in Zinacantan.* Stanford: Stanford University Press, 1965.

Carey, James C. *The Mexican Revolution in Yucatán, 1915–1924.* Boulder: Westview Press, 1984.

Carrillo y Ancona, Crescencio. *El obispado de Yucatán: Historia de su fundación y de sus obispos desde el siglo XVI hasta el XIX.* Mérida: R. Caballero, 1895.

Castillo, Gerónimo. "El indio yucateco. Carácter, costumbres, y condición de los indios, en el departamento de Yucatán." *Registro Yucateco* I (1845), 291–297.

Chamberlain, Robert S. *The Conquest and Colonization of Yucatan, 1517–1550.* New York: Oregon Books, 1966 (orig. 1948).

Chance, John K. *Conquest of the Sierra: Spaniards and Indians in Colonial Oaxaca.* Norman: University of Oklahoma Press, 1989.

Chance, John K., and William B. Taylor. "Cofradías and Cargos: An Historical Perspective on the Mesoamerican Civil-Religious Hierarchy." *American Ethnologist* 12, 1 (1985), 1–26.

Clendinnen, Inga. *Ambivalent Conquests: Maya and Spaniard in Yucatan, 1517–1570.* Cambridge: Cambridge University Press, 1987.

Cline, Howard F. "The 'Aurora Yucateca' and the Spirit of Enterprise in Yucatan, 1821–1847." *Hispanic American Historical Review* 47 (1948), 30–60.

Coe, Michael D. *The Maya.* London: Thames & Hudson, 1987.

Collins, Anne C. "The *Maestros Cantores* in Yucatan." In *Anthropology and History in Yucatan.* Ed. Grant D. Jones. Austin: University of Texas Press, 1977, 233–247.

Cook, Sherburne F. "Francisco Xavier Balmis and the Introduction of Vaccination to Latin America." *Bulletin of the History of Medicine* 11, 5 (1942), 543–560.

———. "Francisco Xavier Balmis and the Introduction of Vaccination to Latin America. Part II." *Bulletin of the History of Medicine* 12, 1 (1942), 70–101.

Cook, Sherburne F., and Woodrow Borah. *Essays in Population History: Mexico and the Caribbean.* 3 vols. Berkeley: University of California Press, 1974.

Costeloe, Michael P. *The Central Republic in Mexico, 1835–1846: Hombres de Bien in the Age of Santa Anna.* Cambridge: Cambridge University Press, 1993.

———. *Church Wealth in Mexico: A Study of the 'Juzgado de Capellanías' in the Archbishopric of Mexico, 1800–1856.* Cambridge: At the University Press, 1967.

DeWalt, Billie R. "Changes in the Cargo System of Mesoamerica." *Anthropological Quarterly* 48, 2 (1975), 90–94.

Diccionario Maya Cordemex. Ed. Alfredo Barrera Vásquez. Mérida: Ediciones Cordemex, 1980.

Dumond, Carol Steichen, and Don E. Dumond, eds. *Demography and Parish Affairs in Yucatan, 1797–1879: Documents from the Archivo de la Mitra Emeritense, Selected by Joaquín de Arrigunaga Peón.* University of Oregon Anthropological Papers no. 27, 1982.

Dumond, Don E. "Independent Maya of the Late Nineteenth Century: Chiefdoms and Power Politics." In *Anthropology and History in Yucatan*. Ed. Grant D. Jones. Austin: University of Texas Press, 1977, 103–138.

———. "The Talking Crosses of Yucatan: A New Look at Their History." *Ethnohistory* 32 (1985), 291–308.

Dunn, Richard S. *Sugar and Slaves: The Rise of the Planter Class in the English West Indies, 1624–1713*. New York: W. W. Norton and Co., 1972.

Edmonson, Munro S., trans. *The Ancient Future of the Itza: The Book of Chilam Balam of Tizimin*. Austin: University of Texas Press, 1982.

———, trans. and annot. *Heaven Born Merida and Its Destiny: The Book of Chilam Balam of Chumayel*. Austin: University of Texas Press, 1986.

Farriss, Nancy M. *Maya Society under Colonial Rule: The Collective Enterprise of Survival*. Princeton: Princeton University Press, 1984.

———. "Remembering the Future, Anticipating the Past: History, Time, and Cosmology among the Maya of Yucatan." *Comparative Studies in Society and History* 29, 3 (1987), 566–593.

Foster, George M. "Peasant Society and the Image of the Limited Good." *American Anthropologist* 67 (1965), 293–315.

Fraginals, Manuel Moreno. *The Sugarmill: The Socioeconomic Complex of Sugar in Cuba, 1760–1860*. Trans. Cedric Belfrage. New York: Monthly Review Press, 1967 (orig. 1964).

Genovese, Eugene. *Roll, Jordan, Roll: The World the Slaves Made*. New York: Vintage Books, 1972.

Gerhard, Peter. *The Southeast Frontier of New Spain*. Princeton: Princeton University Press, 1979; Norman: University of Oklahoma Press, 1993.

Gibson, Charles. *The Aztec under Spanish Rule: A History of the Indians of the Valley of Mexico, 1519–1810*. Stanford: Stanford University Press, 1964.

Goldkind, Victor. "Social Stratification in the Peasant Community: Redfield's Chan Kom Revisited." *American Anthropologist* 67 (1965), 863–884.

González Navarro, Moisés. *Raza y tierra: La guerra de castas y el henequén*. Mexico City: El Colegio de México, 1970.

Goody, Jack, ed. *Literacy in Traditional Societies*. Cambridge: Cambridge University Press, 1968.

Gould, Jeffrey L. *To Lead as Equals: Rural Protest and Political Consciousness in Chinandega, Nicaragua, 1912–1979*. Chapel Hill: University of North Carolina Press, 1990.

Gramsci, Antonio. *Selections from the Prison Notebooks*. Trans. and ed. Quinten Hoare and Geoffrey Nowell Smith. London: Lawrence & Wishart, 1971.

Granado Baeza, Bartolomé José del. "Los indios de Yucatan. Informe dado por el cura de Yaxcabá D. Bartolomé del Granado Baeza, en contestación al interrogatorio de 36 preguntas, circulado por el ministerio de ultramar, sobre el manejo, vida y costumbres de los indios, que acompaño el Illmo. Sr. obispo a la diputación provincial." *Registro Yucateco* I (1845), 165–178.

Guha, Ranajit. *Elementary Aspects of Peasant Insurgency in Colonial India.* Delhi: Oxford University Press, 1983.

Gurr, Ted Robert. *Why Men Rebel.* Princeton: Princeton University Press, 1970.

Handy, Jim. "The Corporate Community, Campesino Organizations, and Agrarian Reform: 1950–1954." *Guatemalan Indians and the State, 1540–1988.* Ed. Carol A. Smith. Austin: University of Texas Press, 1990, 163–182.

Harrison, Peter D. "The Rise of the Bajos and the Fall of the Maya." In *Social Process in Maya Prehistory: Studies in Honor of Sir Eric Thompson.* Ed. Norman Hammond. London: Academic Press, 1977, 469–508.

Hart, John M. *Revolutionary Mexico: The Coming and Process of the Mexican Revolution.* Berkeley: University of California Press, 1987.

Haskett, Robert Stephen. *Indigenous Rulers: An Ethnohistory of Town Government in Colonial Oaxaca.* Albuquerque: University of New Mexico Press, 1991.

Hernández, Juan José. "El indio yucateco." *Registro Yucateco* III (1845), 425–430.

Hill, Robert M., II, and John Monaghan. *Continuities in Highland Maya Social Organization: Ethnohistory in Sacapulas, Guatemala.* Philadelphia: University of Pennsylvania Press, 1987.

House of Commons. Session Paper No. 769. *Commercial Tariffs and Regulations of the Several States of Europe and America, Together with the Commercial Treaties between England and Foreign Countries.* London, 1847.

Hunt, Marta Espejo-Ponce. "The Process of the Development of Yucatan, 1600–1700." *Provinces of Early Mexico.* Ed. Ida Altman and James Lockhart. Los Angeles: University of California Press, 1976, 32–62.

Irigoyen, Renán. "El henequén y la guerra de castas." *Orbe* 4, 15 (1948), 38–45.

———. "Fue el auge del henequén producto de la guerra de castas?" *Orbe* 4, 9 (1947), 62–65.

James, C. L. R. *The Black Jacobins: Toussaint L'Ouverture and the San Domingo Revolution.* New York: Random House, 1963.

Jones, Grant D. "Levels of Settlement Alliance among the San Pedro Maya of Western Belize and Eastern Petén, 1857–1936." In *Anthropology and History in Yucatan.* Ed. Grant D. Jones. Austin: University of Texas Press, 1977, 139–189.

———. *Maya Resistance to Spanish Rule: Time and History on a Colonial Frontier.* Albuquerque: University of New Mexico Press, 1989.

Jones, Grant D. "Revolution and Continuity in Santa Cruz Maya Society." *American Ethnologist* 1 (1974), 659–683.

Joseph, Gilbert M. *Revolution from Without: Yucatán, Mexico, and the United States, 1880–1924.* Cambridge: Cambridge University Press, 1982.

Klein, Herbert S. *Haciendas and Ayllus: Rural Society in the Bolivian Andes in the Eighteenth and Nineteenth Centuries.* Stanford: Stanford University Press, 1993.

Knight, Franklin P. *Slave Society in Cuba during the Nineteenth Century.* Madison: University of Wisconsin Press, 1970.

Konrad, Herman W. "Capitalism on the Tropical-Forest Frontier: Quintana Roo, 1880s to 1930." In *Land, Labor, and Capital in Modern Yucatán: Essays in Regional*

History and Political Economy. Ed. Jeffery T. Brannon and Gilbert M. Joseph. Tuscaloosa: University of Alabama Press, 143–171.

Landa, Diego de. *Relación de las cosas de Yucatán.* Ed. Miguel Rivera Dorado. Madrid: Hermanos García Noblejas, 1985.

Lapointe, Marie. *Los mayas rebeldes de Yucatán.* Zamora: Colegio de Michoacán, 1983.

Lears, T. J. Jackson. "The Concept of Cultural Hegemony: Problems and Possibilities." *American Historical Review* 90, 3 (1985), 567–593.

Lefebvre, Georges. *The Coming of the French Revolution.* Trans. R. R. Palmer. Princeton: Princeton University Press, 1967, orig. 1939.

Levi-Strauss, Claude. *Tristes Tropiques.* Trans. John and Doreen Weightman. New York: Atheneum, 1973.

Lynch, John. *The Spanish American Revolutions, 1808–1826.* New York: W. W. Norton and Co., 1986.

MacLachlan, Colin M. *Criminal Justice in Eighteenth-Century Mexico: A Study of the Tribunal of the Acordada.* Berkeley: University of California Press, 1974.

Mallon, Florencia A. *The Defense of the Community in Peru's Central Highlands: Peasant Struggle and Capitalist Transition, 1860–1940.* Princeton: Princeton University Press, 1983.

McGee, R. Jon. *Life, Ritual, and Religion among the Lacandon Maya.* Belmont, Calif.: Wadsworth Publishing Co., 1990.

Méndez Díaz, Conrado. "La mística del trabajo campesino en Yucatán." *Orbe* 4, 3 (1946), 35–39.

Mintz, Sidney. *Sweetness and Power: The Place of Sugar in Modern History.* New York: Viking, 1985.

Mitchell, William P. *Peasants on the Edge: Crop, Cult, and Crisis in the Andes.* Austin: University of Texas Press, 1991.

Molina Solís, Juan Francisco. *Historia de Yucatán durante la dominación española.* 3 vols. Mérida: Imprenta de la Lotería del Estado, 1904–1913.

Moreno Fraginals, Manuel. *The Sugarmill: The Socioeconomic Complex of Sugar in Cuba, 1760–1870.* Trans. Cedric Belfrage. New York: Monthly Review Press, 1967 (orig. 1964).

El museo yucateco (1841).

Norman, B. A. *Rambles in Yucatan; or, Notes of Travel through the Peninsula, Including a Visit to the Remarkable Ruins of Chi-Chen, Kabah, Zayi, and Uxmal.* New York: J. & H. G. Langley, 1843.

Ojeda, Jorge Victoria. "Arquitectura religiosa en Tihosuco, Quintana Roo. Notas y comentarios sobre este importante conjunto colonial." *Boletín E.C.A.U.D.Y.* 16, 93 (1988), 9–27.

Ortega, Enrique Montalvo. "Revolts and Peasant Mobilizations in Yucatan: Indians, Peones, and Peasants from the Caste War to the Revolution." In *Riot, Rebellion, and Revolution: Rural Social Conflict in Mexico.* Ed. Friedrich Katz. Princeton: Princeton University Press, 1988, 295–317.

Patch, Robert W. "Agrarian Change in Eighteenth-Century Yucatán." *Hispanic American Historical Review* 65, 1 (1985), 21–49.

———. "Decolonization, the Agrarian Problem, and the Origins of the Caste War, 1812–1847." In *Land, Labor, and Capital in Modern Yucatán: Essays in Regional History and Political Economy.* Ed. Jeffery T. Brannon and Gilbert M. Joseph. Tuscaloosa: University of Alabama Press, 1991, 51–82.

———. *Maya and Spaniard in Yucatán, 1648–1812.* Stanford: Stanford University Press, 1993.

Peniche Rivero, Piedad. *Sacerdotes y comerciantes: El poder de los mayas e itzaes de Yucatán en los siglos VII a XVI.* Mexico City: Fondo de Cultura Económica, 1990.

Perera, Victor, and Robert D. Bruce. *The Last Lords of Palenque: The Lacandon Mayas of the Mexican Rain Forest.* Boston: Little, Brown and Company, 1982.

Pérez Toro, Augusto. "El indio maya y la tierra." *Orbe* 4, 7 (1947), 45–50.

Quezada, Sergio. "Encomienda, cabildo, y gubernatura indígena en Yucatán, 1541–1583." *Historia mexicana* 34, 4 (1985), 662–684.

Quintal Martín, Fidelio. "Biografías campesinas del siglo XIX." *Boletín E.C.A.U.D.Y.* 9 (1982), 23–55.

———. *Correspondencia de la guerra de castas.* Mérida: Ediciones de la Universidad Autónoma de Yucatán, 1992.

———, ed. "Proceso y ejecución de Manuel Ay Tec, caudillo campesino de Chichimilá, Yucatán." *Boletín E.C.A.U.D.Y.* 13, 76 (1986), 21–43.

Redfield, Robert. *The Folk Culture of Yucatan.* Chicago: University of Chicago Press, 1941.

Redfield, Robert, and Alfonso Villa Rojas. *Chan Kom: A Maya Village.* Chicago: University of Chicago Press, 1934.

Reed, Nelson. *The Caste War of Yucatan.* Stanford: Stanford University Press, 1964.

El registro yucateco, 4 vols., (1845).

Reid, Paul Joseph. "The Constitution of Cádiz and the Independence of Yucatan." *The Americas* 36, 1 (1979), 22–38.

Reina, Letitia. *Las rebeliones campesinas en México (1819–1906).* Mexico City: Siglo Veintiuno, 1980.

Robertson, William Parish. *A Visit to Mexico, by the West India Islands, Yucatan, and United States, with Observations and Adventures on the Way.* 2 vols. London: Simpkin, Marshall & Co., 1853.

Robinson, David J., and Carolyn G. McGovern. "La migración regional yucateca en la época colonial: El caso de San Francisco de Umán." *Historia Mexicana* 30, 1 (1980), 99–125.

Rodríguez Losa, Salvador. *Geografía política de Yucatán. Tomo I. Censo inédito de 1821, año de la independencia.* Mérida: Universidad Autónoma de Yucatán, 1985.

Roys, Ralph L. *The Indian Background of Colonial Yucatan.* Norman: University of Oklahoma Press, 1972 (orig. 1943).

———. *The Political Geography of the Yucatán Maya.* Washington, D.C.: Carnegie Institute of Washington, 1957.

————. *The Titles of Ebtun.* Washington, D.C.: Carnegie Institute of Washington, 1939.

Rubio Mañé, J. Ignacio. *Los sanjuanistas de Yucatán.* 1971.

Rudé, George. *Ideology and Popular Protest.* New York: Pantheon Books, 1980.

Rus, Jan, and Robert Wasserstrom. "Civil-Religious Hierarchies in Central Chiapas: A Critical Perspective." *American Ethnologist* 7, 3 (1980), 467–472.

Ruz Menéndez, Rodolfo. "Los indios de Yucatán de Bartolomé del Granado Baeza." *Revista de la Universidad de Yucatán* 4, 168 (1989), 52–63.

Ryder, James W. "Internal Migration in Yucatan: Interpretation of Historical Demography and Current Patterns." In *Anthropology and History in Yucatan.* Ed. Grant D. Jones. Austin: University of Texas Press, 1977, 191–231.

Schyrer, Frans. *The Rancheros of Pisaflores: The History of a Peasant Bourgeoisie in Twentieth-Century Mexico.* Toronto: University of Toronto Press, 1980.

Schwartz, Stuart B. *Sugar Plantations in the Formation of Brazilian Society: Bahia, 1550–1835.* Cambridge: Cambridge University Press, 1985.

Scott, James C. *The Moral Economy of the Peasant: Rebellion and Subsistence in Southeast Asia.* New Haven: Yale University Press, 1976.

————. *Weapons of the Weak: Everyday Forms of Peasant Resistance.* New Haven: Yale University Press, 1985.

Seed, Patricia. "'Failing to Marvel': Atahualpa's Encounter with the Word." *Latin American Research Review* 26, 1 (1991), 7–32.

Shattuck, George Cheever. *The Peninsula of Yucatan: Medical, Biological, Meteorological, and Sociological Studies.* Washington, D.C.: Carnegie Institute of Washington, 1933.

Sierra O'Reilly, Justo. *Los indios de Yucatán. Consideraciones históricas sobre la influencia del elemento indígena en la organización social del país.* Ed. Carlos R. Menéndez. 2 vols. Mérida: Compañía Tipográfica Yucateca, 1954.

Silverblatt, Irene. *Moon, Sun, and Witches: Gender Ideologies and Class in Inca and Colonial Peru.* Princeton: Princeton University Press, 1987.

Silverman, Sydel. "The Peasant Concept in Anthropology." *Journal of Peasant Studies* 7, 1 (1979), 49–69.

Skocpol, Theda. *States and Social Revolutions: A Comparative Analysis of France, Russia, and China.* Cambridge University Press, 1979.

Smith, Carol A., ed. *Guatemalan Indians and the State: 1540 to 1988.* Austin: University of Texas Press, 1990.

Smith, Justin H. *The War with Mexico.* 2 vols. New York: Macmillan, 1919.

Smith, Waldemar R. *The Fiesta System and Economic Change.* New York: Columbia University Press, 1977.

Steggerda, Morris. *The Maya Indians of Yucatan.* Washington, D.C.: Carnegie Institute of Washington, 1941.

Stephens, John Lloyd. *Incidents of Travel in Yucatan.* 2 vols. New York: Dover Publications, 1963.

Stern, Steve J. *Peru's Indian Peoples and the Challenge of Spanish Conquest: Huamanga to 1640.* Madison: University of Wisconsin Press, 1982.

Strickon, Arnold. "Hacienda and Plantation in Yucatan: An Historical-Ecological Consideration of the Folk-Urban Continuum in Yucatan." *América Indígena* 25 (1965), 35–65.

Sullivan, Paul. *Unfinished Conversations: Mayas and Foreigners between Two Wars*. Berkeley: University of California Press, 1989.

Taussig, Michael T. *The Devil and Commodity Fetishism in South America*. Chapel Hill: University of North Carolina Press, 1980.

————. *Shamanism, Colonialism, and the Wild Man: A Study in Terror and Healing*. Chicago: University of Chicago Press, 1987.

Taylor, William B. *Drinking, Homicide, and Rebellion in Colonial Mexican Villages*. Stanford: Stanford University Press, 1979.

Thompson, J. E. S. *The Rise and Fall of Maya Civilization*. Norman: University of Oklahoma Press, 1954.

Thompson, Philip C. "The Structure of the Civil Hierarchy in Tekanto, Yucatan: 1785–1820." *Estudios de la cultura maya* 16 (1985), 183–197.

Van Oss, Adriaan C. *Catholic Colonialism: A Parish History of Guatemala, 1524–1821*. Cambridge: Cambridge University Press, 1986.

Van Young, Eric. *Hacienda and Market in Eighteenth-Century Mexico: The Rural Economy of the Guadalajara Region, 1675–1820*. Berkeley: University of California Press, 1981.

"Viaje a Bolonchen-ticul." *Museo yucateco* I (1841), 217–221.

Villa Rojas, Alfonso. *The Maya of East Central Quintana Roo*. Washington, D.C.: Carnegie Institute of Washington, 1943.

Waldeck, Federico de. *Viaje pintoresco y arqueológico a la provincia de Yucatán (América central) durante los años 1834 y 1836*. Trans. Manuel Mestre Ghigliazze. Mérida: Compañía Tipográfica Yucateca, 1930 (orig. 1837).

Wasserstrom, Robert. *Class and Society in Central Chiapas*. Berkeley: University of California Press, 1983.

————. "Revolution in Guatemala: Peasants and Politics under the Arbenz Government." *Comparative Studies in Society and History* 17 (1975), 443–478.

Wells, Alan. *Yucatan's Gilded Age: Haciendas, Henequen, and International Harvester, 1860–1915*. Albuquerque: University of New Mexico Press, 1985.

Wickham-Crowley, Timothy P. *Guerrillas and Revolution in Latin America: A Comparative Study of Insurgents and Regimes since 1956*. Princeton: Princeton University Press, 1992.

Wolf, Eric R. "Closed Corporate Peasant Communities in Mesoamerica and Central Java." *Southwestern Journal of Anthropology* 13 (1957), 1–18.

————. *Europe and the People without History*. Berkeley: University of California Press, 1982.

————. *Peasant Wars of the Twentieth Century*. New York: Harper & Row, 1969.

————. *Peasants*. Englewood Cliffs, N.J.: Prentice-Hall, 1966.

————. *Sons of the Shaking Earth: The People of Mexico and Guatemala—Their Land, History, and Culture*. Chicago: University of Chicago Press, 1959.

Wolf, Eric R., and Sidney W. Mintz. "Haciendas and Plantations in Middle America and the Antilles." *Social and Economic Studies* 6 (1957), 380–412.

Woodward, Ralph Lee. *Central America: A Nation Divided.* New York: Oxford University Press, 1976.

Yrder, James W. "Internal Migration in Yucatán: Interpretation of Historical Demography and Current Patterns." In *Anthropology and History in Yucatan.* Ed. Grant D. Jones. Austin: University of Texas Press, 1977, 191–231.

Index